Modern C++

Modern C++ Programming

Learning Path

How Can You Master C++
with
Modern Best Practices?

MARK JOHN LADO

ISBN: 9798313745862
www.markjohnlado.com

DEDICATION

This book is dedicated to all aspiring programmers and software developers who strive to master C++ and push the boundaries of modern programming. To the students who spend countless hours debugging their code, the professionals who seek to refine their craft, and the enthusiasts who code for the sheer joy of problem-solving—this is for you.

I also dedicate this work to my mentors, teachers, and fellow developers who have shared their knowledge and experience, guiding me through the intricacies of programming. Your insights and encouragement have been invaluable.

To my family and friends, who have provided unwavering support and patience throughout this journey, I am deeply grateful. Your belief in my work has been my greatest motivation.

Finally, to the pioneers of C++ who have shaped the language into what it is today—thank you for building a foundation that empowers innovation. May this book serve as a stepping stone for the next generation of C++ developers.

ACKNOWLEDGMENTS

Writing this book would not have been possible without the contributions, guidance, and support of many individuals.

I sincerely thank the creators and contributors of C++, whose dedication to advancing the language has made it a powerful tool for modern software development. Their work continues to inspire programmers worldwide.

I am also grateful to my mentors, teachers, and colleagues who have shared their expertise, provided feedback, and encouraged my learning. Their insights have been instrumental in shaping this book's content.

To the open-source community and online programming forums, I extend my appreciation. The wealth of knowledge available through discussions, tutorials, and documentation has been invaluable in refining my understanding of C++.

A heartfelt thanks to my family and friends, who have supported me throughout this journey with patience and encouragement. Your unwavering belief in my work has been a constant source of motivation.

Lastly, to the readers—whether you are a beginner or an experienced programmer—I appreciate your trust in this book. May it guide you toward mastering modern C++.

Table of Contents

Chapter 1

Introduction to C++

In the dynamic realm of computer technology, proficiency in programming languages is indispensable. Among the myriad of languages available, C++ stands out as a powerful and versatile tool, essential for both aspiring and seasoned computer technology professionals. This discussion aims to provide a structured introduction to C++, meticulously crafted to meet the academic standards expected of Computer Technology students and educators. We will explore the historical roots and evolutionary journey of C++, delve into its diverse applications, and equip you with the practical knowledge to set up your development environment, ensuring a solid foundation for your C++ programming endeavors. This introduction will not only lay the groundwork for understanding C++ but also address common challenges and questions that may arise as you embark on your learning journey.

1.1 History and Evolution of C++

1.1.1 Origins in C

The genesis of C++ can be traced back to the C programming language, developed by Dennis Ritchie at Bell Labs in the early 1970s. C was revolutionary for its time, offering a balance between high-level programming abstraction and low-level hardware control, making it suitable for system programming and application development alike. As noted by Ritchie himself in "The Development of the C Language," C was designed to be efficient and expressive, traits that would be inherited and expanded upon in its successor, C++ (Ritchie, 1993). The efficiency and portability of C led to its widespread adoption, forming the bedrock upon which C++ would be built.

1.1.2 Birth of C++: C with Classes

In the late 1970s, Bjarne Stroustrup, also at Bell Labs, began working on "C with Classes." Stroustrup aimed to augment C with object-oriented programming (OOP) capabilities, drawing inspiration from Simula67, one of the first object-oriented languages. This initial iteration, "C with Classes," introduced features like classes, derived classes, strong type checking, inlining, and default arguments (Stroustrup, 1980). These additions were intended to facilitate better program organization and code reusability, addressing the growing complexity of software development.

1.1.3 Standardization and Modern C++

"C with Classes" evolved into C++ in 1983, with the addition of virtual functions, function and operator overloading, references, constants, user-controlled free store memory allocation, improved type checking, and single and multiple inheritance (Stroustrup, 1994). The language continued to mature, and in 1998, the first international standard for C++ (ISO/IEC 14882:1998) was published, often referred to as C++98. This standardization was a crucial milestone, providing a stable and well-defined foundation for the language. Subsequent standards, including C++03, C++11, C++14, C++17, C++20, and the ongoing C++23, have introduced significant enhancements, modernizing the language and expanding its capabilities. Each new standard builds upon the last, incorporating features like lambda expressions, move semantics, improved concurrency support, and modules, reflecting the evolving needs of the software development landscape. The continuous evolution of C++ ensures its relevance and power in modern computing, as discussed in Sutter and Alexandrescu's "C++ Coding Standards" which emphasizes the importance of staying updated with the latest standards for effective C++ programming (Sutter & Alexandrescu, 2005).

1.2 Use Cases and Applications

C++'s unique blend of performance and abstraction makes it a language of choice across a vast spectrum of applications. Its efficiency, inherited from C, combined with object-oriented and generic programming paradigms, allows developers to create complex and high-performance systems.

1.2.1 Operating Systems and System Software

Operating systems are foundational software that demand both performance and low-level hardware access. C++ is extensively used in developing operating systems like Microsoft Windows, macOS, and components of Linux distributions. Key system software, including device drivers and file systems, are often written in C++ due to its ability to directly interact with hardware while providing high-level programming constructs. For instance, major parts of Chrome OS, known for its speed and efficiency, are implemented in C++ (Google, n.d.). This highlights C++'s capability in handling resource-intensive tasks at the system level.

1.2.2 Game Development

The gaming industry is another domain where C++ reigns supreme. High-fidelity graphics, real-time physics simulations, and complex game logic require exceptional performance. Game engines like Unreal Engine and Unity (core parts) are built using C++, providing developers with the tools to create visually stunning and highly interactive gaming experiences. As Gregory notes in "Game Engine Architecture," C++'s control over memory management and processor instructions is crucial for optimizing game performance and delivering smooth gameplay (Gregory, 2018).

1.2.3 High-Performance Computing and Finance

In fields like scientific computing, financial modeling, and big data analysis, performance is paramount. C++ is heavily utilized in high-performance computing (HPC) applications, where simulations, complex calculations, and data processing need to be executed rapidly. Financial institutions rely on C++ for building trading platforms and risk management systems that require low latency and high throughput. Libraries like Eigen and Armadillo, written in C++, are widely used for numerical computations in these domains, demonstrating C++'s strength in handling computationally intensive tasks (Eigen, n.d.; Sanderson & Curtin, 2016).

1.2.4 Embedded Systems and IoT

Embedded systems, ranging from microcontrollers in automobiles to IoT devices, often have stringent resource constraints and real-time requirements. C++ is well-suited for embedded programming because of its efficiency and ability to produce optimized machine code. The low-level control offered by C++, combined with its high-level features, allows developers to create sophisticated embedded applications that are both efficient and maintainable. Examples include firmware for network devices, automotive control systems, and various IoT sensors and actuators.

1.3 Installing a Modern C++ Compiler (GCC, Clang, MSVC)

To begin programming in C++, you need a compiler to translate your source code into executable machine code. Modern C++ development often relies on three major compiler families: GCC (GNU Compiler Collection), Clang, and MSVC (Microsoft Visual C++). Each has its strengths and is available on different platforms.

1.3.1 Installing GCC

GCC is a widely used, open-source compiler suite available on virtually all operating systems, including Linux, macOS, and Windows (via MinGW or WSL).

Step-by-step guide for installing GCC on Ubuntu/Debian Linux:

1. **Open a terminal:** Press Ctrl+Alt+T.
2. **Update package lists:** Execute the command sudo apt update.
3. **Install GCC and g++:** Execute sudo apt install g++. This command installs both the C compiler (gcc) and the C++ compiler (g++).
4. **Verify installation:** Run g++ --version to check the installed GCC version. You should see version information printed in the terminal.

Step-by-step guide for installing GCC on macOS:

1. **Install Xcode Command Line Tools:** Open Terminal and run xcode-select --install. Follow the prompts to install. This includes Clang, which on macOS acts as a GCC-compatible compiler.
2. **Verify installation:** Run g++ --version or clang++ --version in the Terminal. You should see version information, indicating successful installation.

Step-by-step guide for installing GCC on Windows (using MinGW-w64):

1. **Download MinGW-w64:** Visit the MinGW-w64 website (https://www.mingw-w64.org/). Navigate to the "Downloads" section.
2. **Run the installer:** Execute the downloaded installer. Choose a suitable installation directory (e.g., C:\mingw64). During installation, you can typically accept the default settings for architecture and exceptions.
3. **Add MinGW-w64 to PATH:** After installation, you need to add the MinGW-w64 bin directory to your system's PATH environment variable.

   - Search for "Environment Variables" in the Windows Start Menu.
   - Click "Edit the system environment variables."
   - Click "Environment Variables..."
   - In "System variables," find and select "Path," then click "Edit..."

- Click "New" and add the path to your MinGW-w64 bin directory (e.g., C:\mingw64\bin).
- Click "OK" on all dialogs to save changes.

4. **Verify installation:** Open Command Prompt and run g++ --version. You should see the GCC version information.

1.3.2 Installing Clang

Clang is another powerful, open-source compiler known for its excellent error messages and modular design. It is often preferred for its diagnostic capabilities and is the default compiler on macOS.

Step-by-step guide for installing Clang on Ubuntu/Debian Linux:

1. **Open a terminal:** Press Ctrl+Alt+T.
2. **Update package lists:** Execute sudo apt update.
3. **Install Clang:** Run sudo apt install clang++.
4. **Verify installation:** Execute clang++ --version to check the installed Clang version.

Step-by-step guide for installing Clang on Windows:

1. **Download Clang for Windows:** Visit the Clang download page on LLVM website (https://releases.llvm.org/download.html). Look for pre-built binaries for Windows (e.g., "LLVM-*-win64.exe").
2. **Run the installer:** Execute the downloaded installer. Choose an installation directory.
3. **Add Clang to PATH:** Similar to MinGW-w64, add the Clang bin directory (e.g., C:\Program Files\LLVM\bin) to your system's PATH environment variable. Follow the same steps as described for MinGW-w64 PATH setup.
4. **Verify installation:** Open Command Prompt and run clang++ --version.

1.3.3 Installing MSVC (Microsoft Visual C++ Compiler)

MSVC is Microsoft's C++ compiler, primarily used on Windows and often integrated with Visual Studio. It's essential for developing Windows-specific applications.

Step-by-step guide for installing MSVC:

1. **Download Visual Studio Community:** Visit the Visual Studio downloads page (https://visualstudio.microsoft.com/downloads/). Download the free "Community" edition.
2. **Run the Visual Studio Installer:** Execute the downloaded installer.
3. **Choose workloads:** During installation, select the "Desktop development with C++" workload. You can choose other workloads as needed, but "Desktop development with C++" is crucial for C++ compilation.
4. **Install:** Click "Install" and wait for the installation to complete.
5. **Verify installation:** Open a "Developer Command Prompt for VS XXXX" (search for it in the Start Menu, where XXXX is your Visual Studio version). In the Developer Command Prompt, run cl. If MSVC is correctly installed, you should see the compiler's help message.

1.4 Setting up an IDE (VS Code, CLion, Code::Blocks)

An Integrated Development Environment (IDE) significantly enhances the coding experience by providing features like code editing, compilation, debugging, and project management. Several IDEs are popular for C++ development, each with its strengths.

1.4.1 VS Code (Visual Studio Code)

VS Code is a lightweight but powerful, cross-platform code editor. With extensions, it becomes a robust C++ IDE.

Step-by-step guide for setting up VS Code for C++:

1. **Install VS Code:** Download and install VS Code from (https://code.visualstudio.com/).
2. **Install C/C++ extension:** Open VS Code, go to the Extensions view (Ctrl+Shift+X or Cmd+Shift+X). Search for "C/C++" by Microsoft and install it. This extension provides IntelliSense, debugging, and code formatting for C++.
3. **Install a compiler (if not already installed):** Follow the GCC, Clang, or MSVC installation steps in section 1.3 based on your operating system. Ensure the compiler's bin directory is in your system PATH.

4. **Configure tasks (optional but recommended):** To compile and run C++ code directly from VS Code, you can configure build tasks. VS Code can often automatically detect your compiler and suggest configurations. You can create tasks.json in a .vscode folder in your project to customize build and run commands. VS Code documentation provides detailed guides on task configuration (https://code.visualstudio.com/docs/cpp/config-msvc).

1.4.2 CLion

CLion is a dedicated C++ IDE by JetBrains, known for its intelligent code assistance, debugging capabilities, and CMake integration. It is a commercial IDE but offers a free trial and educational licenses.

Step-by-step guide for setting up CLion:

1. **Download CLion:** Visit the JetBrains CLion website (https://www.jetbrains.com/clion/) and download the installer.
2. **Install CLion:** Run the installer and follow the on-screen instructions.
3. **Install a compiler (if not already installed):** Ensure you have GCC, Clang, or MSVC installed as described in section 1.3. CLion typically auto-detects installed compilers.
4. **Create a new project:** Launch CLion, and select "New Project." Choose "C++ Executable" or another project type. CLion uses CMake for project management, which it handles seamlessly.
5. **Configure toolchain (if needed):** If CLion doesn't auto-detect your compiler, you may need to configure the toolchain in "Settings/Preferences" -> "Build, Execution, Deployment" -> "Toolchains." Specify the path to your compiler (e.g., GCC, Clang, or MSVC).

1.4.3 Code::Blocks

Code::Blocks is a free, open-source, cross-platform IDE specifically designed for C and C++. It is a more lightweight option compared to CLion but still provides essential IDE features.

Step-by-step guide for setting up Code::Blocks:

1. **Download Code::Blocks:** Visit the Code::Blocks website (http://www.codeblocks.org/) and go to the "Downloads" page.

Choose the download appropriate for your operating system, ideally one that includes a compiler (e.g., "codeblocks-*-mingw-setup.exe" for Windows with MinGW).

2. **Install Code::Blocks:** Run the installer and follow the instructions. If you chose a version with a compiler (like the MinGW version for Windows), it will install GCC as well.
3. **Launch Code::Blocks:** Start Code::Blocks from your applications menu.
4. **Create a new project:** Go to "File" -> "New" -> "Project..." Choose "Console application" and "C++." Follow the wizard to set up your project. Code::Blocks usually auto-detects the installed compiler.

By following these steps, you will have a functional C++ development environment set up, ready for you to start writing and compiling C++ code. Choosing the right compiler and IDE depends on your operating system, project needs, and personal preferences. GCC and Clang are excellent cross-platform compilers, while MSVC is essential for Windows-specific development. VS Code offers flexibility and extensibility, CLion provides powerful C++-specific features, and Code::Blocks is a straightforward, open-source option. As you progress in your C++ journey, experimenting with different tools and configurations will further refine your development workflow.

Chapter 2

Basic Syntax and Data Types

Understanding the basic syntax and data types of C++ is the first critical step in mastering this powerful programming language. Just as grammar and vocabulary form the foundation of human language, syntax and data types are the building blocks of C++ programs. This section will methodically dissect these fundamental concepts, providing a robust understanding essential for any aspiring C++ programmer. We will explore the structure of a C++ program, delve into variables, constants, and fundamental data types, and examine operators and input/output operations. Through clear explanations, real-world examples, and practical code snippets, this discussion aims to equip you with the foundational knowledge needed to write basic C++ programs and understand more complex concepts in subsequent chapters.

2.1 Structure of a C++ Program

Every C++ program adheres to a basic structure that dictates how code is organized and executed. Understanding this structure is crucial for writing correct and maintainable code. A typical C++ program generally consists of several key components, including preprocessor directives, namespace declarations, the main function, and program statements.

2.1.1 The main Function: Entry Point of Execution

At the heart of every executable C++ program lies the main function. This function serves as the entry point where program execution begins. The main function typically has a return type of int, and by convention, a return value of 0 indicates successful program execution, while any other value signals an error. As Stroustrup emphasizes in "The C++ Programming Language," the main function is indispensable; without it, the operating system has no designated starting point for your program (Stroustrup, 2013).

Example: A Minimal C++ Program

```
C++
#include <iostream>

int main() {
  std::cout << "Hello, World!" << std::endl;
  return 0;
}
```

Step-by-step explanation:

1. **#include <iostream>:** This line is a preprocessor directive that includes the iostream header file. This header provides input and output functionalities, allowing us to display text on the console. The #include directive is processed before compilation, effectively copying the contents of iostream into your source code.
2. **int main() { ... }:** This defines the main function. The int keyword specifies that the function returns an integer value. The parentheses () indicate that main is a function, and in this case, it takes no arguments. The curly braces {} enclose the body of the main function, containing the program's executable statements.

3. **std::cout << "Hello, World!" << std::endl;:** This line is a statement that performs output. `std::cout` is the standard output stream object in C++, typically connected to the console. The `<<` operator is the insertion operator, used here to send the string literal `"Hello, World!"` to the output stream. `std::endl` is a manipulator that inserts a newline character and flushes the output stream, ensuring the output is immediately displayed. The `std::` prefix indicates that `cout` and `endl` belong to the standard namespace, which we will discuss next.
4. **return 0;:** This statement returns the integer value `0` from the `main` function, signaling successful execution to the operating system.

2.1.2 Namespaces: Organizing Code

Namespaces are a crucial feature in C++ for organizing code and preventing naming conflicts, especially in larger projects that incorporate multiple libraries or modules. The standard library components, such as `cout` and `endl`, are defined within the `std` namespace. By using `std::cout` and `std::endl`, we explicitly specify that we are using the standard output stream and end-line manipulator from the standard namespace. Alternatively, you can use the `using namespace std;` directive after the `#include` directives to bring all names from the `std` namespace into the current scope, allowing you to use `cout` and `endl` directly without the `std::` prefix. However, for clarity and to avoid potential naming collisions in larger projects, explicitly using `std::` is often considered best practice, as recommended by Meyers in "Effective C++" (Meyers, 2005).

2.2 Variables and Constants

Variables and constants are fundamental to storing and manipulating data in any programming language. C++ offers various ways to declare and use variables and constants, including modern features like `auto` and `constexpr`.

2.2.1 Variables: Named Storage Locations

A variable is a named storage location in memory that can hold a value of a specific data type. In C++, you must declare a variable before you can use it, specifying its data type and name. The data type determines the kind of values the variable can store (e.g., integer, floating-point, character).

Example: Variable Declaration and Assignment

```
C++
#include <iostream>

int main() {
  int age; // Declaration of an integer variable named 'age'
  age = 30; // Assignment of the value 30 to the variable 'age'

  std::cout << "Age: " << age << std::endl;
  return 0;
}
```

Step-by-step explanation:

1. **int age;:** This line declares a variable named `age` of type `int`. At this point, memory is allocated to store an integer value, and the variable `age` is associated with this memory location. However, the variable is not yet initialized with a specific value, and its content is indeterminate until assigned.
2. **age = 30;:** This line assigns the integer value `30` to the variable `age`. Now, the memory location associated with `age` holds the value 30.

2.2.2 Constants: Immutable Values

Constants are values that cannot be changed after their initialization. C++ provides several ways to define constants, including the `const` and `constexpr` keywords.

2.2.2.1 `const` Keyword: Compile-Time and Run-Time Constants

The `const` keyword is used to declare variables whose values are intended to remain constant throughout their scope. `const` variables must be initialized when they are declared, and their values cannot be modified subsequently. `const` can be applied to variables, pointers, and function parameters.

Example: `const` Variable

```
C++
#include <iostream>
```

```
int main() {
    const double PI = 3.14159; // Declaration and initialization of a const
double

    std::cout << "PI: " << PI << std::endl;
    // PI = 3.14; // Error: assignment of read-only variable 'PI' (uncommenting
this line will cause a compilation error)
    return 0;
}
```

Step-by-step explanation:

1. **const double PI = 3.14159;:** This line declares a constant variable named PI of type double and initializes it with the value 3.14159. The const keyword ensures that the value of PI cannot be changed after this initialization.
2. **// PI = 3.14;:** This line is commented out because attempting to reassign a value to PI after its initialization will result in a compilation error. This demonstrates the immutability of const variables.

2.2.2.2 constexpr Keyword: Compile-Time Constants

Introduced in C++11, constexpr (constant expression) is a more powerful way to define constants, ensuring that the value is evaluated at compile time, if possible. This can lead to performance optimizations, especially for values used in templates or as array sizes. constexpr can be used for variables and functions. For functions, it indicates that the function can be evaluated at compile time if the arguments are also compile-time constants. As Vandevoorde, Josuttis, and Gregor note in "C++ Templates," constexpr enhances compile-time programming capabilities, allowing for more efficient and robust code (Vandevoorde et al., 2017).

Example: constexpr Variable and Function

```
C++
#include <iostream>

constexpr int square(int n) {
    return n * n;
}

int main() {
    constexpr int compileTimeSquare = square(5); // Evaluated at compile time
    int runtimeValue = 10;
```

```
    int runTimeSquare = square(runtimeValue); // Evaluated at run time

    std::cout << "Compile-time square: " << compileTimeSquare << std::endl;
    std::cout << "Run-time square: " << runTimeSquare << std::endl;
    return 0;
}
```

Step-by-step explanation:

1. **constexpr int square(int n) { return n * n; }:** This defines a constexpr function named square that takes an integer n and returns its square. Because it is constexpr, if called with a compile-time constant argument, the result can be computed at compile time.
2. **constexpr int compileTimeSquare = square(5);:** Here, square(5) is evaluated at compile time because 5 is a literal constant. The result, 25, is also a compile-time constant and is assigned to compileTimeSquare, which is also declared constexpr.
3. **int runTimeSquare = square(runtimeValue);:** In this case, square(runtimeValue) is evaluated at run time because runtimeValue is a variable whose value is not known at compile time.

2.2.3 auto Keyword: Type Inference

Introduced in C++11, the auto keyword simplifies variable declarations by allowing the compiler to automatically deduce the data type of a variable from its initializer. This is particularly useful for complex types or when the type is immediately obvious from the initialization. However, it's important to use auto judiciously to maintain code readability. As Stroustrup advises, auto should be used when it makes code clearer or safer, especially when dealing with complex template types or lambda expressions (Stroustrup, 2018).

Example: auto Type Inference

```
C++
#include <iostream>
#include <vector>

int main() {
    auto integerValue = 10; // 'integerValue' is inferred as int
    auto doubleValue = 3.14; // 'doubleValue' is inferred as double
```

```
    auto message = "Hello";  // 'message' is inferred as const char* (or
std::string in some contexts, depending on compiler and settings)
    std::vector<int> numbers = {1, 2, 3, 4, 5};
    auto iterator = numbers.begin(); // 'iterator' is inferred as
std::vector<int>::iterator

    std::cout << "Integer value: " << integerValue << std::endl;
    std::cout << "Double value: " << doubleValue << std::endl;
    std::cout << "Message: " << message << std::endl;
    std::cout << "First number in vector: " << *iterator << std::endl;
    return 0;
}
```

Step-by-step explanation:

1. **auto integerValue = 10;:** The compiler infers that integerValue should be of type int because 10 is an integer literal.
2. **auto doubleValue = 3.14;:** The compiler infers that doubleValue should be of type double because 3.14 is a floating-point literal.
3. **auto message = "Hello";:** The compiler infers message to be of type const char* (or potentially std::string depending on compiler settings and context).
4. **auto iterator = numbers.begin();:** Here, auto is particularly useful. The type of numbers.begin() is std::vector<int>::iterator, which is verbose. auto makes the code cleaner and easier to read, especially when dealing with complex iterator types or template instantiations.

2.3 Data Types

C++ offers a rich set of built-in data types to represent different kinds of values. These data types can be broadly categorized into fundamental types, derived types, and user-defined types. This section focuses on the fundamental data types: integers, floating-point numbers, characters, booleans, and strings.

2.3.1 Integer Types (int, short, long, long long)

Integer types are used to represent whole numbers, both positive and negative. C++ provides several integer types that vary in size and range, allowing you to choose the most appropriate type based on your needs and memory considerations. The standard integer types include int, short, long, and long long. The exact size of these types can be platform-dependent, but C++ standards guarantee minimum ranges. For example, int is typically 4 bytes on many modern systems, but its size can vary. short is usually smaller than or equal to int, and long is typically larger than or equal to int. long long (introduced in C++11) is guaranteed to be at least 64 bits, providing a larger range for very large integers. You can also use unsigned versions of these types (e.g., unsigned int, unsigned long) to represent only non-negative integers, effectively doubling the positive range but disallowing negative values.

Example: Integer Types

C++

```
#include <iostream>
#include <limits> // Required for numeric_limits

int main() {
    int integerVar = 100;
    short shortVar = 10;
    long long longLongVar = 123456789012345LL; // LL suffix for long long
literal
    unsigned int unsignedIntVar = 4294967295U; // U suffix for unsigned literal

    std::cout << "Integer: " << integerVar << std::endl;
    std::cout << "Short: " << shortVar << std::endl;
    std::cout << "Long Long: " << longLongVar << std::endl;
    std::cout << "Unsigned Integer: " << unsignedIntVar << std::endl;

    std::cout << "\nSize of int: " << sizeof(int) << " bytes" << std::endl;
    std::cout << "Size of short: " << sizeof(short) << " bytes" << std::endl;
    std::cout << "Size of long long: " << sizeof(long long) << " bytes" <<
std::endl;
    std::cout << "Size of unsigned int: " << sizeof(unsigned int) << " bytes" <<
std::endl;

    std::cout << "\nMaximum value of int: " <<
std::numeric_limits<int>::max() << std::endl;
    std::cout << "Maximum value of unsigned int: " <<
std::numeric_limits<unsigned int>::max() << std::endl;

    return 0;
}
```

Step-by-step explanation:

1. **int integerVar = 100;, short shortVar = 10;, long long longLongVar = 123456789012345LL;, unsigned int unsignedIntVar =**

4294967295U;: These lines declare and initialize variables of different integer types. The LL suffix is used to denote a long long integer literal, and U suffix for unsigned int literal.

2. **sizeof(int), sizeof(short), etc.:** The sizeof operator returns the size (in bytes) of a data type or variable. This demonstrates that different integer types can have different sizes in memory.
3. **std::numeric_limits<int>::max(), std::numeric_limits<unsigned int>::max():** The <limits> header and std::numeric_limits template class provide a way to query the properties of numeric types, such as their maximum and minimum values. This is a portable way to determine the range of integer types, as these ranges can be platform-dependent.

2.3.2 Floating-Point Types (float, double)

Floating-point types are used to represent numbers with fractional parts. C++ provides two primary floating-point types: float and double. float is typically single-precision (usually 32 bits), while double is double-precision (usually 64 bits), offering greater precision and range. double is often the default choice for floating-point calculations due to its higher precision. C++ also has long double for extended precision, though its implementation and precision can vary across compilers and platforms.

Example: Floating-Point Types

```
C++
#include <iostream>
#include <iomanip> // Required for std::setprecision

int main() {
   float floatVar = 3.14159f; // f suffix for float literal
   double doubleVar = 3.141592653589793;

   std::cout << "Float: " << floatVar << std::endl; // Default precision
   std::cout << "Double: " << doubleVar << std::endl; // Default precision

   std::cout << std::fixed << std::setprecision(7) << "Float (7 decimal places): "
<< floatVar << std::endl; // 7 decimal places
   std::cout << std::fixed << std::setprecision(15) << "Double (15 decimal
places): " << doubleVar << std::endl; // 15 decimal places

   std::cout << "\nSize of float: " << sizeof(float) << " bytes" << std::endl;
   std::cout << "Size of double: " << sizeof(double) << " bytes" << std::endl;
```

```
    return 0;
}
```

Step-by-step explanation:

1. **float floatVar = 3.14159f;, double doubleVar = 3.141592653589793;:** These lines declare and initialize variables of type float and double. The f suffix is used to denote a float literal; without it, 3.14159 would be treated as a double literal.
2. **std::cout << std::fixed << std::setprecision(7) << ... and std::cout << std::fixed << std::setprecision(15) << ...:** These lines use manipulators from the <iomanip> header to control the output precision. std::fixed ensures that floating-point numbers are printed in fixed-point notation, and std::setprecision(n) sets the precision to n decimal places. This demonstrates the difference in precision between float and double.

2.3.3 Character Type (char)

The char type is used to represent single characters, such as letters, digits, and symbols. Characters are typically stored as 8-bit integers, and they can be interpreted as characters according to character encoding schemes like ASCII or UTF-8. Character literals are enclosed in single quotes (e.g., 'A', '9', '?').

Example: Character Type

C++

```
#include <iostream>

int main() {
    char charVar = 'A';
    char digitChar = '7';
    char symbolChar = '$';

    std::cout << "Character: " << charVar << std::endl;
    std::cout << "Digit character: " << digitChar << std::endl;
    std::cout << "Symbol character: " << symbolChar << std::endl;
    std::cout << "ASCII value of " << charVar << ": " <<
static_cast<int>(charVar) << std::endl; // Casting char to int to see ASCII
value
    std::cout << "Size of char: " << sizeof(char) << " byte" << std::endl;

    return 0;
```

```
}
```

Step-by-step explanation:

1. **char charVar = 'A';, char digitChar = '7';, char symbolChar = '$';:** These lines declare and initialize char variables with character literals.
2. **static_cast<int>(charVar):** This demonstrates type casting. By casting the char variable charVar to int, we can output its underlying integer representation, which corresponds to its ASCII value.

2.3.4 Boolean Type (bool)

The bool type represents boolean values, which can be either true or false. Boolean variables are often used in conditional statements and logical operations to represent logical states. Boolean literals are true and false. Internally, true is often represented as 1, and false as 0, although you should always use the keywords true and false in your code for clarity.

Example: Boolean Type

C++

```
#include <iostream>

int main() {
  bool isTrue = true;
  bool isFalse = false;

  std::cout << "Is true: " << isTrue << std::endl;
  std::cout << "Is false: " << isFalse << std::endl;
  std::cout << "Size of bool: " << sizeof(bool) << " byte" << std::endl; //
Size might vary depending on compiler and architecture

  return 0;
}
```

Step-by-step explanation:

1. **bool isTrue = true;, bool isFalse = false;:** These lines declare and initialize bool variables with boolean literals true and false.
2. The output demonstrates that true is typically represented as 1 and false as 0 when printed to the console using std::cout.

2.3.5 String Type (std::string)

The std::string type, provided by the C++ Standard Library, is used to represent sequences of characters, or text strings. Unlike C-style strings (character arrays), std::string provides dynamic memory management, making it safer and easier to use. To use std::string, you need to include the <string> header. String literals are enclosed in double quotes (e.g., "Hello, C++!").

Example: String Type

```
C++
#include <iostream>
#include <string> // Required for std::string

int main() {
   std::string message = "Hello, C++!";
   std::string name = "World";
   std::string greeting = "Hello, " + name + "!"; // String concatenation

   std::cout << "Message: " << message << std::endl;
   std::cout << "Greeting: " << greeting << std::endl;
   std::cout << "Length of message: " << message.length() << std::endl; //
Using string member function length()
   std::cout << "Size of string (message variable): " << sizeof(message) << "
bytes" << std::endl; // Size of string object itself, not the string content

   return 0;
}
```

Step-by-step explanation:

1. **#include <string>:** Includes the <string> header, which defines the std::string class.
2. **std::string message = "Hello, C++!";, std::string name = "World";:** These lines declare and initialize std::string variables with string literals.
3. **std::string greeting = "Hello, " + name + "!";:** Demonstrates string concatenation using the + operator. std::string objects can be easily concatenated using +.
4. **message.length():** Calls the length() member function of the std::string object message to get the length of the string.
5. **sizeof(message):** Shows the size of the std::string object itself. Note that sizeof(std::string) typically returns the size of the string

object's internal structure (like pointers and size information), not the size of the dynamically allocated memory that stores the string content. The actual memory used by the string content can vary and is managed dynamically by the std::string class.

2.4 Operators

Operators are special symbols that perform operations on operands (values and variables). C++ provides a rich set of operators, including arithmetic, logical, bitwise, and more. Understanding operators is crucial for performing computations, making decisions, and manipulating data in your programs.

2.4.1 Arithmetic Operators

Arithmetic operators perform mathematical operations. C++ provides the standard arithmetic operators: addition (+), subtraction (-), multiplication (*), division (/), and modulus (%).

Example: Arithmetic Operators

```
C++
#include <iostream>

int main() {
   int a = 10;
   int b = 3;

   std::cout << "Addition: " << a + b << std::endl;      // Output: 13
   std::cout << "Subtraction: " << a - b << std::endl;   // Output: 7
   std::cout << "Multiplication: " << a * b << std::endl; // Output: 30
   std::cout << "Division: " << a / b << std::endl;      // Output: 3 (integer
division)
   std::cout << "Modulus: " << a % b << std::endl;       // Output: 1
(remainder of division)

   double x = 10.0;
   double y = 3.0;
   std::cout << "Double Division: " << x / y << std::endl; // Output:
3.33333... (floating-point division)

   return 0;
}
```

Step-by-step explanation:

1. The code demonstrates the basic arithmetic operators: +, -, *, /, and %.
2. It highlights the difference between integer division (a / b, where both a and b are integers, resulting in integer truncation) and floating-point division (x / y, where x and y are doubles, resulting in a floating-point result).

2.4.2 Logical Operators

Logical operators are used to combine or modify boolean expressions. C++ provides logical AND (&&), logical OR (||), and logical NOT (!).

Example: Logical Operators

```
C++
#include <iostream>

int main() {
  bool condition1 = true;
  bool condition2 = false;

  std::cout << "Logical AND (condition1 && condition2): " << (condition1
&& condition2) << std::endl; // Output: 0 (false)
  std::cout << "Logical OR (condition1 || condition2): " << (condition1 ||
condition2) << std::endl;  // Output: 1 (true)
  std::cout << "Logical NOT (!condition1): " << (!condition1) << std::endl;
// Output: 0 (false)
  std::cout << "Logical NOT (!condition2): " << (!condition2) << std::endl;
// Output: 1 (true)

  return 0;
}
```

Step-by-step explanation:

1. The code demonstrates the logical operators &&, ||, and !.
2. It shows how these operators combine boolean values to produce boolean results according to logical rules (AND, OR, NOT).

2.4.3 Bitwise Operators

Bitwise operators operate on the individual bits of integer operands. C++ provides bitwise AND (&), bitwise OR (|), bitwise XOR (^), bitwise NOT (~), left shift (<<), and right shift (>>). Bitwise operators are often used in low-level programming, hardware interfacing, and performance-critical code where direct manipulation of bits is necessary.

Example: Bitwise Operators

```
C++
#include <iostream>

int main() {
   int a = 6;  // Binary: 0110
   int b = 3;  // Binary: 0011

   std::cout << "Bitwise AND (a & b): " << (a & b) << std::endl;  // Output:
2 (Binary: 0010)
   std::cout << "Bitwise OR (a | b): " << (a | b) << std::endl;   // Output: 7
(Binary: 0111)
   std::cout << "Bitwise XOR (a ^ b): " << (a ^ b) << std::endl;  // Output: 5
(Binary: 0101)
   std::cout << "Bitwise NOT (~a): " << (~a) << std::endl;     // Output: -7
(Binary: ...1001, two's complement)
   std::cout << "Left Shift (a << 1): " << (a << 1) << std::endl;  // Output:
12 (Binary: 1100, shifted left by 1 bit)
   std::cout << "Right Shift (a >> 1): " << (a >> 1) << std::endl; // Output: 3
(Binary: 0011, shifted right by 1 bit)

   return 0;
}
```

Step-by-step explanation:

1. The code demonstrates various bitwise operators. It initializes integers a and b and then applies bitwise operations.
2. The comments show the binary representations and the results of each operation, illustrating how bitwise operators manipulate the bits of the operands. For instance, bitwise AND (&) sets a bit in the result only if the corresponding bits are set in both operands. Bitwise left shift (<<) shifts the bits to the left, effectively multiplying by powers of 2.

2.5 Input/Output Operations

Input/output (I/O) operations are essential for programs to interact with the external world, such as reading data from the user or displaying results. C++ provides the iostream library for standard input and output operations.

2.5.1 Standard Output (std::cout)

We have already used std::cout extensively in previous examples. std::cout is the standard output stream object, typically connected to the console. The insertion operator << is used to send data to std::cout for output. You can output various data types using std::cout, including strings, numbers, and characters.

2.5.2 Standard Input (std::cin)

std::cin is the standard input stream object, typically connected to the keyboard. The extraction operator >> is used to read data from std::cin into variables.

Example: Standard Input with std::cin

```
C++
#include <iostream>
#include <string>

int main() {
    int age;
    std::string name;

    std::cout << "Please enter your name: ";
    std::cin >> name; // Reads a single word (until whitespace)

    std::cout << "Please enter your age: ";
    std::cin >> age; // Reads an integer

    std::cout << "\nHello, " << name << "! You are " << age << " years old."
<< std::endl;

    return 0;
}
```

Step-by-step explanation:

1. **std::cout << "Please enter your name: ";:** Prompts the user to enter their name.
2. **std::cin >> name;:** Reads input from the standard input stream (std::cin) and stores it in the string variable name. std::cin >> name reads input until it encounters whitespace (like a space, tab, or newline). This is important to note: if the user enters "John Doe", only "John" will be read into name.
3. **std::cout << "Please enter your age: ";:** Prompts the user to enter their age.
4. **std::cin >> age;:** Reads integer input from std::cin and stores it in the int variable age.
5. The program then outputs a personalized greeting using the input name and age.

2.5.3 Reading Lines with std::getline()

If you need to read an entire line of input, including whitespace, std::cin >> is insufficient because it stops reading at the first whitespace. The std::getline() function is used to read an entire line of text from an input stream, up to the newline character.

Example: Reading Lines with std::getline()

```
C++
#include <iostream>
#include <string>

int main() {
  std::string fullName;

  std::cout << "Please enter your full name: ";
  std::getline(std::cin, fullName); // Reads the entire line, including spaces

  std::cout << "Hello, " << fullName << "!" << std::endl;

  return 0;
}
```

Step-by-step explanation:

1. **std::getline(std::cin, fullName);:** This line uses the std::getline() function to read an entire line of input from std::cin and store it in the std::string variable fullName. Unlike std::cin >>, std::getline()

reads input until a newline character is encountered, thus reading the entire line, including spaces.

By mastering these basic syntax elements and data types, you are well-prepared to write more complex C++ programs and delve into advanced topics. Understanding variables, constants, data types, operators, and input/output operations forms the bedrock of C++ programming, enabling you to manipulate data, perform calculations, and interact with users effectively. As you continue your learning journey, these fundamental concepts will serve as essential tools in your C++ programming toolkit.

Chapter 3

Control Flow and Functions

Control flow and functions are essential constructs in C++ that dictate the order of execution and modularity of programs. Control flow mechanisms enable programs to make decisions and repeat actions based on conditions, while functions allow for code to be organized into reusable and manageable blocks. This section will delve into these crucial aspects of C++, providing a comprehensive understanding suitable for Computer Technology students and educators. We will explore conditional statements, various types of loops, and the multifaceted nature of functions in C++, including modern features like lambda expressions. Through detailed explanations, practical examples, and real-world analogies, this discussion aims to solidify your grasp of control flow and functions, empowering you to write more sophisticated and efficient C++ programs.

3.1 Conditional Statements

Conditional statements are fundamental control flow structures that allow programs to execute different blocks of code based on whether certain conditions are true or false. C++ provides three primary types of conditional statements: if, else, and switch.

3.1.1 if Statements: Executing Code Conditionally

The if statement is the most basic conditional statement. It executes a block of code only if a specified condition evaluates to true. The condition is typically a boolean expression.

Example: if Statement for Age Check

Imagine a real-world scenario where you are building a program to verify age for access to certain content. An if statement can be used to check if a user's age meets the required threshold.

```
C++
#include <iostream>

int main() {
  int age;
  std::cout << "Enter your age: ";
  std::cin >> age;

  if (age >= 18) {
    std::cout << "Access granted." << std::endl;
  }

  return 0;
}
```

Step-by-step explanation:

1. **int age;**: Declares an integer variable age to store the user's input.
2. **std::cout << "Enter your age: ";**: Prompts the user to enter their age.
3. **std::cin >> age;**: Reads the age entered by the user and stores it in the age variable.

4. **if (age >= 18) { ... }**: This is the if statement. The condition age >= 18 is evaluated. If this condition is true (i.e., if age is 18 or greater), the code block within the curly braces {} is executed.
5. **std::cout << "Access granted." << std::endl;**: This line is executed only if the condition age >= 18 is true, displaying "Access granted." to the console.

3.1.2 if-else Statements: Choosing Between Two Paths

The if-else statement extends the if statement by providing an alternative block of code to execute when the condition in the if statement is false. This allows for a binary choice in program flow.

Example: if-else for Even or Odd Number Check
Consider a scenario where you need to determine if a number is even or odd. An if-else statement is ideal for this binary decision.

```
C++
#include <iostream>

int main() {
  int number;
  std::cout << "Enter an integer: ";
  std::cin >> number;

  if (number % 2 == 0) {
    std::cout << number << " is even." << std::endl;
  } else {
    std::cout << number << " is odd." << std::endl;
  }

  return 0;
}
```

Step-by-step explanation:

1. **int number;**: Declares an integer variable number to store user input.
2. **std::cout << "Enter an integer: ";**: Prompts the user to enter an integer.
3. **std::cin >> number;**: Reads the integer input into the number variable.
4. **if (number % 2 == 0) { ... } else { ... }**: This is the if-else statement.

- **if (number % 2 == 0)**: The condition number % 2 == 0 checks if the remainder of number divided by 2 is 0. If true, the number is even, and the code block within the if block is executed.
- **else { ... }**: If the condition in the if statement is false (i.e., the remainder is not 0), the code block within the else block is executed, indicating the number is odd.

3.1.3 if-else if-else Statements: Handling Multiple Conditions

For situations with more than two possible outcomes, the if-else if-else construct allows you to chain multiple conditions together. The program will evaluate each if and else if condition in order. As soon as a condition is found to be true, its associated block of code is executed, and the rest of the if-else if-else chain is skipped. If none of the if or else if conditions are true, the final else block (if present) is executed.

Example: if-else if-else for Grading System

Consider a grading system where grades are assigned based on score ranges. An if-else if-else structure can efficiently handle multiple grade categories.

```
C++
#include <iostream>

int main() {
  int score;
  std::cout << "Enter your score: ";
  std::cin >> score;

  if (score >= 90) {
    std::cout << "Grade: A" << std::endl;
  } else if (score >= 80) {
    std::cout << "Grade: B" << std::endl;
  } else if (score >= 70) {
    std::cout << "Grade: C" << std::endl;
  } else if (score >= 60) {
    std::cout << "Grade: D" << std::endl;
  } else {
    std::cout << "Grade: F" << std::endl;
  }
```

```
    return 0;
}
```

Step-by-step explanation:

1. **int score;**: Declares an integer variable score to store the student's score.
2. **std::cout << "Enter your score: ";**: Prompts the user to input the score.
3. **std::cin >> score;**: Reads the score from the user input.
4. **if (score >= 90) { ... } else if (score >= 80) { ... } ... else { ... }**: This is the if-else if-else chain.
    - The conditions are evaluated sequentially. For example, first, score >= 90 is checked. If true, "Grade: A" is printed, and the rest of the chain is skipped.
    - If score >= 90 is false, then score >= 80 is checked, and so on.
    - If none of the if or else if conditions are true, the final else block is executed, assigning "Grade: F".

3.1.4 switch Statement: Multi-way Branching

The switch statement provides another way to handle multi-way branching, especially when you need to compare a variable against multiple constant values. It can be more efficient and readable than a long if-else if-else chain when dealing with a fixed set of discrete values. As Eckel notes in "Thinking in C++," switch statements are particularly useful for selecting one of several code paths based on the value of a single expression (Eckel, 2000).

Example: switch Statement for Day of the Week
Imagine a program that outputs the day of the week based on a number input (e.g., 1 for Monday, 2 for Tuesday, etc.). A switch statement is well-suited for this scenario.

```
C++
#include <iostream>

int main() {
    int dayNumber;
    std::cout << "Enter day number (1-7): ";
    std::cin >> dayNumber;
```

```
    switch (dayNumber) {
        case 1:
            std::cout << "Monday" << std::endl;
            break;
        case 2:
            std::cout << "Tuesday" << std::endl;
            break;
        case 3:
            std::cout << "Wednesday" << std::endl;
            break;
        case 4:
            std::cout << "Thursday" << std::endl;
            break;
        case 5:
            std::cout << "Friday" << std::endl;
            break;
        case 6:
            std::cout << "Saturday" << std::endl;
            break;
        case 7:
            std::cout << "Sunday" << std::endl;
            break;
        default:
            std::cout << "Invalid day number." << std::endl;
            break;
    }

    return 0;
}
```

Step-by-step explanation:

1. **int dayNumber;**: Declares an integer variable dayNumber for user input.
2. **std::cout << "Enter day number (1-7): ";**: Prompts the user to enter a day number.
3. **std::cin >> dayNumber;**: Reads the day number from the user.
4. **switch (dayNumber) { ... }**: This is the switch statement. The expression dayNumber is evaluated, and its value is compared against the case labels.
   - **case 1:, case 2:, ..., case 7:**: Each case label represents a constant value to compare against dayNumber. If dayNumber matches a case value, the code block following that case is executed.

- **std::cout << "Monday" << std::endl;, etc.:** These are the code blocks executed for each case.
- **break;:** The break statement is crucial in switch statements. It terminates the execution of the switch block after a case is matched, preventing "fall-through" to the next case.
- **default::** The default case is optional. If provided, it is executed if none of the preceding case values match dayNumber. It's often used to handle invalid or unexpected input values.

3.2 Loops

Loops are control flow structures that enable programs to repeatedly execute a block of code as long as a certain condition remains true, or for a specified number of iterations. C++ offers several types of loops, each suited for different scenarios: for, while, do-while, and the range-based for loop (introduced in C++11).

3.2.1 for Loop: Iterating a Known Number of Times

The for loop is typically used when you know in advance how many times you need to iterate. It consists of three parts: initialization, condition, and increment/decrement, all within the loop header.

Example: for Loop for Counting

Imagine you need to print numbers from 1 to 10. A for loop is a straightforward way to achieve this.

```
C++
#include <iostream>

int main() {
    for (int i = 1; i <= 10; ++i) {
        std::cout << i << " ";
    }
    std::cout << std::endl;

    return 0;
}
```

Step-by-step explanation:

1. for (int i = 1; i <= 10; ++i) { ... }: This is the for loop header.
   - int i = 1; **(Initialization)**: This part is executed only once at the beginning of the loop. It declares and initializes a loop counter variable i to 1.
   - i <= 10; **(Condition)**: This condition is checked before each iteration. As long as i is less than or equal to 10, the loop body will execute.
   - ++i **(Increment/Decrement)**: This part is executed after each iteration of the loop body. ++i increments the value of i by 1.
2. std::cout << i << " ";: This is the loop body. In each iteration, it prints the current value of i followed by a space.

3.2.2 while Loop: Iterating Based on a Condition

The while loop repeatedly executes a block of code as long as a specified condition is true. Unlike the for loop, the while loop is typically used when the number of iterations is not known in advance, and the loop continues until a certain condition is met.

Example: while Loop for User Input Validation

Consider a scenario where you need to repeatedly prompt the user for input until they enter a valid value. A while loop is suitable for this input validation.

```
C++
#include <iostream>

int main() {
  int number;
  bool isValidInput = false;

  while (!isValidInput) {
    std::cout << "Enter a positive integer: ";
    std::cin >> number;

    if (number > 0) {
      isValidInput = true;
    } else {
      std::cout << "Invalid input. Please enter a positive integer." <<
std::endl;
    }
```

```
    }

    std::cout << "You entered: " << number << std::endl;

    return 0;
}
```

Step-by-step explanation:

1. **bool isValidInput = false;**: Initializes a boolean variable isValidInput to false. This variable controls the loop.
2. **while (!isValidInput) { ... }**: This is the while loop. The loop continues to execute as long as the condition !isValidInput (not isValidInput) is true. Initially, isValidInput is false, so !isValidInput is true, and the loop starts.
3. **std::cout << "Enter a positive integer: ";**: Prompts the user for input inside the loop.
4. **std::cin >> number;**: Reads the user's input.
5. **if (number > 0) { isValidInput = true; } else { ... }**: Checks if the entered number is positive.
    - **if (number > 0) { isValidInput = true; }**: If number is positive, isValidInput is set to true. In the next loop condition check, !isValidInput will be false, and the loop will terminate.
    - **else { ... }**: If number is not positive, an error message is displayed, and isValidInput remains false, causing the loop to iterate again, prompting for input again.

3.2.3 do-while Loop: Ensuring at Least One Iteration

The do-while loop is similar to the while loop, but with a crucial difference: the condition is checked *after* the loop body is executed. This guarantees that the loop body is executed at least once, regardless of the initial state of the condition.

Example: do-while Loop for Menu Display

Consider a menu-driven program where you want to display the menu options at least once before checking if the user wants to continue. A do-while loop is suitable for this scenario.

```
C++
#include <iostream>

int main() {
  char choice;

  do {
    std::cout << "\nMenu:" << std::endl;
    std::cout << "1. Option 1" << std::endl;
    std::cout << "2. Option 2" << std::endl;
    std::cout << "3. Exit" << std::endl;
    std::cout << "Enter your choice (1-3): ";
    std::cin >> choice;

    // Process choice (example - could be a switch statement)
    if (choice == '1') {
      std::cout << "Option 1 selected." << std::endl;
    } else if (choice == '2') {
      std::cout << "Option 2 selected." << std::endl;
    } else if (choice == '3') {
      std::cout << "Exiting." << std::endl;
    } else {
      std::cout << "Invalid choice." << std::endl;
    }

  } while (choice != '3'); // Loop continues as long as choice is not '3'

  return 0;
}
```

Step-by-step explanation:

1. **char choice;**: Declares a character variable choice to store the user's menu selection.
2. **do { ... } while (choice != '3');**: This is the do-while loop.
   - **do { ... }**: The code block within the do block is executed at least once, before the condition is checked. This block displays the menu and prompts for user input.
   - **while (choice != '3');**: After the loop body executes, the condition choice != '3' is checked. As long as choice is not equal to '3', the loop continues to iterate, displaying the menu again. If choice is '3', the condition becomes false, and the loop terminates.

3.2.4 Range-Based for Loop (C++11+): Iterating Over Collections

Introduced in C++11, the range-based for loop provides a simplified and more readable way to iterate over elements in collections like arrays, vectors, and other containers. It abstracts away the complexities of iterators and index management, making code cleaner and less error-prone. As Meyers points out, range-based for loops enhance code clarity and reduce the chance of off-by-one errors common in traditional loop constructs (Meyers, 2014).

Example: Range-Based for Loop for Vector Iteration

Imagine you have a vector of numbers and you want to process each number. A range-based for loop simplifies this iteration.

```
C++
#include <iostream>
#include <vector>

int main() {
  std::vector<int> numbers = {10, 20, 30, 40, 50};

  for (int number : numbers) { // Range-based for loop
    std::cout << number << " ";
  }
  std::cout << std::endl;

  return 0;
}
```

Step-by-step explanation:

1. **std::vector<int> numbers = {10, 20, 30, 40, 50};**: Creates a std::vector named numbers and initializes it with integer values.
2. **for (int number : numbers) { ... }**: This is the range-based for loop.
    - **int number**: Declares a loop variable number of type int. In each iteration, number will take on the value of the current element in the numbers collection.
    - **: numbers**: Specifies the range to iterate over, which is the numbers vector in this case.
    - In each iteration, the loop automatically retrieves the next element from the numbers vector and assigns it to number, then executes the loop body. This continues for all elements in numbers.

3.3 Functions

Functions are fundamental building blocks of modular and reusable code in C++. A function is a self-contained block of code that performs a specific task. Functions help in breaking down complex programs into smaller, more manageable, and reusable units, improving code organization, readability, and maintainability.

3.3.1 Function Declaration and Definition

A function in C++ must be declared before it can be used. The declaration, also known as the function prototype, specifies the function's name, return type, and parameters. The definition provides the actual implementation of the function—the code that is executed when the function is called. Separating declaration from definition allows the compiler to know about the function's interface before encountering its implementation, which is crucial for modular programming and separate compilation.

Example: Function Declaration and Definition

```
C++
#include <iostream>

// Function declaration (prototype)
int add(int a, int b);

int main() {
    int sum = add(5, 3); // Function call
    std::cout << "Sum: " << sum << std::endl;
    return 0;
}

// Function definition
int add(int a, int b) {
    return a + b;
}
```

Step-by-step explanation:

1. **// Function declaration (prototype)**: This comment indicates the function declaration section.
2. **int add(int a, int b);**: This is the function declaration or prototype.
    - **int**: Specifies the return type of the function (it returns an integer).
    - **add**: Is the name of the function.
    - **(int a, int b)**: Specifies the parameter list. The function takes two integer parameters, a and b.
    - The semicolon ; at the end signifies that this is a declaration, not a definition.
3. **int sum = add(5, 3);**: This line in main calls the add function with arguments 5 and 3. The return value from add is stored in the sum variable.
4. **// Function definition**: Comment indicating the function definition section.
5. **int add(int a, int b) { ... }**: This is the function definition. It provides the actual implementation of the add function.
    - The header int add(int a, int b) is the same as the declaration (except for the semicolon).
    - The code block { return a + b; } is the function body. It calculates the sum of a and b and returns the result using the return statement.

3.3.2 Function Overloading: Multiple Functions with the Same Name

C++ supports function overloading, which allows you to define multiple functions with the same name but different parameter lists (different number of parameters, or different types of parameters, or different order of parameter types). The compiler distinguishes between overloaded functions based on the arguments passed during the function call. Function overloading enhances code flexibility and readability by allowing you to use the same function name for operations that are conceptually similar but operate on different data types. As Stroustrup explains, overloading is a key feature of C++ that supports polymorphism and simplifies the interface for users of a class or a set of related functions (Stroustrup, 1994).

Example: Function Overloading for add Function
Consider a scenario where you need to add both integers and doubles. Function overloading allows you to use the same function name add for both operations.

```
C++
#include <iostream>

// Overloaded functions named 'add'
int add(int a, int b) {
    std::cout << "Adding integers: ";
    return a + b;
}

double add(double a, double b) {
    std::cout << "Adding doubles: ";
    return a + b;
}

int main() {
    int sumInt = add(5, 3);        // Calls add(int, int)
    double sumDouble = add(5.5, 3.3); // Calls add(double, double)

    std::cout << sumInt << std::endl;
    std::cout << sumDouble << std::endl;
    return 0;
}
```

Step-by-step explanation:

1. **int add(int a, int b) { ... }**: Defines the first version of the add function, which takes two integer parameters and returns an integer sum.
2. **double add(double a, double b) { ... }**: Defines the second version of the add function, also named add, but it takes two double parameters and returns a double sum. The parameter lists are different (different types), so this is a valid overload.
3. **int sumInt = add(5, 3);**: When add(5, 3) is called, the compiler selects the add(int, int) function because the arguments 5 and 3 are integers.
4. **double sumDouble = add(5.5, 3.3);**: When add(5.5, 3.3) is called, the compiler selects the add(double, double) function because the arguments 5.5 and 3.3 are doubles.
5. The output shows that the correct overloaded function is called based on the argument types, and the appropriate "Adding integers" or "Adding doubles" message is printed.

3.3.3 Default Arguments: Providing Optional Parameters

Default arguments allow you to specify default values for function parameters in the function declaration. When calling a function with default arguments, you can omit arguments for parameters that have default values. If you omit an argument, the default value is used. Default arguments provide flexibility in function calls and can simplify function interfaces, especially for functions with many parameters where some parameters often take on the same value.

Example: Function with Default Arguments

Consider a function to greet a user, where the greeting message can be customized, but a default message is available if no custom message is provided.

```
C++
#include <iostream>
#include <string>

// Function with a default argument for greeting message
void greet(std::string name, std::string message = "Hello") {
    std::cout << message << ", " << name << "!" << std::endl;
```

```
}

int main() {
  greet("Alice");         // Uses default message "Hello"
  greet("Bob", "Good morning"); // Uses custom message "Good morning"
  return 0;
}
```

Step-by-step explanation:

1. **void greet(std::string name, std::string message = "Hello") { ... }:** Defines the greet function.
   - **std::string message = "Hello":** Specifies a default argument for the message parameter. If no value is provided for message when calling greet, it will default to "Hello".
2. **greet("Alice");:** Calls greet with only one argument, "Alice". The message parameter is omitted, so it takes its default value "Hello".
3. **greet("Bob", "Good morning");:** Calls greet with two arguments. "Bob" is passed for name, and "Good morning" is passed for message, overriding the default message.

3.3.4 Inline Functions: Suggesting Compiler Optimization

Inline functions are a compiler directive to request the compiler to replace a function call with the actual function code at the point of call, rather than performing a function call. This can potentially improve performance by reducing function call overhead, especially for small, frequently called functions. However, the compiler is not obligated to inline a function, and may choose not to inline it based on various factors like function complexity and optimization settings. As Sutter and Alexandrescu advise, inline functions should be used judiciously, primarily for very small, performance-critical functions (Sutter & Alexandrescu, 2005).

Example: Inline Function for Square Calculation
Consider a simple function to calculate the square of a number, which is a good candidate for inlining due to its simplicity and potential frequency of use.

```
C++
#include <iostream>

// Inline function to calculate square
inline int square(int n) {
    return n * n;
}

int main() {
    int result = square(7); // Inline function call (compiler may inline)
    std::cout << "Square: " << result << std::endl;
    return 0;
}
```

Step-by-step explanation:

1. **inline int square(int n) { ... }**: Defines an inline function square. The inline keyword is a request to the compiler to consider inlining this function.
2. **int result = square(7);**: When square(7) is called, the compiler *may* replace this call with the actual code of the square function, effectively making the code as if it were written directly as int result = 7 * 7;. Whether inlining actually happens is up to the compiler's optimization decisions.

3.3.5 Lambda Expressions (C++11+): Anonymous Functions

Lambda expressions, introduced in C++11, provide a way to create anonymous functions—functions without a name—directly within the code where they are needed. Lambdas are particularly useful for short, localized operations, often used with algorithms from the Standard Library or as callbacks. They enhance code conciseness and expressiveness, especially when dealing with functional programming paradigms in C++. As Josuttis notes in "C++ Standard Library Tutorial and Reference," lambda expressions are a powerful addition to C++, enabling more functional style programming and simplifying many common programming tasks (Josuttis, 2012).

Example: Lambda Expression for Sorting with a Custom Comparator

Imagine you need to sort a vector of pairs based on the second element of each pair. A lambda expression can be used to define a custom comparison function inline for the sorting algorithm.

```
C++
#include <iostream>
#include <vector>
#include <algorithm> // Required for std::sort
#include <string>    // Required for std::string and std::pair

int main() {
   std::vector<std::pair<std::string, int>> items = {
      {"ItemA", 30},
      {"ItemB", 10},
      {"ItemC", 20}
   };

   // Sort items based on the second element of the pair (integer value) using a
lambda expression
   std::sort(items.begin(), items.end(), [](const std::pair<std::string, int>& a,
const std::pair<std::string, int>& b) {
      return a.second < b.second; // Compare based on the second element
   });

   std::cout << "Sorted items based on value:" << std::endl;
   for (const auto& item : items) {
      std::cout << item.first << ": " << item.second << std::endl;
   }

   return 0;
}
```

Step-by-step explanation:

1. **std::vector<std::pair<std::string, int>> items = { ... };**: Creates a vector of pairs, where each pair contains a std::string (item name) and an int (item value).
2. **std::sort(items.begin(), items.end(), [](const std::pair<std::string, int>& a, const std::pair<std::string, int>& b) { ... });**: Calls the std::sort algorithm to sort the items vector.
   - **items.begin(), items.end()**: Specify the range to be sorted (from the beginning to the end of the items vector).

- [](const std::pair<std::string, int>& a, const std::pair<std::string, int>& b) { ... }: This is the lambda expression. It is passed as the third argument to std::sort to provide a custom comparison function.
    - [] **(Capture list)**: In this case, the capture list is empty [], meaning the lambda does not capture any variables from its surrounding scope.
    - (const std::pair<std::string, int>& a, const std::pair<std::string, int>& b) **(Parameter list)**: Defines the parameters for the lambda function. It takes two constant references to std::pair<std::string, int> objects, named a and b.
    - { return a.second < b.second; } **(Lambda body)**: The body of the lambda function. It compares the second elements (.second) of the two pairs a and b. It returns true if a.second is less than b.second, indicating that a should come before b in the sorted order.

3. The loop then prints the sorted items, demonstrating that they are now sorted based on their integer values (second element of the pairs).

By understanding and utilizing conditional statements, loops, and functions effectively, you gain the ability to control the flow of your C++ programs and organize your code into reusable and modular components. These control flow and function constructs are fundamental to writing robust, efficient, and maintainable C++ applications. As you advance in your C++ studies, these concepts will be indispensable tools in your programming arsenal.

Chapter 4

Pointers and Memory Management

Pointers and memory management are among the most critical and often challenging aspects of C++ programming. Mastering these concepts is essential for writing efficient, robust, and performant applications, especially in system-level programming, game development, and high-performance computing. This section provides a detailed exploration of pointers and memory management in C++, tailored for Computer Technology students and educators. We will begin with the fundamentals of pointers, progress to dynamic memory allocation using `new` and `delete`, introduce smart pointers as a modern solution for memory management, discuss Resource Acquisition Is Initialization (RAII), and finally address memory leaks and debugging tools. Through real-world analogies, practical examples, and step-by-step guides, this discussion aims to demystify these complex topics and equip you with the knowledge and skills to manage memory effectively in your C++ programs.

4.1 Basics of Pointers

Pointers are a powerful feature in C++ that provide direct memory access. Understanding pointers is crucial for grasping dynamic memory allocation and many advanced C++ concepts. A pointer is a variable that stores the memory address of another variable. Think of a pointer as an address in the real world; just as an address tells you where a house is located, a pointer tells you where a variable is located in memory.

4.1.1 Declaring Pointers

To declare a pointer, you use the asterisk * symbol along with the data type that the pointer will point to. The syntax is dataType *pointerName;. For example, int *ptr; declares a pointer named ptr that can store the address of an integer variable. It's important to note that the pointer itself is a variable that occupies memory, and its data type (e.g., int*) specifies the type of data it points to, not the type of the pointer itself. As Josuttis notes in "C++ Standard Library Tutorial and Reference," the type of the pointer is crucial for pointer arithmetic and dereferencing (Josuttis, 2012).

Example: Pointer Declaration and Initialization

```
C++
#include <iostream>

int main() {
    int number = 10; // Declare an integer variable
    int *ptr;        // Declare a pointer to an integer

    ptr = &number;  // Initialize ptr with the address of number

    std::cout << "Value of number: " << number << std::endl;
    std::cout << "Address of number: " << &number << std::endl;
    std::cout << "Value of ptr: " << ptr << std::endl;
    std::cout << "Value pointed to by ptr: " << *ptr << std::endl;

    return 0;
}
```

Step-by-step explanation:

1. **int number = 10;**: Declares an integer variable number and initializes it with the value 10.
2. **int *ptr;**: Declares a pointer variable named ptr that is intended to point to an integer. At this point, ptr is uninitialized and does not point to any valid memory location.
3. **ptr = &number;**: This line initializes ptr with the address of number. The & operator is the address-of operator, which returns the memory address of number. Now, ptr holds the memory address where number is stored.
4. **std::cout << "Address of number: " << &number << std::endl;**: Prints the memory address of the number variable using the & operator.
5. **std::cout << "Value of ptr: " << ptr << std::endl;**: Prints the value stored in ptr, which is the memory address of number. You will observe that this address is the same as the address of number printed in the previous line.
6. **std::cout << "Value pointed to by ptr: " << *ptr << std::endl;**: Prints the value at the memory location pointed to by ptr. The * operator, when used with a pointer, is the dereference operator. It accesses the value stored at the memory address held by the pointer. In this case, *ptr accesses the value of number, which is 10.

4.1.2 Dereferencing and Address-of Operator

As demonstrated in the example, C++ provides two key operators for working with pointers: the address-of operator (&) and the dereference operator (*).

- **Address-of Operator (&):** When placed before a variable name, the & operator returns the memory address of that variable. For example, &number gives the memory address of the variable number.
- **Dereference Operator (*):** When placed before a pointer variable, the * operator accesses the value stored at the memory address held by the pointer. For example, if ptr holds the address of number, then *ptr gives the value of number.

Understanding the distinction between these operators is crucial for effectively using pointers. The address-of operator gets you the memory location, while the dereference operator gets you the value at that location.

4.2 Dynamic Memory Allocation (new and delete)

Dynamic memory allocation is a powerful feature in C++ that allows you to allocate memory during program execution (run-time) rather than at compile time. This is particularly useful when you don't know the size of memory you will need in advance, such as when dealing with user input, variable-sized data structures, or objects created based on runtime conditions. C++ provides the new and delete operators for dynamic memory management.

4.2.1 new Operator: Allocating Memory

The new operator is used to allocate memory dynamically from the heap. When you use new, it reserves a block of memory of the specified size and returns a pointer to the beginning of that block. If memory allocation is successful, new returns a valid pointer; if it fails (e.g., due to insufficient memory), it throws a std::bad_alloc exception (or returns a null pointer in older versions of C++ or when using new(std::nothrow)). As Stroustrup emphasizes in "The C++ Programming Language," dynamic memory allocation is essential for creating flexible and adaptable programs, but it also introduces the responsibility of manual memory management (Stroustrup, 2013).

Example: Dynamic Memory Allocation using new

```
C++
#include <iostream>

int main() {
  int *dynamicNumberPtr;

  dynamicNumberPtr = new int; // Dynamically allocate memory for an
integer

  if (dynamicNumberPtr == nullptr) { // Check if allocation failed (important
in older C++ standards, less critical in modern C++)
      std::cerr << "Memory allocation failed!" << std::endl;
      return 1; // Indicate error
  }
```

```
    *dynamicNumberPtr = 25; // Assign value to the dynamically allocated
integer

    std::cout << "Value at dynamic memory: " << *dynamicNumberPtr <<
std::endl;
    std::cout << "Address of dynamic memory: " << dynamicNumberPtr <<
std::endl;

    // Memory deallocation using delete is needed later

    return 0;
}
```

Step-by-step explanation:

1. **int *dynamicNumberPtr;**: Declares a pointer dynamicNumberPtr to an integer.
2. **dynamicNumberPtr = new int;**: This is where dynamic memory allocation happens. new int allocates enough memory to store an integer from the heap and returns a pointer to this newly allocated memory. This pointer is then assigned to dynamicNumberPtr.
3. **if (dynamicNumberPtr == nullptr) { ... }**: This is a crucial error check, especially in older C++ standards. After new in older standards, if memory allocation fails, it might return a null pointer. Checking for nullptr (or NULL in older code) ensures that you handle potential allocation failures gracefully. In modern C++, new throws an exception on failure, but checking for nullptr is still good practice for robustness, especially when dealing with external libraries or older code.
4. ***dynamicNumberPtr = 25;**: Dereferences dynamicNumberPtr to access the dynamically allocated memory and assigns the value 25 to it.
5. The code then prints the value and address of the dynamically allocated memory.
6. **// Memory deallocation using delete is needed later**: This comment is a critical reminder. Memory allocated with new must be explicitly deallocated using delete to prevent memory leaks. This is the responsibility of the programmer when using new and delete.

4.2.2 delete Operator: Deallocating Memory

The delete operator is used to deallocate memory that was previously allocated using new. When you are finished using dynamically allocated memory, you *must* use delete to free it back to the heap. Failing to do so results in memory leaks, where allocated memory is no longer accessible to the program but is not returned to the system, leading to resource exhaustion over time. It's essential to pair every new with a corresponding delete to ensure proper memory management.

Example: Dynamic Memory Allocation and Deallocation
Extending the previous example, let's add memory deallocation using delete.

```
C++
#include <iostream>

int main() {
  int *dynamicNumberPtr = new int; // Dynamically allocate memory

  if (dynamicNumberPtr == nullptr) {
    std::cerr << "Memory allocation failed!" << std::endl;
    return 1;
  }

  *dynamicNumberPtr = 25;
  std::cout << "Value at dynamic memory: " << *dynamicNumberPtr <<
std::endl;

  delete dynamicNumberPtr; // Deallocate the dynamically allocated memory
  dynamicNumberPtr = nullptr; // Good practice: set pointer to nullptr after
delete

  // dynamicNumberPtr is now a dangling pointer if not set to nullptr.
Dereferencing it after delete is undefined behavior.

  return 0;
}
```

Step-by-step explanation:

1. The code is similar to the previous example, allocating memory with new and assigning a value.

2. **delete dynamicNumberPtr;**: This line is crucial. It deallocates the memory that dynamicNumberPtr was pointing to, freeing it back to the heap. After this line, the memory block is no longer considered allocated to the program.
3. **dynamicNumberPtr = nullptr;**: This is a best practice after using delete. Setting dynamicNumberPtr to nullptr explicitly makes it clear that the pointer is no longer pointing to valid memory. This helps prevent accidental dangling pointer dereferences. A dangling pointer is a pointer that points to memory that has been deallocated. Dereferencing a dangling pointer leads to undefined behavior, which can cause crashes, data corruption, or unpredictable program behavior.

4.3 Smart Pointers

Manual memory management using new and delete is error-prone and can lead to memory leaks, dangling pointers, and other memory-related issues. To address these problems, C++ introduced smart pointers in C++11. Smart pointers are RAII wrappers around raw pointers that automatically manage memory deallocation. They ensure that dynamically allocated memory is automatically freed when the smart pointer goes out of scope, thus preventing memory leaks and reducing the burden of manual memory management. C++ provides several types of smart pointers, including unique_ptr, shared_ptr, and weak_ptr, each with different ownership semantics.

4.3.1 unique_ptr: Exclusive Ownership

unique_ptr provides exclusive ownership of dynamically allocated memory. This means that only one unique_ptr can point to a given memory location at any time. When a unique_ptr goes out of scope, the memory it manages is automatically deallocated. unique_ptr is lightweight and efficient, and it is the preferred smart pointer for exclusive ownership scenarios. As Meyers recommends, prefer unique_ptr by default for single ownership because of its efficiency and clear ownership semantics (Meyers, 2014).

Example: unique_ptr for Exclusive Ownership

```
C++
#include <iostream>
#include <memory> // Required for smart pointers

int main() {
   std::unique_ptr<int> uniquePtr(new int); // Create a unique_ptr managing
dynamically allocated int

   if (uniquePtr == nullptr) { // unique_ptr will not be nullptr after successful
allocation, nullptr check is not strictly necessary here.
      std::cerr << "Memory allocation failed!" << std::endl;
      return 1;
   }

   *uniquePtr = 42;
   std::cout << "Value managed by unique_ptr: " << *uniquePtr << std::endl;

   // Memory is automatically deallocated when uniquePtr goes out of scope at
the end of main()

   return 0;
}
```

Step-by-step explanation:

1. **#include <memory>**: Includes the <memory> header, which defines smart pointer classes like unique_ptr.
2. **std::unique_ptr<int> uniquePtr(new int);**: Creates a unique_ptr named uniquePtr that manages a dynamically allocated integer.
   - std::unique_ptr<int>: Specifies that uniquePtr is a smart pointer that will manage an integer.
   - (new int): Dynamically allocates memory for an integer using new int. The pointer returned by new int is then passed to the unique_ptr constructor. The unique_ptr now takes ownership of this dynamically allocated memory.
3. **if (uniquePtr == nullptr) { ... }**: While unique_ptr itself won't be nullptr after successful allocation, checking for null after new int *before* constructing the unique_ptr was a common pattern in older C++ when new could return null. In modern C++, new throws an exception on allocation failure, making this null check less critical *for the unique_ptr itself*. However, if you were

to handle the raw pointer before constructing the unique_ptr, such a check could be relevant. In this example, it's included for illustrative purposes and for robustness in potentially older or error-handling contexts.

4. ***uniquePtr = 42;**: Dereferences uniquePtr to access the managed integer and assigns the value 42.
5. **// Memory is automatically deallocated when uniquePtr goes out of scope at the end of main()**: This is the key benefit of unique_ptr. When uniquePtr goes out of scope (at the end of the main function in this case), its destructor is automatically called. The destructor of unique_ptr automatically deallocates the memory it manages using delete. You do not need to explicitly call delete.

Transferring Ownership with std::move

Because unique_ptr represents exclusive ownership, you cannot copy a unique_ptr. However, you can transfer ownership to another unique_ptr using std::move. std::move transfers ownership from one unique_ptr to another, leaving the source unique_ptr in a valid but empty state (it no longer manages any memory).

Example: Moving unique_ptr Ownership

```
C++
#include <iostream>
#include <memory>

std::unique_ptr<int> createUniquePtr() {
  std::unique_ptr<int> localPtr(new int(100));
  return localPtr; // Ownership is moved when returning
}

int main() {
  std::unique_ptr<int> ptr1 = createUniquePtr(); // Ownership moved from
localPtr to ptr1
  std::cout << "Value in ptr1: " << *ptr1 << std::endl;

  std::unique_ptr<int> ptr2 = std::move(ptr1); // Ownership moved from
ptr1 to ptr2
  std::cout << "Value in ptr2: " << *ptr2 << std::endl;
  // std::cout << "Value in ptr1 after move: " << *ptr1 << std::endl; //
Error: ptr1 is now empty, dereferencing would be undefined behavior.
```

```
    // Memory managed by ptr2 will be deallocated when ptr2 goes out of scope

    return 0;
}
```

Step-by-step explanation:

1. **std::unique_ptr<int> createUniquePtr() { ... }**: Defines a function createUniquePtr that creates a unique_ptr and returns it.
2. **std::unique_ptr<int> localPtr(new int(100));**: Inside createUniquePtr, a unique_ptr localPtr is created, managing a dynamically allocated integer initialized to 100.
3. **return localPtr;**: When localPtr is returned, ownership of the managed memory is *moved* to the receiving unique_ptr in main. localPtr is no longer managing the memory after the return.
4. **std::unique_ptr<int> ptr1 = createUniquePtr();**: In main, ptr1 receives the unique_ptr returned by createUniquePtr. Ownership is transferred from localPtr to ptr1.
5. **std::unique_ptr<int> ptr2 = std::move(ptr1);**: std::move(ptr1) explicitly moves ownership from ptr1 to ptr2. After this move, ptr1 becomes empty and no longer manages the memory. ptr2 now owns the memory.
6. **// std::cout << "Value in ptr1 after move: " << *ptr1 << std::endl;**: This line is commented out because attempting to dereference ptr1 after the move is undefined behavior. ptr1 is now in a valid but empty state.

4.3.2 shared_ptr: Shared Ownership

shared_ptr provides shared ownership of dynamically allocated memory. Multiple shared_ptrs can point to the same memory location, and the memory is deallocated only when the last shared_ptr pointing to it goes out of scope. shared_ptr uses reference counting to track the number of shared_ptrs sharing ownership. When the reference count drops to zero, the memory is automatically deleted. shared_ptr is useful in scenarios where multiple parts of a program need to share ownership of a resource, such as in complex data structures or concurrent programming. As Abrahams and Gurtovoy explain in "C++ Template Metaprogramming," shared_ptr facilitates resource management in complex ownership scenarios, but it's important to be mindful of potential overhead and circular dependencies (Abrahams & Gurtovoy, 2004).

Example: shared_ptr for Shared Ownership

```
C++
#include <iostream>
#include <memory>

void useSharedPtr(std::shared_ptr<int> ptr) {
  std::cout << "Value inside function: " << *ptr << std::endl;
  std::cout << "Reference count inside function: " << ptr.use_count() <<
std::endl;
} // ptr goes out of scope here, reference count decreases

int main() {
  std::shared_ptr<int> sharedPtr1 = std::make_shared<int>(50); // Create a
shared_ptr using make_shared (recommended)
  std::cout << "Initial reference count: " << sharedPtr1.use_count() <<
std::endl;

  std::shared_ptr<int> sharedPtr2 = sharedPtr1; // Copy shared_ptr,
ownership is shared
  std::cout << "Reference count after copy: " << sharedPtr1.use_count() <<
std::endl;

  useSharedPtr(sharedPtr1); // Pass shared_ptr to a function, ownership is
shared
  std::cout << "Reference count after function call: " <<
sharedPtr1.use_count() << std::endl;

  // sharedPtr1 and sharedPtr2 go out of scope, reference count decreases,
memory deallocated when count reaches zero.

  return 0;
}
```

Step-by-step explanation:

1. **#include <memory>**: Includes the <memory> header for smart pointers.
2. **std::shared_ptr<int> sharedPtr1 = std::make_shared<int>(50);**: Creates a shared_ptr named sharedPtr1 managing a dynamically allocated integer initialized to 50. std::make_shared is generally recommended over std::shared_ptr<int>(new int(50)) for efficiency and exception safety.

3. **std::cout << "Initial reference count: " << sharedPtr1.use_count() << std::endl;**: sharedPtr1.use_count() returns the current reference count for the managed memory. Initially, it is 1 because only sharedPtr1 owns the memory.
4. **std::shared_ptr<int> sharedPtr2 = sharedPtr1;**: Copies sharedPtr1 to sharedPtr2. This does *not* create a copy of the managed integer. Instead, both sharedPtr1 and sharedPtr2 now point to the *same* dynamically allocated integer, and the reference count is incremented.
5. **std::cout << "Reference count after copy: " << sharedPtr1.use_count() << std::endl;**: The reference count is now 2 because two shared_ptrs share ownership.
6. **useSharedPtr(sharedPtr1);**: Calls the useSharedPtr function, passing sharedPtr1 as an argument. Inside useSharedPtr, the parameter ptr also shares ownership of the memory.
7. **std::cout << "Reference count inside function: " << ptr.use_count() << std::endl;**: Inside useSharedPtr, the reference count is 3 because sharedPtr1, sharedPtr2, and ptr (inside the function) all share ownership.
8. **// ptr goes out of scope here, reference count decreases**: When useSharedPtr returns, the local shared_ptr parameter ptr goes out of scope. Its destructor is called, and the reference count is decremented.
9. **std::cout << "Reference count after function call: " << sharedPtr1.use_count() << std::endl;**: Back in main, after the function call, the reference count is back to 2 because ptr is no longer in scope.
10. **// sharedPtr1 and sharedPtr2 go out of scope, reference count decreases, memory deallocated when count reaches zero.**: When sharedPtr1 and sharedPtr2 go out of scope at the end of main, their destructors are called. The reference count is decremented twice, eventually reaching zero. When the reference count becomes zero, the memory managed by the shared_ptr is automatically deallocated using delete.
11.

Circular Dependencies and weak_ptr

While shared_ptr is powerful, it can lead to issues with circular dependencies. If two or more objects own shared_ptrs to each other, their reference counts may never reach zero, even if they are no longer accessible from the rest of the program, causing a memory leak. weak_ptr is designed to break such circular dependencies.

4.3.3 weak_ptr: Non-Owning Reference

weak_ptr is a smart pointer that provides a non-owning, "weak" reference to an object managed by a shared_ptr. A weak_ptr does not increment the reference count and does not prevent the managed object from being deallocated when the last shared_ptr goes out of scope. weak_ptr is typically used to observe an object managed by shared_ptr without participating in ownership, often to break circular dependencies or to check if an object still exists before accessing it. As Meyers advises, use weak_ptr to break cycles of shared_ptrs and to observe objects without extending their lifetime (Meyers, 2014).

Example: weak_ptr to Break Circular Dependency
Consider a scenario where class A and class B have shared_ptrs to each other, creating a circular dependency. Using weak_ptr in one direction can break this cycle.

```
C++
#include <iostream>
#include <memory>

class B; // Forward declaration of class B

class A {
public:
  std::shared_ptr<B> bPtr; // A owns a shared_ptr to B
  ~A() { std::cout << "A destructor called" << std::endl; }
};

class B {
public:
  std::weak_ptr<A> aPtr; // B holds a weak_ptr to A (non-owning)
  ~B() { std::cout << "B destructor called" << std::endl; }
};

int main() {
  std::shared_ptr<A> a = std::make_shared<A>();
  std::shared_ptr<B> b = std::make_shared<B>();

  a->bPtr = b;
  b->aPtr = a; // Circular dependency created

  // a and b go out of scope, destructors will be called because weak_ptr
doesn't prevent deallocation.
```

```
    return 0;
}
```

Step-by-step explanation:

1. **class B;**: Forward declaration of class B is needed because class A refers to B before B is fully defined.
2. **class A { public: std::shared_ptr<B> bPtr; ... };**: Class A has a shared_ptr member bPtr that points to an object of type B. This represents ownership from A to B.
3. **class B { public: std::weak_ptr<A> aPtr; ... };**: Class B has a weak_ptr member aPtr that points to an object of type A. Crucially, weak_ptr does *not* represent ownership from B to A.
4. **std::shared_ptr<A> a = std::make_shared<A>();, std::shared_ptr<B> b = std::make_shared<B>();**: Creates shared_ptrs a and b managing objects of type A and B respectively.
5. **a->bPtr = b;, b->aPtr = a;**: Creates the circular dependency. a points to b via a shared_ptr, and b points back to a via a weak_ptr. 6. **// a and b go out of scope, destructors will be called because weak_ptr doesn't prevent deallocation.**: When a and b go out of scope at the end of main, their destructors are called, and the destructors of objects of class A and B are also called. This is because the weak_ptr from B to A does not contribute to the reference count, so the reference counts of both objects eventually become zero, allowing for deallocation. If b->aPtr were also a shared_ptr, the reference counts would never reach zero due to the circular ownership, and the destructors would not be called, leading to a memory leak.

Using weak_ptr::lock() to Access the Managed Object

Because weak_ptr is non-owning and does not prevent deallocation, the object it points to might be deleted. To safely access the object pointed to by a weak_ptr, you must convert it to a shared_ptr using the lock() method. lock() returns a shared_ptr that shares ownership of the object if the object still exists. If the object has been deleted, lock() returns a null shared_ptr.

Example: Using weak_ptr::lock()

C++

```
#include <iostream>
#include <memory>

int main() {
    std::shared_ptr<int> sharedPtr = std::make_shared<int>(100);
    std::weak_ptr<int> weakPtr = sharedPtr; // Create a weak_ptr pointing to
the same memory

    {
        std::shared_ptr<int> lockedPtr = weakPtr.lock(); // Try to lock weak_ptr
to get a shared_ptr
        if (lockedPtr) { // Check if lock was successful (object still exists)
            std::cout << "Value from locked weak_ptr: " << *lockedPtr <<
std::endl;
        } else {
            std::cout << "Object no longer exists." << std::endl;
        }
    } // lockedPtr goes out of scope here, but sharedPtr and weakPtr still exist

    sharedPtr.reset(); // Release ownership of sharedPtr, object might be deleted
if no other shared_ptr owns it.

    {
        std::shared_ptr<int> lockedPtr = weakPtr.lock(); // Try to lock weak_ptr
again after sharedPtr.reset()
        if (lockedPtr) {
            std::cout << "Value from locked weak_ptr (after reset): " <<
*lockedPtr << std::endl; // This will not be executed
        } else {
            std::cout << "Object no longer exists after sharedPtr reset." <<
std::endl; // This will be executed
        }
    }

    return 0;
}
```

Step-by-step explanation:

1. **std::shared_ptr<int> sharedPtr = std::make_shared<int>(100);:** Creates a shared_ptr sharedPtr managing an integer.
2. **std::weak_ptr<int> weakPtr = sharedPtr;:** Creates a weak_ptr weakPtr that points to the same memory as sharedPtr. Note that this does not increase the reference count.
3. **std::shared_ptr<int> lockedPtr = weakPtr.lock();:** Attempts to lock weakPtr to obtain a shared_ptr named lockedPtr. If the object

still exists (i.e., the reference count is greater than zero), lock() returns a valid shared_ptr that shares ownership. If the object has been deleted, lock() returns a null shared_ptr.

4. **if (lockedPtr) { ... } else { ... }**: Checks if lockedPtr is not null (i.e., lock was successful). If successful, the value is accessed and printed.
5. **sharedPtr.reset();**: Explicitly releases ownership of sharedPtr. If weakPtr were the only remaining pointer (which it is in this example after sharedPtr is reset), the managed object would be deallocated at this point.
6. The second lock() attempt after sharedPtr.reset() will now fail because the object might have been deleted (in this case, it will be). The else block is executed, indicating that the object no longer exists.

4.4 RAII (Resource Acquisition Is Initialization)

Resource Acquisition Is Initialization (RAII) is a fundamental C++ programming idiom that ties resource management to object lifetime. In RAII, resources (like memory, file handles, network connections, mutexes, etc.) are acquired during object initialization and automatically released in the object's destructor. This ensures that resources are properly managed and released, even if exceptions occur, leading to more robust and exception-safe code. Smart pointers are a prime example of RAII in action for memory management. As Meyers highlights, RAII is a cornerstone of exception-safe C++ programming, ensuring resource leaks are minimized and code reliability is enhanced (Meyers, 2005).

Example: RAII with Smart Pointers for Memory Management
Smart pointers (unique_ptr, shared_ptr) embody the RAII principle for dynamic memory.

```
C++
#include <iostream>
#include <memory>
#include <fstream> // For file handling

class FileManager {
public:
```

```
    FileManager(const std::string& filename) : filePtr_(new
std::ofstream(filename)) {
        if (!filePtr_->is_open()) {
            throw std::runtime_error("Failed to open file: " + filename);
        }
        std::cout << "File opened successfully." << std::endl;
    }

    ~FileManager() {
        filePtr_->close(); // Resource release in destructor
        std::cout << "File closed." << std::endl;
    }

    void writeToFile(const std::string& data) {
        if (filePtr_->is_open()) {
            *filePtr_ << data << std::endl;
        } else {
            throw std::runtime_error("File is not open for writing.");
        }
    }

private:
    std::unique_ptr<std::ofstream> filePtr_; // unique_ptr manages file resource
(ofstream)
};

int main() {
    try {
        FileManager manager("output.txt"); // Resource acquired in constructor
        manager.writeToFile("Hello RAII!");
        manager.writeToFile("More data.");
        // File resource will be automatically released when manager goes out of
scope, even if exceptions occur after this point.
    } catch (const std::exception& e) {
        std::cerr << "Exception: " << e.what() << std::endl;
        return 1;
    }

    return 0;
} // Destructor of manager is called here, releasing file resource
```

Step-by-step explanation:

1. **#include <fstream>**: Includes the <fstream> header for file input/output operations.
2. **class FileManager { ... };**: Defines a class FileManager to manage file operations using RAII.

3. **std::unique_ptr<std::ofstream> filePtr_;**: FileManager uses a unique_ptr named filePtr_ to manage a dynamically allocated std::ofstream object. This is the RAII principle in action: the file resource (std::ofstream) is managed by a smart pointer.
4. **FileManager(const std::string& filename) : filePtr_(new std::ofstream(filename)) { ... }**: Constructor of FileManager.
   - **filePtr_(new std::ofstream(filename))**: In the constructor's initializer list, a new std::ofstream object is dynamically allocated to open the file specified by filename. The unique_ptr filePtr_ is initialized to manage this dynamically allocated std::ofstream object. Resource acquisition happens during object initialization.
   - **Error handling:** The constructor checks if the file was opened successfully using !filePtr_->is_open(). If not, it throws a std::runtime_error exception, preventing the object from being fully constructed if resource acquisition fails.
5. **~FileManager() { ... }**: Destructor of FileManager.
   - **filePtr_->close();**: In the destructor, the file is closed using filePtr_->close(). Resource release happens in the destructor. Because filePtr_ is a unique_ptr, the dynamically allocated std::ofstream object (and thus the file resource) will be automatically deallocated when the FileManager object is destroyed (when it goes out of scope or is explicitly deleted).
6. **writeToFile(const std::string& data)**: A member function to write data to the managed file.
7. **int main() { try { ... } catch (const std::exception& e) { ... } }**: The main function demonstrates the use of FileManager within a try-catch block to handle potential exceptions during file operations.
8. **FileManager manager("output.txt");**: Creates a FileManager object named manager. The constructor is called, attempting to open "output.txt". If successful, the file is opened and managed by manager.
9. **manager.writeToFile("Hello RAII!");, manager.writeToFile("More data.");**: Writes data to the file using the FileManager object.
10. **// File resource will be automatically released when manager goes out of scope...**: When manager goes out of scope at the end of the try block (or if an exception is thrown within the try

block), the destructor of manager is automatically called. This ensures that the file is closed and resources are released, regardless of whether exceptions occurred.

4.5 Memory Leaks and Debugging Tools (Valgrind, AddressSanitizer)

Memory leaks are a common and insidious problem in C++ programs that use dynamic memory allocation. A memory leak occurs when dynamically allocated memory is no longer reachable by the program but is not deallocated using delete. Over time, memory leaks can accumulate, leading to increased memory usage, performance degradation, and eventually program crashes. Detecting and fixing memory leaks is a crucial part of C++ development. Tools like Valgrind and AddressSanitizer are invaluable for identifying memory-related errors, including leaks.

4.5.1 Memory Leaks: Causes and Consequences

Memory leaks typically occur due to programmer errors in managing dynamically allocated memory. Common causes include:

- **Forgetting to use delete:** Allocating memory with new but not freeing it with delete when it's no longer needed.
- **Exceptions preventing delete:** If an exception is thrown between new and delete and not properly caught, the delete call might be skipped, leading to a leak. RAII (smart pointers) helps prevent this.
- **Lost pointers:** Overwriting a pointer variable that holds the address of dynamically allocated memory before deallocating it, making the memory unreachable.
- **Circular references with shared_ptr:** As discussed earlier, circular dependencies in shared_ptr ownership can prevent deallocation.

The consequences of memory leaks can range from gradual performance slowdown to application crashes, especially in long-running programs or systems with limited memory resources.

4.5.2 Valgrind: Memory Error Detector

Valgrind is a powerful, open-source memory debugging and profiling tool. It can detect a wide range of memory errors, including memory leaks, invalid memory accesses (e.g., reading or writing freed memory, accessing memory outside allocated blocks), and thread errors. Valgrind runs your program in a virtual environment and monitors memory operations, providing detailed reports of errors. It is widely used on Linux and macOS platforms. As Turner notes in "Effective Performance Engineering," Valgrind is an indispensable tool for performance analysis and memory error detection in C++ applications (Turner, 2018).

Step-by-step guide for using Valgrind to detect memory leaks (on Linux/macOS):

1. **Install Valgrind (if not already installed):** On Debian/Ubuntu: `sudo apt-get install valgrind`. On macOS (using Homebrew): `brew install valgrind`.
2. **Compile your C++ program:** Compile your program with debugging information (e.g., using `g++ -g your_program.cpp -o your_program`). The `-g` flag includes debugging symbols, which Valgrind uses to provide more informative error messages.
3. **Run your program under Valgrind:** Execute the command `valgrind --leak-check=full ./your_program`. `--leak-check=full` enables detailed leak checking. Replace `./your_program` with the path to your executable.
4. **Analyze Valgrind output:** Valgrind will run your program and produce a report after the program exits. The report will detail any memory errors detected, including memory leaks, invalid reads/writes, etc. Look for sections like "LEAK SUMMARY" in the output to identify potential memory leaks.

Example: Detecting Memory Leak with Valgrind

Let's introduce a memory leak into our dynamic allocation example and detect it with Valgrind.

```
C++
#include <iostream>

int main() {
  int *leakyPtr = new int; // Memory allocated, but no delete
```

```
    *leakyPtr = 100;
    std::cout << "Value: " << *leakyPtr << std::endl;

    // Intentional memory leak: delete leakyPtr; is commented out

    return 0; // leakyPtr goes out of scope, but allocated memory is leaked
}
```

Running Valgrind on this program:

```bash
valgrind --leak-check=full ./leaky_program
```

Valgrind Output (Example - output details may vary slightly):

```
==12345== Memcheck, a memory error detector
==12345== Copyright (C) 2002-2017, and GNU GPL'd, by Julian Seward et al.
==12345== Using Valgrind-3.13.0 and LibVEX; rerun with -h for copyright info
==12345== Command: ./leaky_program
==12345==
Value: 100
==12345==
==12345== HEAP SUMMARY:
==12345==     in use at exit: 4 bytes in 1 blocks
==12345==   total heap usage: 1 allocs, 0 frees, 4 bytes allocated
==12345==
==12345== 4 bytes in 1 blocks are definitely lost in loss record 1 of 1
==12345==    at 0x4C2FB0F: operator new(unsigned long) (in /usr/lib/valgrind/memcheck-amd64-linux.so)
==12345==    by 0x109179: main (in /path/to/leaky_program/leaky_program)
==12345==
==12345== LEAK SUMMARY:
==12345==    definitely lost: 4 bytes in 1 blocks
==12345==      possibly lost: 0 bytes in 0 blocks
==12345==    still reachable: 0 bytes in 0 blocks
==12345==         suppressed: 0 bytes in 0 blocks
==12345==
==12345== For counts of detected and suppressed errors, rerun with: -v
==12345== ERROR SUMMARY: 1 errors from 1 contexts (suppressed: 0 from 0)
```

Analyzing Valgrind Output:

- HEAP SUMMARY: in use at exit: 4 bytes in 1 blocks: Indicates that at the program's exit, 4 bytes of memory in 1 block are still allocated on the heap but not freed.
- 4 bytes in 1 blocks are definitely lost in loss record 1 of 1: This is the key leak message. "Definitely lost" means Valgrind is certain that this memory is leaked (not reachable and not freed). It also provides the allocation site: operator new(unsigned long) called from main function in leaky_program.cpp.
- LEAK SUMMARY: definitely lost: 4 bytes in 1 blocks: Summarizes the leak information.
- ERROR SUMMARY: 1 errors from 1 contexts: Indicates that Valgrind detected 1 error (a memory leak) in 1 context.

This Valgrind output clearly points to a memory leak of 4 bytes in the leaky_program, helping you identify and fix the issue by adding delete leakyPtr;.

4.5.3 AddressSanitizer (ASan): Fast Memory Error Detection

AddressSanitizer (ASan) is another powerful memory error detection tool, often considered faster than Valgrind for many types of errors. ASan is integrated into modern compilers like GCC and Clang. It uses compile-time instrumentation and run-time checks to detect memory errors such as heap buffer overflows, stack buffer overflows, use-after-free, and memory leaks. ASan is particularly effective for catching errors early in the development cycle due to its speed and ease of use. As Patterson and Hennessy note in "Computer Organization and Design," tools like ASan are critical for ensuring memory safety and program correctness, especially in complex software systems (Patterson & Hennessy, 2020).

Step-by-step guide for using AddressSanitizer to detect memory errors (using GCC/Clang):

1. **Compile your C++ program with ASan flags:** When compiling your C++ program using GCC or Clang, add the -fsanitize=address flag to both the compilation and linking stages. For example: g++ -fsanitize=address -g your_program.cpp -o your_program.

2. **Run your program:** Execute your compiled program as usual: ./your_program.
3. **Analyze ASan output (if errors are detected):** If ASan detects a memory error during program execution, it will print a detailed error report to standard error and typically abort the program. The report will indicate the type of error, the memory address involved, and the location in the code where the error occurred.

Example: Detecting Heap Use-After-Free with AddressSanitizer
Let's create a program with a heap use-after-free error and detect it using ASan.

```
C++
#include <iostream>

int main() {
   int *ptr = new int;
   *ptr = 10;
   delete ptr;

   *ptr = 20; // Use-after-free error: accessing memory after it has been freed

   std::cout << "Value: " << *ptr << std::endl; // This line might or might not
execute before ASan error is reported

   return 0;
}
```

Compiling and running with ASan:

```
Bash
g++ -fsanitize=address -g use_after_free.cpp -o use_after_free
./use_after_free
```

ASan Output (Example - output details may vary slightly):

```
==12346==ERROR: AddressSanitizer: heap-use-after-free on address
0x602000000010 at pc 0x7ffff7a7b82b bp 0x7fffffffdf80 sp 0x7fffffffdf78
WRITE of size 4 at 0x602000000010 thread T0
   #0 0x7ffff7a7b82a in main /path/to/use_after_free/use_after_free.cpp:8
   #1 0x7ffff7a7c0b2 in __libc_start_main (/lib/x86_64-linux-
gnu/libc.so.6+0x270b2)
   #2 0x41907d in _start (/path/to/use_after_free/use_after_free+0x1907d)

Address 0x602000000010 is located in heap block of size 4, freed by:
```

```
    #0 0x7ffff7ad15cf in operator delete(void*) (/lib/x86_64-linux-gnu/libasan.so.4+0x9d5cf)
    #1 0x7ffff7a7b812 in main /path/to/use_after_free/use_after_free.cpp:7
    #2 0x7ffff7a7c0b2 in __libc_start_main (/lib/x86_64-linux-gnu/libc.so.6+0x270b2)
    #3 0x41907d in _start (/path/to/use_after_free/use_after_free+0x1907d)

SUMMARY: AddressSanitizer: heap-use-after-free
(/path/to/use_after_free/use_after_free+0x100000000000) in main
Shadow bytes around soon-to-be-freed memory:
  000000000000: fa fa fa fa fa fa fa fa fa fa fa fa fa fa fa fa
  000000000010: fd fd fd fd fd fd fd fd fd fd fd fd fd fd fd fd
=>000000000020: fd fd fd fd fd fd fd fd fd fd fd fd fd fd fd fd
  000000000030: fa fa fa fa fa fa fa fa fa fa fa fa fa fa fa fa
  000000000040: 00 00 00 00 00 00 00 00 00 00 00 00 00 00 00 00
Shadow byte legend (one shadow byte represents 8 application bytes):
  Addressable:           00
  Partially addressable: 01 02 03 04 05 06 07
  Heap left redzone:       fa
  Freed heap region:       fd
  Stack left redzone:     f1
  Stack mid redzone:       f2
  Stack right redzone:    f3
  Stack after return:    f5
  Stack use after scope:  f8
  Global redzone:         f9
  Redzone after globals:  f

==12346== ABORTING
```

Analyzing ASan Output:

- **==12346==ERROR: AddressSanitizer: heap-use-after-free on address 0x602000000010 ...**: This is the main error message, clearly indicating a heap-use-after-free error. It provides the memory address where the error occurred (`0x602000000010`).
- **WRITE of size 4 at 0x602000000010 thread T0**: Specifies that the error was a write operation of size 4 bytes at the given address.
- **#0 0x7ffff7a7b82a in main /path/to/use_after_free/use_after_free.cpp:8**: Provides the source code location of the error: line 8 of `use_after_free.cpp` in the `main` function. * **Address 0x602000000010 is located in heap block of size 4, freed by: ... #1 0x7ffff7a7b812 in main /path/to/use_after_free/use_after_free.cpp:7**: Indicates where

the memory was originally allocated and then freed. Line 7 of use_after_free.cpp in main is where delete ptr; was called.

ASan's detailed output pinpoints the exact location of the use-after-free error (line 8) and where the memory was freed (line 7), making it very easy to diagnose and fix the problem.

By using smart pointers and adhering to RAII principles, you can significantly reduce the risk of memory leaks and other memory management errors in your C++ programs. When manual memory management is necessary or when debugging existing code, tools like Valgrind and AddressSanitizer are essential for detecting and diagnosing memory-related issues, ensuring the reliability and stability of your software.

Chapter 5

Object-Oriented Programming (OOP)

Object-Oriented Programming (OOP) represents a paradigm shift in software development, moving away from procedural approaches to organizing code around "objects" that encapsulate both data and behavior. This approach promotes modularity, reusability, and maintainability, making it a cornerstone of modern software engineering. For Computer Technology students and educators, understanding OOP principles in C++ is crucial for developing complex and scalable applications. This section will delve into the core concepts of OOP in C++, including classes, objects, inheritance, polymorphism, and related features, providing a comprehensive and academically rigorous discussion. We will explore these concepts through real-world analogies, practical code examples, and step-by-step explanations, ensuring a deep and practical understanding of OOP in C++.

5.1 Classes and Objects: Blueprints and Instances

At the heart of OOP lie classes and objects. A class can be thought of as a blueprint or a template that defines the characteristics (data) and behaviors (functions) of a particular type of entity. An object, on the other hand, is a concrete instance of a class. Imagine a blueprint for a house (the class); the actual houses built from that blueprint are the objects. Each house (object) will share the same basic design (defined by the class) but may have different specific attributes, such as paint color or address. As Lippman, Lajoie, and Moo explain in "C++ Primer," classes are user-defined types that serve as the foundation for object-oriented programming in C++ (Lippman, Lajoie, & Moo, 2012).

5.1.1 Defining Classes

In C++, you define a class using the `class` keyword followed by the class name and curly braces `{}` enclosing the class members (data and functions).

Example: Defining a Car Class

```
C++
#include <iostream>
#include <string>

class Car {
public: // Access specifier: public members are accessible from outside the class
   std::string model; // Data member (attribute)
   std::string color; // Data member (attribute)

   void startEngine() { // Member function (method)
      std::cout << "Engine started for " << color << " " << model << std::endl;
   }
};
```

Step-by-step explanation:

1. **#include <iostream> and #include <string>**: Include necessary headers for input/output operations and string manipulation.
2. **class Car { ... };**: Declares a class named Car. The class definition is enclosed in curly braces {} and terminated by a semicolon ;.
3. **public:**: This is an access specifier. Members declared after public: are accessible from anywhere, both inside and outside the class.
4. **std::string model; and std::string color;**: These are data members or attributes of the Car class. model and color are variables of type std::string that will store the car's model and color, respectively.
5. **void startEngine() { ... }**: This is a member function or method of the Car class. startEngine is a function that belongs to the Car class and defines a behavior of a Car object. It prints a message to the console indicating that the engine has started, including the car's color and model.

5.1.2 Creating Objects

Once a class is defined, you can create objects (instances) of that class. To create an object, you declare a variable of the class type, just like you would declare a variable of built-in types like int or string.

Example: Creating Car Objects

```
C++
#include <iostream>
#include <string>

class Car { // Class definition from previous example
public:
    std::string model;
    std::string color;

    void startEngine() {
        std::cout << "Engine started for " << color << " " << model <<
std::endl;
    }
};

int main() {
    Car car1; // Create a Car object named car1
```

```
    car1.model = "Sedan"; // Access and set data member
    car1.color = "Red"; // Access and set data member
    car1.startEngine(); // Call member function

    Car car2; // Create another Car object named car2
    car2.model = "SUV";
    car2.color = "Blue";
    car2.startEngine();

    return 0;
}
```

Step-by-step explanation:

1. **Car car1;**: Creates an object named car1 of the class Car. This is similar to declaring an integer variable int x;. car1 is now an instance of the Car blueprint.
2. **car1.model = "Sedan"; and car1.color = "Red";**: Accesses the public data members model and color of the car1 object using the dot operator .. Values "Sedan" and "Red" are assigned to these data members, respectively.
3. **car1.startEngine();**: Calls the public member function startEngine() on the car1 object using the dot operator .. This executes the code defined in the startEngine() function, which will print a message specific to car1's color and model.
4. **Car car2;**: Creates another object car2 of the Car class.
5. Similar steps are repeated for car2 to set its model, color, and call its startEngine() function. Each object (car1, car2) is independent and has its own set of data members.

5.2 Constructors and Destructors: Object Lifecycle Management

Constructors and destructors are special member functions that are automatically called during the creation and destruction of objects, respectively. They play a crucial role in managing the lifecycle of objects, particularly in initialization and cleanup tasks. As Stroustrup points out in "The C++ Programming Language," constructors and destructors are fundamental for ensuring proper object initialization and resource management in C++ (Stroustrup, 2013).

5.2.1 Constructors: Object Initialization

A constructor is a special member function with the same name as the class itself. It is automatically invoked when an object of the class is created. Constructors are used to initialize the object's data members and perform any setup operations required when an object comes into existence. C++ supports different types of constructors, including default constructors, parameterized constructors, and copy constructors.

Example: Constructors for Car Class

```
C++
#include <iostream>
#include <string>

class Car {
public:
   std::string model;
   std::string color;

   // Default constructor (no arguments)
   Car() {
      std::cout << "Default constructor called for Car" << std::endl;
      model = "Unknown";
      color = "Unknown";
   }

   // Parameterized constructor (takes model and color arguments)
   Car(std::string carModel, std::string carColor) : model(carModel),
color(carColor) { // Initializer list for efficiency
      std::cout << "Parameterized constructor called for " << color << " " <<
model << std::endl;
   }

   void startEngine() {
      std::cout << "Engine started for " << color << " " << model <<
std::endl;
   }
};

int main() {
   Car defaultCar; // Calls default constructor
   std::cout << "Default Car: " << defaultCar.color << " " <<
defaultCar.model << std::endl;
```

```
    Car myCar("Sedan", "Silver"); // Calls parameterized constructor
    std::cout << "My Car: " << myCar.color << " " << myCar.model <<
std::endl;

    return 0;
}
```

Step-by-step explanation:

1. **Car() { ... }**: This is the default constructor. It has the same name as the class (Car) and takes no arguments. It is called when an object is created without any explicit arguments, like Car defaultCar;. Inside the default constructor, model and color are initialized to "Unknown".
2. **Car(std::string carModel, std::string carColor) : model(carModel), color(carColor) { ... }**: This is a parameterized constructor. It also has the same name as the class (Car) but takes two arguments: carModel and carColor. It is called when an object is created with arguments, like Car myCar("Sedan", "Silver");.
    - **: model(carModel), color(carColor)**: This is an initializer list. It's an efficient way to initialize data members in the constructor. It initializes model with the value of carModel and color with the value of carColor.
3. **Car defaultCar;**: Creates an object defaultCar. Since no arguments are provided, the default constructor Car() is called.
4. **Car myCar("Sedan", "Silver");**: Creates an object myCar. Arguments "Sedan" and "Silver" are provided, so the parameterized constructor Car(std::string, std::string) is called.
5. The output demonstrates that the appropriate constructor is called based on how the object is created, and the data members are initialized accordingly.

5.2.2 Destructors: Object Cleanup

A destructor is another special member function, also with the same name as the class, but prefixed with a tilde ~ (e.g., ~Car()). It is automatically called when an object is about to be destroyed (e.g., when it goes out of scope or is explicitly deleted if dynamically allocated). Destructors are used to perform cleanup operations, such as releasing dynamically allocated memory, closing files, or releasing other resources held by the object. Destructors are crucial for implementing RAII and preventing resource leaks.

Example: Destructor for Car Class

```
C++
#include <iostream>
#include <string>

class Car {
public:
   std::string model;
   std::string color;

   Car(std::string carModel, std::string carColor) : model(carModel),
color(carColor) {
      std::cout << "Parameterized constructor called for " << color << " " <<
model << std::endl;
   }

   ~Car() { // Destructor
      std::cout << "Destructor called for " << color << " " << model <<
std::endl;
   }

   void startEngine() {
      std::cout << "Engine started for " << color << " " << model <<
std::endl;
   }
};

int main() {
   Car myCar("Sedan", "Silver"); // Object created, constructor called
   myCar.startEngine();

   // myCar object goes out of scope at the end of main(), destructor ~Car() is
automatically called here.

   return 0;
}
```

Step-by-step explanation:

1. **~Car() { ... }**: This is the destructor for the Car class. It has the name ~Car() (tilde followed by the class name) and takes no arguments. It is automatically called when a Car object is destroyed.

2. **Car myCar("Sedan", "Silver");**: Creates a Car object myCar. The parameterized constructor is called.
3. **// myCar object goes out of scope at the end of main(), destructor ~Car() is automatically called here.**: When the main function reaches its end, the local object myCar goes out of scope. At this point, the destructor ~Car() for myCar is automatically called.
4. The output will show the constructor message when myCar is created and the destructor message when myCar is destroyed at the end of main, demonstrating the automatic invocation of constructors and destructors.

5.3 Access Specifiers: Controlling Member Visibility

Access specifiers in C++ control the visibility and accessibility of class members (data members and member functions) from outside the class and from derived classes (in inheritance). C++ provides three main access specifiers: public, private, and protected. Encapsulation, a key OOP principle, is achieved through the use of access specifiers. As Gamma, Helm, Johnson, and Vlissides emphasize in "Design Patterns," encapsulation is fundamental to reducing dependencies and managing complexity in object-oriented systems (Gamma, Helm, Johnson, & Vlissides, 1995).

5.3.1 public: Accessible Everywhere

Members declared as public are accessible from anywhere: from within the class itself, from outside the class through objects, and from derived classes. Public members define the interface of the class, representing the operations and data that are intended to be used by external code.

5.3.2 private: Accessible Only Within the Class

Members declared as private are the most restrictive. They are accessible only from within the class itself (i.e., by other member functions of the same class). Private members are not accessible from outside the class or from derived classes. Private access is used to implement data hiding and encapsulation, protecting the internal implementation details of a class from external modification or direct access.

5.3.3 protected: Accessible Within Class and Derived Classes

Members declared as protected are in between public and private in terms of accessibility. They are accessible from within the class itself and from derived classes (classes that inherit from this class). However, protected members are not accessible from outside the class or from unrelated classes. protected access is useful in inheritance hierarchies, allowing base classes to provide members that are intended to be used by derived classes but not by arbitrary external code.

Example: Access Specifiers in BankAccount Class

Consider a BankAccount class where account balance should be private and only accessible through controlled public methods, while account number might be protected if we plan to create specialized account types through inheritance.

```
C++
#include <iostream>
#include <string>

class BankAccount {
private: // Private members - only accessible within the class
    double balance; // Private data member: balance is hidden from outside
access

protected: // Protected members - accessible within class and derived classes
    std::string accountNumber; // Protected data member: accessible in derived
classes

public: // Public members - accessible from anywhere
    BankAccount(std::string accNumber, double initialBalance) :
accountNumber(accNumber), balance(initialBalance) {
        std::cout << "Account " << accountNumber << " created with balance: "
<< balance << std::endl;
    }

    void deposit(double amount) {
        if (amount > 0) {
            balance += amount;
```

```
        std::cout << "Deposited " << amount << ". New balance: " <<
balance << std::endl;
      } else {
        std::cout << "Invalid deposit amount." << std::endl;
      }
    }

  void withdraw(double amount) {
    if (amount > 0 && balance >= amount) {
      balance -= amount;
      std::cout << "Withdrawn " << amount << ". New balance: " <<
balance << std::endl;
    } else {
      std::cout << "Insufficient balance or invalid withdrawal amount." <<
std::endl;
    }
  }

  double getBalance() const { // Public getter method to access balance (read-
only)
    return balance; // Accessing private member from within a public
member function is allowed
  }

  void displayAccountNumber() const { // Public method to display account
number
    std::cout << "Account Number: " << accountNumber << std::endl; //
Accessing protected member from within a public member function is allowed
  }
};

int main() {
  BankAccount account("1234567890", 1000.0);
  account.deposit(500.0);
  account.withdraw(200.0);
  std::cout << "Current Balance: " << account.getBalance() << std::endl;
  account.displayAccountNumber();

  // Error: Attempting to access private member 'balance' from outside the
class:
  // std::cout << "Balance: " << account.balance << std::endl; // This line
would cause a compile-time error

  // Error: Attempting to access protected member 'accountNumber' from
outside the class:
```

```
    // std::cout << "Account Number: " << account.accountNumber <<
std::endl; // This line would also cause a compile-time error

    return 0;
}
```

Step-by-step explanation:

1. **private: double balance;**: Declares balance as a private data member. It can only be accessed from within the BankAccount class itself.
2. **protected: std::string accountNumber;**: Declares accountNumber as a protected data member. It can be accessed from within BankAccount and any classes derived from BankAccount.
3. **public: ...**: Declares public member functions: BankAccount (constructor), deposit, withdraw, getBalance, and displayAccountNumber. These are the public interface of the BankAccount class.
4. **getBalance() const**: A public getter method that returns the private balance. This provides controlled read-only access to the balance from outside the class, respecting encapsulation.
5. **displayAccountNumber() const**: A public method to display the protected accountNumber.
6. In main(), you can call the public methods (deposit, withdraw, getBalance, displayAccountNumber) on the account object.
7. The commented-out lines attempting to directly access account.balance and account.accountNumber would result in compile-time errors because balance is private and accountNumber is protected, and they are being accessed from outside the class. This demonstrates access control and encapsulation.

5.4 Inheritance: Creating Hierarchies of Classes

Inheritance is a fundamental OOP mechanism that allows you to create new classes (derived classes or child classes) based on existing classes (base classes or parent classes). Inheritance establishes an "is-a" relationship between classes, where a derived class inherits properties (data and functions) from its base class and can extend or modify them. Inheritance promotes code reuse, reduces redundancy, and facilitates the creation of class hierarchies. As Martin explains in "Clean Code," inheritance is a powerful tool for organizing code and representing hierarchical relationships, but it should be used judiciously to avoid overly complex hierarchies (Martin, 2008).

5.4.1 Single Inheritance

Single inheritance is the simplest form of inheritance where a derived class inherits from only one base class.

Example: Single Inheritance - SavingsAccount inheriting from BankAccount

Let's create a SavingsAccount class that inherits from the BankAccount class. A savings account is a specialized type of bank account and naturally "is-a" BankAccount.

```
C++
#include <iostream>
#include <string>

class BankAccount { // Base class (from previous example)
private:
   double balance;
protected:
   std::string accountNumber;
public:
   BankAccount(std::string accNumber, double initialBalance) :
accountNumber(accNumber), balance(initialBalance) {
      std::cout << "BankAccount constructor called for account: " <<
accountNumber << std::endl;
   }
   ~BankAccount() {
      std::cout << "BankAccount destructor called for account: " <<
accountNumber << std::endl;
   }
   void deposit(double amount) {
      if (amount > 0) {
         balance += amount;
         std::cout << "BankAccount deposit: " << amount << ". New balance:
" << balance << std::endl;
      } else {
         std::cout << "BankAccount Invalid deposit amount." << std::endl;
      }
   }
```

```
    void withdraw(double amount) {
        if (amount > 0 && balance >= amount) {
            balance -= amount;
            std::cout << "BankAccount withdraw: " << amount << ". New
balance: " << balance << std::endl;
        } else {
            std::cout << "BankAccount Insufficient balance or invalid withdrawal
amount." << std::endl;
        }
    }
    double getBalance() const { return balance; }
    void displayAccountNumber() const { std::cout << "BankAccount Account
Number: " << accountNumber << std::endl; }
};

class SavingsAccount : public BankAccount { // Derived class inheriting
publicly from BankAccount
private:
    double interestRate;
public:
    SavingsAccount(std::string accNumber, double initialBalance, double rate) //
Constructor for SavingsAccount
        : BankAccount(accNumber, initialBalance), interestRate(rate) { // Call
base class constructor using initializer list
        std::cout << "SavingsAccount constructor called for account: " <<
accountNumber << std::endl;
    }
    ~SavingsAccount() {
        std::cout << "SavingsAccount destructor called for account: " <<
accountNumber << std::endl;
    }

    void applyInterest() {
        double interest = getBalance() * interestRate; // Accessing base class
public member function
        deposit(interest); // Calling base class public member function
        std::cout << "Interest applied: " << interest << ". New balance: " <<
getBalance() << std::endl;
    }

    void displayInterestRate() const {
        std::cout << "Interest Rate: " << interestRate << std::endl;
    }
};

int main() {
```

```
    SavingsAccount savings("SA123", 1000.0, 0.05); // Create a SavingsAccount
object
    savings.deposit(500.0); // Inherited deposit method
    savings.applyInterest(); // SavingsAccount specific method
    std::cout << "Savings Account Balance: " << savings.getBalance() <<
std::endl; // Inherited getBalance method
    savings.displayAccountNumber(); // Inherited displayAccountNumber
method
    savings.displayInterestRate(); // SavingsAccount specific method

    return 0;
}
```

Step-by-step explanation:

1. **class SavingsAccount : public BankAccount { ... };**: Declares SavingsAccount as a derived class that publicly inherits from BankAccount. The : public BankAccount part specifies public inheritance.
2. **SavingsAccount(std::string accNumber, double initialBalance, double rate) : BankAccount(accNumber, initialBalance), interestRate(rate) { ... }**: Constructor for SavingsAccount.
   - **: BankAccount(accNumber, initialBalance)**: This is crucial. It calls the constructor of the base class BankAccount in the initializer list, passing accNumber and initialBalance. This ensures that the base class part of the SavingsAccount object is properly initialized.
   - **, interestRate(rate)**: Initializes the SavingsAccount's own data member interestRate.
3. **void applyInterest() { ... }**: A method specific to SavingsAccount to apply interest.
   - **getBalance() and deposit()**: Inside applyInterest, it calls getBalance() and deposit(), which are *public* member functions inherited from the BankAccount base class. Derived classes can directly access public and protected members of the base class.
4. In main(), a SavingsAccount object savings is created. You can call methods inherited from BankAccount (like deposit, getBalance, displayAccountNumber) as well as methods specific to SavingsAccount (like applyInterest, displayInterestRate).
5. The output demonstrates that when a SavingsAccount object is created, both the BankAccount constructor and the SavingsAccount constructor are called. Similarly, both

destructors are called when the SavingsAccount object is destroyed, in reverse order of constructor calls (derived class destructor then base class destructor).

5.4.2 Multiple Inheritance

Multiple inheritance allows a derived class to inherit from more than one base class. This can be useful for combining features from multiple sources, but it can also introduce complexities, such as the diamond problem (ambiguity when inheriting from a common ancestor through multiple paths). Careful design and understanding of the inheritance hierarchy are crucial when using multiple inheritance.

Example: Multiple Inheritance - ElectricCar inheriting from Car and ElectricVehicle

Let's assume we have a Car class and an ElectricVehicle interface (or class). We can create an ElectricCar class that inherits from both.

```
C++
#include <iostream>
#include <string>

class Car { // Base class 1
public:
   std::string model;
   std::string color;
   Car(std::string carModel, std::string carColor) : model(carModel),
color(carColor) {
      std::cout << "Car constructor called for " << color << " " << model <<
std::endl;
   }
   ~Car() {
      std::cout << "Car destructor called for " << color << " " << model <<
std::endl;
   }
   void startEngine() {
      std::cout << "Car Engine started for " << color << " " << model <<
std::endl;
   }
};

class ElectricVehicle { // Base class 2 (could be interface or abstract class in
more complex scenarios)
public:
```

```
    int batteryCapacity;
    ElectricVehicle(int capacity) : batteryCapacity(capacity) {
        std::cout << "ElectricVehicle constructor called, capacity: " <<
batteryCapacity << std::endl;
    }
    ~ElectricVehicle() {
        std::cout << "ElectricVehicle destructor called, capacity: " <<
batteryCapacity << std::endl;
    }
    void chargeBattery() {
        std::cout << "Battery charging started, capacity: " << batteryCapacity <<
std::endl;
    }
};

class ElectricCar : public Car, public ElectricVehicle { // Derived class
inheriting from both Car and ElectricVehicle
public:
    ElectricCar(std::string carModel, std::string carColor, int capacity)
        : Car(carModel, carColor), ElectricVehicle(capacity) { // Call constructors
of both base classes
        std::cout << "ElectricCar constructor called for " << color << " " <<
model << ", capacity: " << batteryCapacity << std::endl;
    }
    ~ElectricCar() {
        std::cout << "ElectricCar destructor called for " << color << " " <<
model << ", capacity: " << batteryCapacity << std::endl;
    }
    void driveElectric() {
        std::cout << "Driving electric " << color << " " << model << ", battery
capacity: " << batteryCapacity << std::endl;
    }
};

int main() {
    ElectricCar tesla("Model S", "Black", 100); // Create an ElectricCar object
    tesla.startEngine(); // Inherited from Car
    tesla.chargeBattery(); // Inherited from ElectricVehicle
    tesla.driveElectric(); // ElectricCar specific method
    std::cout << "Electric Car Model: " << tesla.model << ", Color: " <<
tesla.color << ", Battery Capacity: " << tesla.batteryCapacity << std::endl; //
Accessing members from both base classes

    return 0;
}
```

Step-by-step explanation:

1. **class ElectricCar : public Car, public ElectricVehicle { ... };**: Declares ElectricCar inheriting publicly from both Car and ElectricVehicle. This is multiple inheritance.
2. **ElectricCar(std::string carModel, std::string carColor, int capacity) : Car(carModel, carColor), ElectricVehicle(capacity) { ... }**: Constructor of ElectricCar.
   - **: Car(carModel, carColor), ElectricVehicle(capacity)**: In the initializer list, it calls the constructors of *both* base classes, Car and ElectricVehicle, ensuring both base class parts are initialized. The order of base class constructors in the initializer list determines the order of their execution.
3. In main(), an ElectricCar object tesla is created. It can call methods and access members inherited from both Car (like startEngine, model, color) and ElectricVehicle (like chargeBattery, batteryCapacity), as well as its own methods (like driveElectric).
4. The output shows that constructors of all three classes (Car, ElectricVehicle, ElectricCar) are called in the order of inheritance and object creation, and destructors are called in reverse order when tesla goes out of scope.

5.4.3 Virtual Inheritance (Addressing Diamond Problem)

Virtual inheritance is used in multiple inheritance scenarios to address the diamond problem. The diamond problem arises when a class inherits from two classes that share a common base class. Without virtual inheritance, the derived class would inherit two copies of the common base class's members, leading to ambiguity and potential issues. Virtual inheritance ensures that only one instance of the shared base class is inherited, resolving the ambiguity. As Vandevoorde and Josuttis explain in "C++ Templates," virtual inheritance is a mechanism to control the structure of inheritance hierarchies and manage shared base classes in multiple inheritance (Vandevoorde & Josuttis, 2003).

Note: A detailed example of virtual inheritance and the diamond problem is complex and often more relevant in advanced OOP discussions. For introductory purposes, understanding the concept and purpose of virtual inheritance is key. A simpler example demonstrating the ambiguity without virtual inheritance and how virtual inheritance resolves it would be beneficial for Computer Technology students. However, for conciseness and to maintain focus on core OOP concepts, a detailed code example of virtual inheritance is omitted here but its purpose and relevance in resolving the diamond problem is highlighted.

5.5 Polymorphism: "Many Forms"

Polymorphism, meaning "many forms," is a core OOP principle that allows objects of different classes to be treated as objects of a common type. Polymorphism enables writing code that can work with objects of various types in a uniform way, enhancing flexibility and extensibility. C++ supports polymorphism through mechanisms like function overriding (in inheritance) and virtual functions (for runtime polymorphism). As Meyer describes in "Object-Oriented Software Construction," polymorphism is a cornerstone of object-oriented design, enabling code to be more adaptable and resilient to change (Meyer, 1997).

5.5.1 Function Overriding: Redefining Base Class Behavior

Function overriding occurs in inheritance when a derived class provides a different implementation for a member function that is already defined in its base class. To enable overriding, the base class function should be declared as `virtual`. When you call a virtual function through a base class pointer or reference, the actual function implementation that gets executed is determined by the *dynamic type* of the object (the type of the object at runtime), not the *static type* (the type of the pointer or reference at compile time). This is runtime polymorphism.

Example: Function Overriding with Virtual Functions
Let's consider our `BankAccount` and `SavingsAccount` classes. We can make the `withdraw` function virtual in `BankAccount` and override it in `SavingsAccount` to add specific behavior for savings accounts (e.g., limit withdrawals).

```
C++
#include <iostream>
#include <string>

class BankAccount { // Base class
private:
   double balance;
protected:
   std::string accountNumber;
public:
   BankAccount(std::string accNumber, double initialBalance) :
accountNumber(accNumber), balance(initialBalance) {
      std::cout << "BankAccount constructor called for account: " <<
accountNumber << std::endl;
   }
   ~BankAccount() {
      std::cout << "BankAccount destructor called for account: " <<
accountNumber << std::endl;
   }
   virtual void deposit(double amount) { // Virtual deposit function
      if (amount > 0) {
         balance += amount;
         std::cout << "BankAccount deposit: " << amount << ". New balance:
" << balance << std::endl;
      } else {
         std::cout << "BankAccount Invalid deposit amount." << std::endl;
      }
   }
   virtual void withdraw(double amount) { // Virtual withdraw function - base
class implementation
      if (amount > 0 && balance >= amount) {
         balance -= amount;
         std::cout << "BankAccount withdraw: " << amount << ". New
balance: " << balance << std::endl;
      } else {
         std::cout << "BankAccount Insufficient balance or invalid withdrawal
amount." << std::endl;
      }
   }
   double getBalance() const { return balance; }
   void displayAccountNumber() const { std::cout << "BankAccount Account
Number: " << accountNumber << std::endl; }
};

class SavingsAccount : public BankAccount { // Derived class
private:
```

```
    double interestRate;
public:
    SavingsAccount(std::string accNumber, double initialBalance, double rate)
        : BankAccount(accNumber, initialBalance), interestRate(rate) {
        std::cout << "SavingsAccount constructor called for account: " <<
accountNumber << std::endl;
    }
    ~SavingsAccount() {
        std::cout << "SavingsAccount destructor called for account: " <<
accountNumber << std::endl;
    }
    void applyInterest() {
        double interest = getBalance() * interestRate;
        deposit(interest);
        std::cout << "Interest applied: " << interest << ". New balance: " <<
getBalance() << std::endl;
    }
    void displayInterestRate() const {
        std::cout << "Interest Rate: " << interestRate << std::endl;
    }

    void withdraw(double amount) override { // Overriding withdraw function
in SavingsAccount - specific implementation
        if (amount > 0 && getBalance() >= amount && amount <= 500) { //
Savings account specific withdrawal limit
            BankAccount::withdraw(amount); // Call base class withdraw
implementation using scope resolution
            std::cout << "SavingsAccount withdraw: " << amount << ". New
balance: " << getBalance() << std::endl;
        } else {
            std::cout << "SavingsAccount Withdrawal limit exceeded or insufficient
balance/invalid amount." << std::endl;
        }
    }
};

int main() {
    BankAccount* basePtr1 = new BankAccount("BA123", 1000.0); // Base
class pointer to base class object
    BankAccount* basePtr2 = new SavingsAccount("SA456", 1500.0, 0.03); //
Base class pointer to derived class object

    basePtr1->withdraw(300.0); // Calls BankAccount::withdraw() - base class
implementation
    basePtr2->withdraw(600.0); // Calls SavingsAccount::withdraw() - derived
class overridden implementation (polymorphism in action)
```

```
    delete basePtr1;
    delete basePtr2;

    return 0;
}
```

Step-by-step explanation:

1. **virtual void withdraw(double amount); in BankAccount:** Declares the withdraw function as virtual in the base class. This is essential for enabling runtime polymorphism.
2. **void withdraw(double amount) override; in SavingsAccount:** Overrides the withdraw function in the SavingsAccount class. The override keyword (C++11 and later) is optional but recommended; it explicitly indicates that this function is intended to override a base class virtual function, helping catch errors if the override is not valid.
3. **BankAccount::withdraw(amount); in SavingsAccount::withdraw:** Inside the overridden SavingsAccount::withdraw, BankAccount::withdraw(amount) is called using scope resolution ::. This explicitly calls the base class implementation of withdraw from within the derived class's overridden version. This allows you to reuse the base class functionality and extend it in the derived class.
4. **BankAccount* basePtr1 = new BankAccount("BA123", 1000.0); and BankAccount* basePtr2 = new SavingsAccount("SA456", 1500.0, 0.03);:** Creates base class pointers basePtr1 and basePtr2. basePtr1 points to a BankAccount object, and basePtr2 points to a SavingsAccount object. This is polymorphism—a base class pointer can point to objects of derived classes.
5. **basePtr1->withdraw(300.0);:** Calls withdraw through basePtr1. Since basePtr1 points to a BankAccount object, BankAccount::withdraw() is called (base class implementation).
6. **basePtr2->withdraw(600.0);:** Calls withdraw through basePtr2. Since basePtr2 points to a SavingsAccount object, and withdraw is virtual and overridden, SavingsAccount::withdraw() is called (derived class overridden implementation). This is runtime polymorphism in action—the function called depends on the object's actual type at runtime, not the pointer's type at compile time.

5.5.2 Virtual Functions: Enabling Runtime Polymorphism

Virtual functions are member functions declared with the virtual keyword in the base class. They are the cornerstone of runtime polymorphism in C++. When a virtual function is called through a base class pointer or reference, the C++ runtime system determines the actual type of the object being pointed to (dynamic type) and calls the version of the virtual function that is appropriate for that object's type. This dynamic dispatch mechanism is what enables polymorphism. Virtual functions are essential for creating flexible and extensible class hierarchies, allowing you to write generic code that can work with objects of different derived classes in a polymorphic manner.

5.6 Encapsulation and Abstraction: Hiding Complexity and Simplifying Interfaces

Encapsulation and abstraction are two closely related OOP principles that aim to manage complexity and improve code organization.

5.6.1 Encapsulation: Data Hiding

Encapsulation is the principle of bundling data (attributes) and methods (functions) that operate on that data within a single unit (an object). Encapsulation also involves data hiding, which means restricting direct access to the internal data of an object and exposing it only through well-defined public interfaces (methods). Access specifiers (private, protected, public) are the primary mechanism for achieving encapsulation in C++. Encapsulation protects the integrity of data by preventing unauthorized or direct modification and promotes modularity by hiding implementation details.

5.6.2 Abstraction: Simplifying Interfaces

Abstraction involves presenting only essential information to the outside world and hiding complex implementation details. Abstraction focuses on "what" an object does rather than "how" it does it. In C++, abstraction is achieved through classes and interfaces. Public methods of a class provide an abstract interface to interact with objects, while the private and protected members and the implementation details are hidden, providing a simplified view for users of the class. Abstraction reduces cognitive load, makes code easier to understand and use, and allows for implementation changes without affecting the external interface.

Example: Encapsulation and Abstraction in Television Class

Consider a Television class. Encapsulation would involve making the internal state of the TV (like channel, volume, power state) private, and providing public methods like powerOn(), powerOff(), changeChannel(), adjustVolume() to interact with the TV. Abstraction means that the user of the Television class interacts with these simple public methods without needing to know the complex internal workings of the TV (how signals are processed, how the display works, etc.).

```
C++
#include <iostream>
#include <string>

class Television {
private: // Encapsulated data - hidden implementation details
   bool isOn;
   int currentChannel;
   int currentVolume;
   int maxVolume;
   int minChannel;
   int maxChannel;

public: // Abstract interface - simplified public methods
   Television(int maxVol = 100, int minCh = 1, int maxCh = 100) : isOn(false),
currentChannel(minCh), currentVolume(0), maxVolume(maxVol),
minChannel(minCh), maxChannel(maxCh) {
      std::cout << "Television object created." << std::endl;
   }

   void powerOn() {
      isOn = true;
      std::cout << "Television powered ON." << std::endl;
   }

   void powerOff() {
      isOn = false;
```

```
        std::cout << "Television powered OFF." << std::endl;
    }

    void changeChannel(int channel) {
        if (isOn && channel >= minChannel && channel <= maxChannel) {
            currentChannel = channel;
            std::cout << "Channel changed to " << currentChannel << std::endl;
        } else if (!isOn) {
            std::cout << "Television is off. Power it on first." << std::endl;
        } else {
            std::cout << "Invalid channel number." << std::endl;
        }
    }

    void adjustVolume(int volumeChange) {
        if (isOn) {
            currentVolume += volumeChange;
            if (currentVolume < 0) currentVolume = 0;
            if (currentVolume > maxVolume) currentVolume = maxVolume;
            std::cout << "Volume adjusted to " << currentVolume << std::endl;
        } else {
            std::cout << "Television is off. Power it on first." << std::endl;
        }
    }

    void displayStatus() const {
        std::cout << "Television Status: ";
        if (isOn) {
            std::cout << "ON, Channel: " << currentChannel << ", Volume: " <<
currentVolume << std::endl;
        } else {
            std::cout << "OFF" << std::endl;
        }
    }
};

int main() {
    Television tv; // Create a Television object
    tv.powerOn();
    tv.changeChannel(5);
    tv.adjustVolume(20);
    tv.displayStatus();
    tv.adjustVolume(-30); // Attempt to decrease volume below minimum
    tv.displayStatus();
    tv.powerOff();
    tv.displayStatus();
```

```
    tv.changeChannel(10); // Attempt to change channel when off

    return 0;
}
```

Step-by-step explanation:

1. **private: bool isOn; int currentChannel; ...**: Declares data members (isOn, currentChannel, currentVolume, maxVolume, minChannel, maxChannel) as private. These represent the internal state of the Television and are encapsulated (hidden from direct external access).
2. **public: Television(int maxVol = 100, ...)**: Public constructor and public methods (powerOn, powerOff, changeChannel, adjustVolume, displayStatus) are declared as public. These provide the abstract interface to interact with the Television object.
3. The public methods provide a simplified and controlled way to interact with the Television. For example, changeChannel handles input validation (checking if the TV is on and if the channel number is valid) and updates the currentChannel internally. The user of the Television class only needs to call tv.changeChannel(5) without worrying about the internal details of channel management.
4. The main function demonstrates interacting with the Television object through its public interface. It powers on the TV, changes channels, adjusts volume, and displays status, all using the abstract public methods. The internal state (isOn, currentChannel, currentVolume) is managed by the Television object itself and is not directly accessed or modified from main. This exemplifies encapsulation and abstraction.

5.7 Operator Overloading: Customizing Operator Behavior

Operator overloading allows you to redefine the behavior of standard C++ operators (like +, -, *, /, ==, !=, <, >, etc.) for user-defined types (classes). Operator overloading enables you to make objects of your classes work with operators in a natural and intuitive way, similar to how built-in types work. It enhances code readability and expressiveness, especially for classes that represent mathematical or logical entities. As Koenig and Moo explain in "Accelerated C++," operator overloading allows user-defined types to integrate seamlessly with the syntax and semantics of built-in types (Koenig & Moo, 2000).

Example: Operator Overloading for Vector2D Class

Let's create a Vector2D class to represent 2D vectors and overload the + operator for vector addition.

```
C++
#include <iostream>

class Vector2D {
public:
   double x, y;

   Vector2D(double xVal = 0.0, double yVal = 0.0) : x(xVal), y(yVal) {}

   // Overloading the + operator for vector addition
   Vector2D operator+(const Vector2D& other) const { // Returns a new
Vector2D object as result
      return Vector2D(x + other.x, y + other.y);
   }

   // Overloading the output stream operator << to print Vector2D objects
   friend std::ostream& operator<<(std::ostream& os, const Vector2D& v) {
// Friend function for output stream
      os << "(" << v.x << ", " << v.y << ")";
      return os;
   }
};

int main() {
   Vector2D v1(1.0, 2.0);
   Vector2D v2(3.0, 4.0);

   Vector2D v3 = v1 + v2; // Using overloaded + operator for vector addition

   std::cout << "Vector v1: " << v1 << std::endl; // Using overloaded <<
operator
   std::cout << "Vector v2: " << v2 << std::endl;
   std::cout << "Vector v3 (v1 + v2): " << v3 << std::endl;

   return 0;
}
```

Step-by-step explanation:

1. **`class Vector2D { ... };`**: Defines a class `Vector2D` to represent 2D vectors with `x` and `y` components.
2. **`Vector2D operator+(const Vector2D& other) const { ... }`**: This is the operator overloading function for the `+` operator.
    - **`Vector2D operator+`**: Declares that we are overloading the `+` operator.
    - **`(const Vector2D& other)`**: Specifies the parameter. For binary operators like `+`, the left operand is the object on which the operator is called (`v1` in `v1 + v2`), and the right operand is passed as the parameter (`v2` in `v1 + v2`). `const Vector2D&` is used for efficiency and to prevent modification of the right operand.
    - **`const` (after parameter list)**: Indicates that this operator overload function is a `const` member function, meaning it does not modify the object on which it is called (`v1` in `v1 + v2`).
    - **`return Vector2D(x + other.x, y + other.y);`**: The function body creates a new `Vector2D` object whose `x` component is the sum of the `x` components of the two operands (`x + other.x`), and similarly for the `y` component. This new `Vector2D` object, representing the vector sum, is returned as the result of the `+` operation.
3. **`friend std::ostream& operator<<(std::ostream& os, const Vector2D& v) { ... }`**: This overloads the output stream operator `<<` to enable printing `Vector2D` objects directly using `std::cout << v1;`.
    - **`friend std::ostream& operator<<`**: Declares a friend function that overloads the `<<` operator. It's a friend function because the left operand of `<<` is an `ostream` object (like `std::cout`), not a `Vector2D` object, so it cannot be a member function of `Vector2D`.
    - **`(std::ostream& os, const Vector2D& v)`**: Specifies the parameters: `std::ostream& os` (the output stream) and `const Vector2D& v` (the `Vector2D` object to be printed).
    - **`os << "(" << v.x << ", " << v.y << ")"; return os;`**: Formats the `Vector2D` object's `x` and `y` components into a string representation like `(x, y)` and inserts it into the output stream `os`. The function returns the modified output stream `os` to allow for chaining (e.g., `std::cout << v1 << v2;`).

4. **Vector2D v3 = v1 + v2;**: In main(), vector addition is performed using the overloaded + operator. This looks natural and readable because of operator overloading.
5. **std::cout << "Vector v1: " << v1 << std::endl;**: Prints Vector2D objects directly using std::cout thanks to the overloaded << operator.

5.8 Move Semantics and Rvalue References: Efficient Resource Transfer

Move semantics and rvalue references are modern C++ features (introduced in C++11) designed to improve performance, particularly when dealing with objects that manage resources (like dynamically allocated memory). Move semantics enable efficient transfer of resources from one object to another, avoiding unnecessary deep copies and improving efficiency, especially for temporary objects or objects that are no longer needed in their original location. As Sutter and Alexandrescu highlight, move semantics and rvalue references are crucial for writing modern, high-performance C++ code, enabling significant performance gains in resource management (Sutter & Alexandrescu, 2005).

5.8.1 Rvalue References: Identifying Temporary Objects

Rvalue references are a new type of reference in C++, denoted by && (double ampersand). They are designed to bind to rvalues, which are temporary objects, literals, or expressions that are about to be destroyed or are not intended to persist beyond their current scope. Rvalue references allow you to distinguish between lvalues (objects that have names and persistent locations) and rvalues, enabling move semantics.

5.8.2 Move Constructor and Move Assignment Operator

Move constructors and move assignment operators are special member functions that are invoked when an object is initialized or assigned from an rvalue. Instead of performing a deep copy (copying all resources), move constructors and move assignment operators *move* resources from the source object to the destination object. This typically involves transferring ownership of dynamically allocated memory or other resources, leaving the source object in a valid but "moved-from" state.

Example: Move Constructor and Move Assignment for String **Class**

Let's create a simplified String class that manages dynamically allocated character arrays and implement move constructor and move assignment operator to demonstrate move semantics.

```
C++
#include <iostream>
#include <cstring> // For strcpy, strlen, delete[]

class String {
public:
   char* data; // Pointer to dynamically allocated character array
   size_t length;

   // Default constructor
   String() : data(nullptr), length(0) {
      std::cout << "String Default Constructor" << std::endl;
   }

   // Constructor from C-style string
   String(const char* str) : length(std::strlen(str)) {
      std::cout << "String Parameterized Constructor from C-string" <<
std::endl;
      data = new char[length + 1]; // Allocate memory for string + null
terminator
      std::strcpy(data, str);      // Copy string content
   }

   // Copy constructor (deep copy)
   String(const String& other) : length(other.length) {
      std::cout << "String Copy Constructor" << std::endl;
      data = new char[length + 1]; // Allocate new memory
      std::strcpy(data, other.data); // Copy content from other string
   }

   // Move constructor (move resources)
```

```
    String(String&& other) noexcept : data(other.data), length(other.length) { //
noexcept for exception safety
        std::cout << "String Move Constructor" << std::endl;
        other.data = nullptr; // Set source object's data pointer to nullptr to
prevent double deletion
        other.length = 0;
    }

    // Copy assignment operator (deep copy)
    String& operator=(const String& other) {
        std::cout << "String Copy Assignment Operator" << std::endl;
        if (this != &other) { // Prevent self-assignment
            delete[] data;     // Deallocate existing data
            length = other.length;
            data = new char[length + 1];
            std::strcpy(data, other.data);
        }
        return *this;
    }

    // Move assignment operator (move resources)
    String& operator=(String&& other) noexcept {
        std::cout << "String Move Assignment Operator" << std::endl;
        if (this != &other) { // Prevent self-assignment
            delete[] data;     // Deallocate existing data
            data = other.data; // Steal data pointer
            length = other.length;
            other.data = nullptr; // Set source object's data pointer to nullptr
            other.length = 0;
        }
        return *this;
    }

    ~String() { // Destructor
        std::cout << "String Destructor" << std::endl;
        delete[] data; // Deallocate dynamically allocated memory
    }

    friend std::ostream& operator<<(std::ostream& os, const String& s) {
        os << (s.data ? s.data : "(null)"); // Handle null data pointer
        return os;
    }
};

String createString() { // Function returning a String object (rvalue)
    String temp("Hello from createString");
```

```
    return temp; // NRVO (Named Return Value Optimization) might happen, but move semantics are still relevant in general cases.
}

int main() {
    String str1 = "Initial String"; // Parameterized constructor
    String str2 = str1;         // Copy constructor (deep copy)
    String str3 = createString(); // Move constructor (move, not copy, from rvalue return)
    str2 = str3;              // Copy assignment operator (deep copy)
    str1 = createString();       // Move assignment operator (move, not copy, from rvalue return)

    std::cout << "str1: " << str1 << std::endl;
    std::cout << "str2: " << str2 << std::endl;
    std::cout << "str3: " << str3 << std::endl;

    return 0;
}
```

Step-by-step explanation:

1. **class String { ... };**: Defines a String class that manages a dynamically allocated character array (char* data).
2. **String(String&& other) noexcept : data(other.data), length(other.length) { ... }**: This is the move constructor. It takes an rvalue reference String&& other as input.
    - **String(String&& other) noexcept**: String(String&& other) is the move constructor declaration. noexcept specifier indicates that this constructor will not throw exceptions, which is important for certain optimizations and exception safety.
    - **: data(other.data), length(other.length)**: In the initializer list, it *moves* resources: it directly copies the data pointer and length from the other object to the newly constructed object. It does *not* allocate new memory or copy the string content.
    - **other.data = nullptr; other.length = 0;**: Crucially, it sets other.data to nullptr and other.length to 0. This is essential to leave the source object (other) in a valid but "moved-from" state. When other's destructor is called later, it will not attempt to delete[] nullptr, preventing double deletion.

3. **String& operator=(String&& other) noexcept { ... }**: This is the move assignment operator. It also takes an rvalue reference String&& other.
    - It first checks for self-assignment (if (this != &other)).
    - It deallocates any existing data in the current object (delete[] data;).
    - It then *moves* resources from other to the current object, similar to the move constructor: data = other.data; length = other.length; other.data = nullptr; other.length = 0;.
4. **String createString() { ... }**: This function returns a String object. The returned String object is an rvalue (a temporary object).
5. **String str3 = createString();**: When str3 is initialized with the return value of createString(), the *move constructor* is called (if available and applicable, as in this case). This is because the return value of createString() is an rvalue. Move constructor efficiently transfers ownership of the dynamically allocated string from the temporary object returned by createString() to str3, avoiding a deep copy.
6. **str1 = createString();**: When str1 is assigned the return value of createString(), the *move assignment operator* is called for the same reason (assignment from an rvalue). Move assignment efficiently transfers ownership of the string from the temporary object to str1.
7. In contrast, String str2 = str1; and str2 = str3; call the *copy constructor* and *copy assignment operator*, respectively, because str1 and str3 are lvalues (named objects). Copy operations perform deep copies, allocating new memory and copying content.

8. The output will show messages indicating which constructor and assignment operator are called in each case, demonstrating the invocation of move constructor and move assignment operator when dealing with rvalues, leading to more efficient resource management.

By mastering OOP concepts like classes, objects, inheritance, polymorphism, encapsulation, abstraction, operator overloading, and move semantics, Computer Technology students and educators can develop sophisticated, maintainable, and efficient C++ software solutions. These principles provide a powerful framework for organizing code, managing complexity, and building robust applications in various domains.

Chapter 6

The Standard Library (STL)

The Standard Template Library (STL) is a cornerstone of modern C++ programming, providing a rich set of templates for containers, algorithms, and iterators. It embodies the principles of generic programming, enabling developers to write efficient, reusable, and highly adaptable code. For Computer Technology students and educators, a deep understanding of the STL is indispensable, as it significantly simplifies complex programming tasks and promotes best practices in software development. This section will explore key components of the STL, including containers, iterators, algorithms, functional programming utilities, regular expressions, multi-threading support, and file handling, offering a comprehensive overview with practical examples and academic insights. We will delve into each component, elucidating its purpose, usage, and real-world applicability, ensuring a robust understanding of the STL's capabilities and its role in creating efficient and maintainable C++ applications.

6.1 Containers: Organizing Data Efficiently

Containers are fundamental building blocks of the STL, providing various ways to store and organize collections of data. These are template classes designed to hold elements of any type, offering different data structures optimized for specific operations and use cases. As Josuttis notes in "The C++ Standard Library: A Tutorial and Reference," the STL containers are designed with efficiency and flexibility in mind, allowing developers to choose the most appropriate data structure for their needs (Josuttis, 2012). Understanding the characteristics of different containers is crucial for efficient data management in C++ programs.

6.1.1 Sequence Containers: Ordered Data Storage

Sequence containers store elements in a linear sequence, maintaining the order of insertion or a specific order defined by the container itself. Key sequence containers in the STL include `vector`, `array`, and `list`.

6.1.1.1 `vector`: Dynamic Arrays

`std::vector` is a dynamic array, providing contiguous storage for elements and allowing efficient random access. Vectors can grow or shrink in size dynamically at runtime, making them highly versatile for collections where the size is not known in advance or changes frequently.

Example: Using `std::vector`

```C++
#include <iostream>
#include <vector>

int main() {
    std::vector<int> numbers; // Declare a vector of integers

    // Add elements to the vector
    numbers.push_back(10);
    numbers.push_back(20);
    numbers.push_back(30);
```

```
    // Access elements using index (random access)
    std::cout << "Vector elements: ";
    for (size_t i = 0; i < numbers.size(); ++i) {
        std::cout << numbers[i] << " ";
    }
    std::cout << std::endl;

    // Iterate through the vector using range-based for loop
    std::cout << "Vector elements (range-based loop): ";
    for (int number : numbers) {
        std::cout << number << " ";
    }
    std::cout << std::endl;

    // Check size and capacity
    std::cout << "Vector size: " << numbers.size() << std::endl;
    std::cout << "Vector capacity: " << numbers.capacity() << std::endl; // Capacity might be larger than size

    return 0;
}
```

Step-by-step explanation:

1. **#include <vector>**: Includes the header file for std::vector.
2. **std::vector<int> numbers;**: Declares a vector named numbers that will store integers.
3. **numbers.push_back(10);, numbers.push_back(20);, numbers.push_back(30);**: push_back() is a member function of std::vector that adds elements to the end of the vector, dynamically increasing its size if necessary.
4. **for (size_t i = 0; i < numbers.size(); ++i) { ... }**: Iterates through the vector using a traditional index-based loop. numbers.size() returns the current number of elements in the vector. numbers[i] accesses the element at index i (random access).
5. **for (int number : numbers) { ... }**: Iterates through the vector using a range-based for loop, a more concise way to iterate over all elements in a container.
6. **numbers.size()**: Returns the number of elements currently in the vector.
7. **numbers.capacity()**: Returns the total number of elements that the vector has allocated memory for. Capacity is often greater than or equal to size, as vectors typically allocate extra memory

to accommodate future growth, reducing the frequency of reallocations.

8.

Real-world scenario: std::vector is widely used for storing lists of items, such as storing frames in video processing, managing lists of users in a system, or holding data read from a file where the number of items is not known beforehand.

6.1.1.2 array: Fixed-Size Arrays

std::array is a fixed-size array, providing contiguous storage like std::vector but with a size fixed at compile time. std::array is essentially a safer and more feature-rich alternative to traditional C-style arrays, offering bounds checking and STL compatibility.

Example: Using std::array

```
C++
#include <iostream>
#include <array>

int main() {
   std::array<int, 5> fixedNumbers = {1, 2, 3, 4, 5}; // Declare and initialize a
fixed-size array of 5 integers

   // Access elements using index
   std::cout << "Array elements: ";
   for (size_t i = 0; i < fixedNumbers.size(); ++i) {
      std::cout << fixedNumbers[i] << " ";
   }
   std::cout << std::endl;

   // Iterate using range-based for loop
   std::cout << "Array elements (range-based loop): ";
   for (int number : fixedNumbers) {
      std::cout << number << " ";
   }
   std::cout << std::endl;

   // Check size (fixed size)
   std::cout << "Array size: " << fixedNumbers.size() << std::endl; // Size is
fixed at compile time

   // Access element using at() for bounds checking
   try {
```

```
        std::cout << "Element at index 6: " << fixedNumbers.at(6) << std::endl;
// Attempt to access out-of-bounds element
    } catch (const std::out_of_range& e) {
        std::cerr << "Out of range exception caught: " << e.what() << std::endl;
// at() throws exception for out-of-bounds access
    }

    return 0;
}
```

Step-by-step explanation:

1. **#include <array>**: Includes the header for std::array.
2. **std::array<int, 5> fixedNumbers = {1, 2, 3, 4, 5};**: Declares and initializes an std::array named fixedNumbers. <int, 5> specifies that it will store integers and have a fixed size of 5. Initialization is done using an initializer list {1, 2, 3, 4, 5}.
3. Iteration and access using index and range-based for loop are similar to std::vector.
4. **fixedNumbers.size()**: Returns the fixed size of the array, which is 5 in this case. Unlike std::vector, std::array's size is constant and determined at compile time.
5. **fixedNumbers.at(6)**: at() is a member function that provides bounds-checked access to elements. If you try to access an element outside the valid range (0 to size-1), at() throws an std::out_of_range exception. This is a safety feature compared to direct index access [], which does not perform bounds checking and can lead to undefined behavior for out-of-bounds access.
6. **try { ... } catch (const std::out_of_range& e) { ... }**: Demonstrates exception handling using try-catch to catch the std::out_of_range exception thrown by at(6).

Real-world scenario: std::array is suitable for situations where the size of the collection is known at compile time and does not need to change, such as representing fixed-size buffers, matrices of a known dimension in mathematical computations, or storing a fixed number of configuration parameters.

6.1.1.3 list: Doubly Linked Lists

std::list is a doubly linked list, providing non-contiguous storage where each element points to both the previous and next elements in the sequence. Lists excel at efficient insertion and deletion of elements at any position, but they do not offer efficient random access like vectors or arrays.

Example: Using std::list

```
C++
#include <iostream>
#include <list>

int main() {
   std::list<std::string> names; // Declare a list of strings

   // Add elements to the list
   names.push_back("Alice");
   names.push_front("Bob"); // Add to the front
   names.push_back("Charlie");

   // Iterate through the list
   std::cout << "List elements: ";
   for (const std::string& name : names) { // Use const& for efficiency and to
avoid copying strings
      std::cout << name << " ";
   }
   std::cout << std::endl;

   // Insert element in the middle using iterators
   std::list<std::string>::iterator it = ++names.begin(); // Get iterator to the
second element
   names.insert(it, "David"); // Insert "David" before the element pointed to by
'it'

   std::cout << "List elements after insertion: ";
   for (const std::string& name : names) {
      std::cout << name << " ";
   }
   std::cout << std::endl;

   // Remove element from the front
   names.pop_front();

   std::cout << "List elements after pop_front: ";
   for (const std::string& name : names) {
      std::cout << name << " ";
   }
   std::cout << std::endl;


   return 0;
}
```

Step-by-step explanation:

1. **#include <list>**: Includes the header for std::list.
2. **std::list<std::string> names;**: Declares a list named names to store strings.
3. **names.push_back("Alice");**, **names.push_front("Bob");**, **names.push_back("Charlie");**: push_back() adds to the end, push_front() adds to the beginning. Lists support efficient insertion at both ends.
4. **for (const std::string& name : names) { ... }**: Iterates through the list using a range-based for loop. Note that random access using indices (like names[i]) is *not* efficient for std::list. Iteration typically uses iterators or range-based loops.
5. **std::list<std::string>::iterator it = ++names.begin();**: Gets an iterator to the second element of the list.
    - **names.begin()**: Returns an iterator pointing to the first element.
    - **++names.begin()**: Increments the iterator to point to the next element (the second element).
    - **std::list<std::string>::iterator it**: Declares an iterator it of the appropriate type for std::list<std::string>. Iterators are essential for navigating and manipulating elements in lists and other STL containers.
6. **names.insert(it, "David");**: insert(iterator position, value) inserts a new element ("David") *before* the position indicated by the iterator it. Insertion in a list is efficient because it only involves adjusting pointers, not shifting elements like in a vector.
7. **names.pop_front();**: pop_front() removes the element from the beginning of the list. Lists support efficient removal from both ends (pop_front() and pop_back()).

Real-world scenario: std::list is suitable when frequent insertions and deletions are needed, especially in the middle of the sequence, and random access is not a primary requirement. Examples include managing playlists where songs might be added or removed frequently, implementing undo/redo functionality in an editor, or representing queues or stacks where elements are added and removed primarily from the front or back.

6.1.2 Associative Containers: Key-Value Pairs and Sets

Associative containers store elements in a way that allows efficient retrieval based on keys. They typically maintain elements in a sorted order (or hashed order in the case of unordered associative containers). Key associative containers in the STL include set, map, and unordered_map.

6.1.2.1 set: Unique Sorted Elements

std::set is an associative container that stores unique elements in a sorted order (by default, using < operator). Sets are efficient for checking for the presence of an element, removing duplicates, and maintaining sorted collections.

Example: Using std::set

```
C++
#include <iostream>
#include <set>

int main() {
  std::set<int> uniqueNumbers; // Declare a set of integers

  // Insert elements into the set (duplicates are automatically ignored)
  uniqueNumbers.insert(30);
  uniqueNumbers.insert(10);
  uniqueNumbers.insert(20);
  uniqueNumbers.insert(10); // Duplicate insertion - will be ignored

  // Iterate through the set (elements are automatically sorted)
  std::cout << "Set elements (sorted and unique): ";
  for (int number : uniqueNumbers) {
    std::cout << number << " ";
  }
  std::cout << std::endl;

  // Check if an element exists using count()
  if (uniqueNumbers.count(20)) {
    std::cout << "Set contains 20" << std::endl;
  } else {
    std::cout << "Set does not contain 20" << std::endl;
  }

  // Find an element using find()
```

```
    std::set<int>::iterator it = uniqueNumbers.find(20);
    if (it != uniqueNumbers.end()) {
        std::cout << "Found element: " << *it << std::endl;
    } else {
        std::cout << "Element not found" << std::endl;
    }

    return 0;
}
```

Step-by-step explanation:

1. **#include <set>**: Includes the header for std::set.
2. **std::set<int> uniqueNumbers;**: Declares a set named uniqueNumbers to store integers.
3. **uniqueNumbers.insert(30);, uniqueNumbers.insert(10);, uniqueNumbers.insert(20);, uniqueNumbers.insert(10);**: insert() adds elements to the set. Duplicate insertions (like the second 10) are automatically ignored; sets only store unique elements.
4. **for (int number : uniqueNumbers) { ... }**: Iterates through the set using a range-based for loop. Elements in a set are automatically stored in sorted order (ascending order by default for integers).
5. **uniqueNumbers.count(20)**: count(value) returns the number of times a value appears in the set. For std::set, it will be either 1 (if the element is present) or 0 (if not present), because sets store only unique elements. It's an efficient way to check for element existence.
6. **std::set<int>::iterator it = uniqueNumbers.find(20);**: find(value) searches for a value in the set and returns an iterator to the element if found, or uniqueNumbers.end() if not found.
7. **if (it != uniqueNumbers.end()) { ... }**: Checks if the iterator returned by find() is not equal to uniqueNumbers.end(). If it's not equal, it means the element was found, and *it dereferences the iterator to get the value of the element.

Real-world scenario: std::set is useful for maintaining unique collections of items, such as storing unique user IDs, managing sets of keywords, or implementing mathematical sets. Sets are also used when you need to efficiently check for the presence of an element or iterate through elements in sorted order.

6.1.2.2 map: Key-Value Pairs (Sorted)

std::map is an associative container that stores key-value pairs, where each key is unique and is associated with a value. Maps maintain key-value pairs in a sorted order based on the keys (by default, using < operator on keys). Maps are efficient for looking up values based on their keys, implementing dictionaries, and storing data with key-based access.

Example: Using std::map

```
C++
#include <iostream>
#include <map>
#include <string>

int main() {
   std::map<std::string, int> ages; // Declare a map where keys are strings
(names) and values are integers (ages)

   // Insert key-value pairs into the map
   ages["Alice"] = 30;
   ages["Bob"] = 25;
   ages["Charlie"] = 35;

   // Access value by key using [] operator
   std::cout << "Age of Alice: " << ages["Alice"] << std::endl;

   // Iterate through the map (key-value pairs are sorted by key)
   std::cout << "Map elements (sorted by key): " << std::endl;
   for (const auto& pair : ages) { // Use auto& for convenience and efficiency
      std::cout << pair.first << ": " << pair.second << std::endl; // pair.first is
the key, pair.second is the value
   }

   // Check if a key exists using count()
   if (ages.count("Bob")) {
      std::cout << "Map contains key 'Bob'" << std::endl;
   } else {
      std::cout << "Map does not contain key 'Bob'" << std::endl;
   }

   // Find an element using find()
   std::map<std::string, int>::iterator it = ages.find("Charlie");
   if (it != ages.end()) {
      std::cout << "Found key: " << it->first << ", value: " << it->second <<
std::endl; // it->first accesses key, it->second accesses value
```

```
    } else {
        std::cout << "Key not found" << std::endl;
    }

    return 0;
}
```

Step-by-step explanation:

1. **#include <map>**: Includes the header for std::map.
2. **std::map<std::string, int> ages;**: Declares a map named ages. <std::string, int> specifies that keys will be of type std::string and values will be of type int.
3. **ages["Alice"] = 30;, ages["Bob"] = 25;, ages["Charlie"] = 35;**: Inserts key-value pairs into the map using the [] operator. If the key already exists, its value is updated; if it doesn't exist, a new key-value pair is inserted.
4. **ages["Alice"]**: Accesses the value associated with the key "Alice" using the [] operator. If the key is not found, it will insert a new key with a default-constructed value (for integer, it would be 0), which might not be the desired behavior in all cases. For safer access, use find() or at().
5. **for (const auto& pair : ages) { ... }**: Iterates through the map using a range-based for loop. Each element in a map is a std::pair object, where pair.first is the key and pair.second is the value. Elements are iterated in sorted order of keys. auto& is used for convenience and efficiency.
6. **ages.count("Bob")**: count(key) returns the number of times a key appears in the map. For std::map, it will be either 1 (if the key exists) or 0 (if not), as keys in a map are unique.
7. **std::map<std::string, int>::iterator it = ages.find("Charlie");**: find(key) searches for a key in the map and returns an iterator to the key-value pair if found, or ages.end() if the key is not found.
8. **it->first and it->second**: If the iterator it is valid (not ages.end()), it->first accesses the key part of the pair, and it->second accesses the value part.

Real-world scenario: std::map is extensively used for implementing dictionaries, symbol tables in compilers, configuration settings where values are accessed by names, and any scenario where you need to associate keys with values and efficiently look up values based on keys in a sorted order.

6.1.2.3 unordered_map: Key-Value Pairs (Hashed)

std::unordered_map is similar to std::map in that it stores key-value pairs, but it uses a hash table for storage instead of a sorted tree structure. This results in average constant-time complexity for insertion, deletion, and lookup operations, making unordered_map generally faster than std::map for these operations, especially when order is not important. However, elements in unordered_map are not stored in any particular order.

Example: Using std::unordered_map

```
C++
#include <iostream>
#include <unordered_map>
#include <string>

int main() {
   std::unordered_map<std::string, int> wordCounts; // Declare an
unordered_map to count word occurrences

   // Count word frequencies
   wordCounts["apple"]++;
   wordCounts["banana"]++;
   wordCounts["apple"]++;
   wordCounts["orange"]++;
   wordCounts["banana"]++;
   wordCounts["banana"]++;

   // Access count by key
   std::cout << "Count of 'apple': " << wordCounts["apple"] << std::endl;
   std::cout << "Count of 'banana': " << wordCounts["banana"] << std::endl;
   std::cout << "Count of 'orange': " << wordCounts["orange"] << std::endl;

   // Iterate through the unordered_map (order is not guaranteed)
   std::cout << "Unordered_map elements (order not guaranteed): " <<
std::endl;
   for (const auto& pair : wordCounts) {
      std::cout << pair.first << ": " << pair.second << std::endl;
   }

   // Check if a key exists using count()
   if (wordCounts.count("grape")) {
      std::cout << "Map contains key 'grape'" << std::endl;
   } else {
```

```
        std::cout << "Map does not contain key 'grape'" << std::endl;
    }

    return 0;
}
```

Step-by-step explanation:

1. **#include <unordered_map>**: Includes the header for std::unordered_map.
2. **std::unordered_map<std::string, int> wordCounts;**: Declares an unordered_map named wordCounts to store word counts (keys are strings, values are integers).
3. **wordCounts["apple"]++;**, etc.: Increments the count for words. If a word is encountered for the first time, it's inserted into the unordered_map with a default value of 0, and then incremented to 1. Subsequent increments update the count.
4. Accessing values by key using [] and checking key existence using count() are similar to std::map.
5. **for (const auto& pair : wordCounts) { ... }**: Iterates through the unordered_map. The order of elements in an unordered_map is not guaranteed to be sorted or related to the insertion order; it depends on the hash function and internal organization of the hash table.

Real-world scenario: std::unordered_map is highly efficient for tasks like frequency counting, implementing caches, symbol tables where order is not important but fast lookup is crucial, and general-purpose key-value storage where performance is prioritized over sorted order.

6.2 Iterators and Algorithms: Working with Container Elements

Iterators and algorithms are essential components of the STL that work together to provide a powerful and flexible way to manipulate data stored in containers. Iterators are objects that act like pointers, allowing you to traverse elements in containers, while algorithms are functions that perform operations on ranges of elements defined by iterators. As Meyers emphasizes in "Effective STL," understanding iterators and algorithms is key to leveraging the full power of the STL and writing efficient and generic C++ code (Meyers, 2001).

6.2.1 Iterators: Navigating Containers

Iterators provide a consistent way to access elements in different types of containers. They abstract away the underlying container implementation, allowing algorithms to work generically with various container types. Iterators support operations like incrementing to move to the next element, dereferencing to access the current element's value, and comparing iterators.

6.2.2 Algorithms: Performing Operations on Ranges

STL algorithms are generic functions that operate on ranges of elements defined by iterators. They are decoupled from specific container types and can work with any container that provides compatible iterators. Algorithms cover a wide range of operations, including searching, sorting, transforming, copying, and numerical operations.

6.2.2.1 find: Searching for an Element

The std::find algorithm searches for the first occurrence of a specific value within a range defined by iterators.

Example: Using std::find with std::vector

```
C++
#include <iostream>
#include <vector>
#include <algorithm> // For std::find

int main() {
   std::vector<int> numbers = {10, 20, 30, 40, 50};

   // Search for value 30 in the vector
   std::vector<int>::iterator it = std::find(numbers.begin(), numbers.end(), 30);
// find(begin_iterator, end_iterator, value_to_find)

   if (it != numbers.end()) {
      std::cout << "Value 30 found at position: " <<
std::distance(numbers.begin(), it) << std::endl; // std::distance to get index
   } else {
      std::cout << "Value 30 not found in the vector" << std::endl;
   }
```

```
    // Search for value 60 (not present)
    it = std::find(numbers.begin(), numbers.end(), 60);
    if (it != numbers.end()) {
        std::cout << "Value 60 found" << std::endl;
    } else {
        std::cout << "Value 60 not found in the vector" << std::endl;
    }

    return 0;
}
```

Step-by-step explanation:

1. **#include <algorithm>**: Includes the header for STL algorithms, including std::find.
2. **std::vector<int>::iterator it = std::find(numbers.begin(), numbers.end(), 30);**: Calls std::find.
   - **numbers.begin()**: Returns an iterator to the beginning of the numbers vector (the start of the range to search).
   - **numbers.end()**: Returns an iterator to one position past the end of the numbers vector (the end of the range to search; end() iterator itself does not point to a valid element).
   - **30**: The value to search for.
   - **std::find(...)**: Searches for the first occurrence of 30 within the range [numbers.begin(), numbers.end()). It returns an iterator to the element if found, or numbers.end() if not found.
   - **std::vector<int>::iterator it**: Declares an iterator it to store the result of std::find.
3. **if (it != numbers.end()) { ... }**: Checks if the iterator it is not equal to numbers.end(). If it's not equal, it means std::find found the value.
4. **std::distance(numbers.begin(), it)**: std::distance is an STL algorithm that calculates the distance (number of elements) between two iterators. In this case, it calculates the index of the found element by finding the distance from the beginning iterator to the iterator pointing to the found element.

Real-world scenario: std::find is used in various search operations, such as finding a specific user in a list, locating a particular record in a data collection, or searching for a substring within a string.

6.2.2.2 sort: Sorting Elements

The std::sort algorithm sorts elements within a range defined by iterators. By default, it sorts elements in ascending order using the < operator, but you can provide a custom comparison function or function object to define a different sorting order.

Example: Using std::sort with std::vector

```
C++
#include <iostream>
#include <vector>
#include <algorithm> // For std::sort

int main() {
   std::vector<int> unsortedNumbers = {30, 10, 50, 20, 40};

   std::cout << "Unsorted vector: ";
   for (int number : unsortedNumbers) {
      std::cout << number << " ";
   }
   std::cout << std::endl;

   // Sort the vector in ascending order
   std::sort(unsortedNumbers.begin(), unsortedNumbers.end()); //
sort(begin_iterator, end_iterator) - default ascending order

   std::cout << "Sorted vector (ascending): ";
   for (int number : unsortedNumbers) {
      std::cout << number << " ";
   }
   std::cout << std::endl;

   // Sort in descending order using a custom comparator (lambda function)
   std::sort(unsortedNumbers.begin(), unsortedNumbers.end(),
std::greater<int>()); // sort(begin, end, comparator) - descending order using
std::greater

   std::cout << "Sorted vector (descending): ";
   for (int number : unsortedNumbers) {
      std::cout << number << " ";
   }
   std::cout << std::endl;

   return 0;
}
```

Step-by-step explanation:

1. **std::sort(unsortedNumbers.begin(), unsortedNumbers.end());:** Calls std::sort to sort the unsortedNumbers vector in ascending order.
   - **unsortedNumbers.begin(), unsortedNumbers.end():** Define the range to be sorted (the entire vector).
   - **std::sort(...):** Sorts the elements within the specified range using the default comparison operator <.
2. **std::sort(unsortedNumbers.begin(), unsortedNumbers.end(), std::greater<int>());:** Calls std::sort with a custom comparator std::greater<int>() to sort in descending order.
   - **std::greater<int>():** This is a function object (functor) from the <functional> header (implicitly included by <algorithm>). It provides a comparison function that returns true if the first argument is greater than the second, effectively reversing the sorting order to descending.

Real-world scenario: std::sort is fundamental for ordering data, such as sorting search results by relevance, ordering items in a list alphabetically or numerically, and preparing data for efficient searching or processing.

6.2.2.3 transform: Applying a Function to a Range

The std::transform algorithm applies a given function to each element in an input range and stores the results in an output range. It is useful for performing element-wise operations on containers.

Example: Using std::transform with std::vector

```
C++
#include <iostream>
#include <vector>
#include <algorithm> // For std::transform
#include <cmath>     // For std::sqrt

int main() {
    std::vector<double> numbers = {1.0, 4.0, 9.0, 16.0};
    std::vector<double> squareRoots(numbers.size()); // Output vector, same
size as input
```

```
    std::cout << "Original vector: ";
    for (double number : numbers) {
        std::cout << number << " ";
    }
    std::cout << std::endl;

    // Transform each element to its square root
    std::transform(numbers.begin(), numbers.end(), squareRoots.begin(),
std::sqrt); // transform(input_begin, input_end, output_begin, function)

    std::cout << "Square roots: ";
    for (double root : squareRoots) {
        std::cout << root << " ";
    }
    std::cout << std::endl;

    return 0;
}
```

Step-by-step explanation:

1. **#include <cmath>**: Includes the header for mathematical functions, specifically std::sqrt (square root).
2. **std::vector<double> squareRoots(numbers.size());**: Declares an output vector squareRoots of the same size as the input vector numbers. The output vector needs to be pre-allocated to hold the transformed elements.
3. **std::transform(numbers.begin(), numbers.end(), squareRoots.begin(), std::sqrt);**: Calls std::transform.
    - **numbers.begin(), numbers.end()**: Define the input range (the entire numbers vector).
    - **squareRoots.begin()**: Defines the beginning of the output range (where the transformed elements will be stored).
    - **std::sqrt**: The function to be applied to each element. std::sqrt is a function from <cmath> that calculates the square root of a number.
    - **std::transform(...)**: Applies std::sqrt to each element in the input range [numbers.begin(), numbers.end()) and stores the result in the output range starting at squareRoots.begin().

Real-world scenario: std::transform is useful for applying operations to entire datasets, such as scaling data values, converting units, applying mathematical functions to signal processing data, or performing element-wise transformations on image pixels.

6.2.2.4 for_each: Applying a Function to Each Element

The std::for_each algorithm applies a given function to each element in a range defined by iterators. It is similar to std::transform but is typically used when you want to perform an action on each element (like printing or modifying in-place) without creating a new output range.

Example: Using std::for_each with std::vector

```
C++
#include <iostream>
#include <vector>
#include <algorithm> // For std::for_each

// Function to print each number (function object - functor)
struct NumberPrinter {
   void operator()(int number) const { // Overloaded function call operator -
makes NumberPrinter a functor
       std::cout << "Number: " << number << std::endl;
   }
};

int main() {
   std::vector<int> data = {10, 20, 30, 40};

   std::cout << "Processing elements using for_each: " << std::endl;

   // Apply NumberPrinter functor to each element
   std::for_each(data.begin(), data.end(), NumberPrinter()); //
for_each(begin_iterator, end_iterator, function_object)

   std::cout << std::endl;

   // Apply lambda function to each element (more concise way)
   std::cout << "Processing elements using for_each with lambda: " <<
std::endl;
   std::for_each(data.begin(), data.end(), [](int number){ // Lambda function as
function object
       std::cout << "Value: " << number * 2 << std::endl; // Example: double
each number and print
   });

   return 0;
```

}

Step-by-step explanation:

1. **struct NumberPrinter { ... };**: Defines a function object (functor) named NumberPrinter.
   - **void operator()(int number) const { ... }**: Overloads the function call operator (). This makes NumberPrinter an object that can be called like a function. When a NumberPrinter object is called with an integer argument, this operator() function will be executed, printing the number.
2. **std::for_each(data.begin(), data.end(), NumberPrinter());**: Calls std::for_each with the NumberPrinter functor.
   - **NumberPrinter()**: Creates a temporary instance of the NumberPrinter functor.
   - **std::for_each(...)**: Applies the operator() of the NumberPrinter object to each element in the range [data.begin(), data.end()).
3. **std::for_each(data.begin(), data.end(), [](int number){ ... });**: Calls std::for_each using a lambda function as the function object.
   - **[](int number){ ... }**: This is a lambda expression. It defines an anonymous function object inline. This lambda function takes an integer number as input and prints its double. Lambda functions provide a concise way to define function objects directly where they are needed.

Real-world scenario: std::for_each is useful for performing actions on every item in a collection, such as printing all items in a list, applying a validation function to each data entry, or triggering an event for each object in a game world.

6.3 Functional Programming with <functional>: Enhancing Algorithm Flexibility

The <functional> header in C++ provides tools for functional programming, allowing you to treat functions as objects and compose them in flexible ways. Key components in <functional> for use with STL algorithms include function objects (functors), function adapters, and lambda expressions. These tools enhance the expressiveness and adaptability of STL algorithms. As Abrahams and Gurtovoy explain in "C++ Template Metaprogramming," functional programming techniques, enabled by `<functional>`, significantly enhance the power and flexibility of generic programming in C++ (Abrahams & Gurtovoy, 2004).

6.3.1 Function Objects (Functors): Objects Behaving Like Functions

Function objects, or functors, are objects of classes that overload the function call operator `operator()`. This allows objects to be called as if they were functions. Functors can encapsulate state and provide more flexible behavior than regular functions when used with STL algorithms. We already saw an example of a functor `NumberPrinter` in the `std::for_each` example.

6.3.2 Lambda Expressions: Concise Anonymous Functions

Lambda expressions, introduced in C++11, provide a concise way to define anonymous function objects inline. They are particularly useful for creating short, localized function objects to be used with STL algorithms, making code more readable and reducing boilerplate. We also saw an example of a lambda function in the `std::for_each` example.

6.3.3 Function Adapters: Combining and Modifying Function Objects

Function adapters are templates that allow you to modify or combine existing function objects to create new ones. Examples include `std::bind`, `std::not1`, `std::not2`, which can be used to bind arguments to functions, negate predicates, or compose function objects. (Note: `std::bind` has been partially superseded by lambdas in modern C++ for many use cases, but understanding its concept is still valuable).

Example: Using `std::bind` (Function Adapter) with `std::for_each`

```
C++
#include <iostream>
#include <vector>
```

```
#include <algorithm> // For std::for_each
#include <functional> // For std::bind, std::placeholders

// Function to add two numbers and print the result
void addAndPrint(int a, int b) {
  std::cout << a << " + " << b << " = " << a + b << std::endl;
}

int main() {
  std::vector<int> numbers = {1, 2, 3, 4};
  int baseValue = 10;

  std::cout << "Using std::bind with for_each: " << std::endl;

  // Use std::bind to create a function object that calls addAndPrint with
baseValue as the first argument
  std::for_each(numbers.begin(), numbers.end(), std::bind(addAndPrint,
baseValue, std::placeholders::_1)); // bind(function, fixed_arg1,
placeholder_for_arg2)

  return 0;
}
```

Step-by-step explanation:

1. **#include <functional>**: Includes the header for <functional>, which contains std::bind and placeholders.
2. **void addAndPrint(int a, int b) { ... }**: Defines a regular function addAndPrint that takes two integers and prints their sum.
3. **std::bind(addAndPrint, baseValue, std::placeholders::_1)**: Uses std::bind to create a new function object.
   - **addAndPrint**: The function to be bound.
   - **baseValue**: The first argument to addAndPrint is fixed to baseValue (which is 10).
   - **std::placeholders::_1**: A placeholder indicating that the second argument to addAndPrint will be taken from the argument passed to the function object created by std::bind. _1 represents the first argument passed to the bound function object.
   - **std::bind(...)**: Returns a function object. When this function object is called with one argument, it will call addAndPrint(baseValue, argument).
4. **std::for_each(numbers.begin(), numbers.end(), ...)**: std::for_each applies the function object created by std::bind to each element

in the numbers vector. For each element in numbers, the bound function object is called, effectively calling addAndPrint(baseValue, element).

Real-world scenario: Functional programming techniques with <functional> and STL algorithms enhance code flexibility and reusability. They are used for creating complex data processing pipelines, event handling systems, and situations where you need to customize algorithm behavior dynamically or compose functions for more complex operations. While lambdas often provide a more modern and concise alternative for many use cases, understanding function objects and adapters like std::bind is still valuable for comprehending the evolution of functional programming in C++ and for working with legacy code or situations where more complex function object manipulations are required.

6.4 Regular Expressions <regex>: Pattern Matching and Text Processing

The <regex> library in C++ provides support for regular expressions, a powerful tool for pattern matching and text processing. Regular expressions allow you to define search patterns using a special syntax to match, search, and manipulate strings based on complex rules. The <regex> library enables tasks like input validation, data extraction, text parsing, and search-and-replace operations with sophisticated pattern matching capabilities. As Friedl details in "Mastering Regular Expressions," regular expressions are an indispensable tool for text processing and pattern matching in computer science (Friedl, 2006).

Example: Using <regex> for Email Validation

```
C++
#include <iostream>
#include <string>
#include <regex> // For std::regex, std::regex_match

int main() {
    std::string email1 = "test@example.com";
    std::string email2 = "invalid-email";
    std::string emailRegex = R"([a-zA-Z0-9._%+-]+@[a-zA-Z0-9.-]+\.[a-zA-
Z]{2,})"; // Raw string literal for regex pattern
```

```
    std::regex pattern(emailRegex); // Create a regex object from the pattern

    // Match email1 against the regex pattern
    if (std::regex_match(email1, pattern)) { // regex_match(string, regex_object)
- checks if entire string matches
        std::cout << "'" << email1 << "' is a valid email address" << std::endl;
    } else {
        std::cout << "'" << email1 << "' is not a valid email address" <<
std::endl;
    }

    // Match email2 against the regex pattern
    if (std::regex_match(email2, pattern)) {
        std::cout << "'" << email2 << "' is a valid email address" << std::endl;
    } else {
        std::cout << "'" << email2 << "' is not a valid email address" <<
std::endl;
    }

    return 0;
}
```

Step-by-step explanation:

1. **#include <regex>**: Includes the header for the <regex> library.
2. **std::string emailRegex = R"([a-zA-Z0-9._%+-]+@[a-zA-Z0-9.-]+\.[a-zA-Z]{2,})";**: Defines a regular expression pattern for email validation as a raw string literal.
    - **R"(...)"**: Raw string literal. Characters within raw string literals are not escaped, making it convenient to write regex patterns that often contain backslashes.
    - [a-zA-Z0-9._%+-]+: Matches one or more alphanumeric characters, dots, underscores, percent signs, plus or minus signs (for the username part of the email).
    - @: Matches the "@" symbol.
    - [a-zA-Z0-9.-]+: Matches one or more alphanumeric characters, dots, or hyphens (for the domain part).
    - \.: Matches a literal dot (escaped with a backslash because . has a special meaning in regex).
    - [a-zA-Z]{2,}: Matches two or more alphabetic characters (for the top-level domain, like "com", "org", "net").

3. **std::regex pattern(emailRegex);:** Creates a std::regex object named pattern from the string emailRegex. This compiles the regex pattern into an internal representation that can be used for matching.
4. **std::regex_match(email1, pattern):** std::regex_match attempts to match the *entire* input string (email1) against the regex pattern (pattern). It returns true if the entire string matches the pattern, and false otherwise.
5. The code then uses if statements to check the return value of std::regex_match and print whether each email string is considered valid or not based on the regex pattern.

Real-world scenario: Regular expressions are widely used for input validation (email, phone numbers, URLs, etc.), data extraction from text files or web pages (parsing log files, web scraping), text search and replace in editors and IDEs, and any text processing task requiring pattern-based manipulation.

6.5 Multi-threading <thread>, <mutex>, <atomic>: Concurrent Execution

The <thread>, <mutex>, and <atomic> headers in C++ provide support for multi-threading, allowing you to create programs that can execute multiple threads concurrently. Multi-threading enables parallelism, improving performance for tasks that can be divided into independent subtasks. The <thread> library provides tools for creating and managing threads, <mutex> for synchronizing access to shared resources to prevent data races, and <atomic> for atomic operations on variables, ensuring thread-safe operations without explicit locks in certain cases. As Williams explains in "C++ Concurrency in Action," mastering multi-threading is essential for developing high-performance and responsive applications in modern computing environments (Williams, 2019).

Example: Basic Multi-threading with <thread> and <mutex>

```
C++
#include <iostream>
#include <thread>   // For std::thread
```

```
#include <mutex>   // For std::mutex
#include <string>

std::mutex consoleMutex; // Mutex to protect console output (shared resource)

// Function to be executed by a thread
void printMessage(const std::string& message, int threadID) {
  for (int i = 0; i < 5; ++i) {
    std::lock_guard<std::mutex> lock(consoleMutex); // Acquire mutex lock
- RAII style
    std::cout << "Thread " << threadID << ": " << message << " (iteration
" << i << ")" << std::endl;
  }
} // Mutex lock automatically released when lock_guard goes out of scope

int main() {
  std::thread thread1(printMessage, "Hello from thread 1", 1); // Create thread
1, passing function and arguments
  std::thread thread2(printMessage, "Hello from thread 2", 2); // Create thread
2

  thread1.join(); // Wait for thread 1 to finish
  thread2.join(); // Wait for thread 2 to finish

  std::cout << "Main thread finished" << std::endl;

  return 0;
}
```

Step-by-step explanation:

1. **#include <thread>, #include <mutex>**: Includes headers for <thread> and <mutex>.
2. **std::mutex consoleMutex;**: Declares a mutex object named consoleMutex. A mutex (mutual exclusion) is used to protect shared resources from concurrent access by multiple threads, preventing data races. In this example, consoleMutex is used to protect console output (std::cout), as simultaneous output from multiple threads can become garbled.
3. **void printMessage(const std::string& message, int threadID) { ... }**: Defines the function that will be executed by each thread.
   - **std::lock_guard<std::mutex> lock(consoleMutex);**: Creates a std::lock_guard object named lock, associating it with consoleMutex. std::lock_guard is a RAII (Resource Acquisition Is Initialization) wrapper for mutexes.

When lock_guard is constructed, it automatically acquires the lock on consoleMutex. When lock_guard goes out of scope (at the end of the printMessage function or if an exception is thrown), its destructor is automatically called, which releases the lock on consoleMutex. This ensures that the mutex is always released, even in case of exceptions, preventing deadlocks.

   - **std::cout << ...**: The code inside the lock_guard's scope is protected by the mutex. Only one thread can execute this code at a time, ensuring that console output is synchronized and readable.
4. **std::thread thread1(printMessage, "Hello from thread 1", 1);**: Creates a new thread named thread1.
   - **std::thread thread1(...)**: Constructs a std::thread object. The first argument is the function to be executed in the new thread (printMessage), and subsequent arguments are the arguments to be passed to that function ("Hello from thread 1" and 1).
5. **std::thread thread2(printMessage, "Hello from thread 2", 2);**: Creates another thread thread2, also executing printMessage with different arguments.
6. **thread1.join();, thread2.join();**: join() is a member function of std::thread. Calling thread1.join() makes the main thread wait for thread1 to complete its execution before continuing. Similarly, thread2.join() waits for thread2. Calling join() ensures that the main thread waits for all created threads to finish before the program exits.

Real-world scenario: Multi-threading is crucial for improving performance in applications that can benefit from parallelism, such as image processing, video encoding/decoding, game engines, web servers, and any application that needs to perform multiple tasks concurrently to improve responsiveness or throughput. Mutexes and atomic operations are essential for writing thread-safe code when multiple threads access shared resources, preventing data corruption and ensuring program correctness in concurrent environments.

6.6 File Handling fstream, ifstream, ofstream: Persistent Data Storage

The <fstream>, <ifstream>, and <ofstream> headers in C++ provide classes for file handling, allowing you to read data from and write data to files. fstream provides general-purpose file stream functionality, ifstream is specialized for input file streams (reading from files), and ofstream for output file streams (writing to files). File handling is essential for data persistence, configuration management, and interacting with external data sources. As Prata describes in "C++ Primer Plus," file I/O is a fundamental aspect of programming, allowing programs to interact with external storage and data sources (Prata, 2014).

Example: File Reading and Writing with ofstream and ifstream

```
C++
#include <iostream>
#include <fstream> // For file streams
#include <string>

int main() {
   std::string filename = "example.txt";

   // Write to a file using ofstream
   { // Scope for ofstream object - file will be closed automatically when it goes
out of scope
      std::ofstream outputFile(filename); // Create an ofstream object and open
file for writing

      if (outputFile.is_open()) { // Check if file opened successfully
         outputFile << "Hello, File I/O!" << std::endl; // Write data to the file
         outputFile << "This is a second line." << std::endl;
         outputFile.close(); // Explicitly close the file (RAII also closes it when
outputFile goes out of scope)
         std::cout << "Data written to file: " << filename << std::endl;
      } else {
         std::cerr << "Error opening file for writing: " << filename <<
std::endl;
      }
   } // outputFile automatically closed here due to RAII

   // Read from a file using ifstream
```

```
  { // Scope for ifstream object
    std::ifstream inputFile(filename); // Create an ifstream object and open file for reading
    std::string line;

    if (inputFile.is_open()) {
      std::cout << "Reading data from file: " << filename << std::endl;
      while (std::getline(inputFile, line)) { // Read line by line until end of file
        std::cout << "Line: " << line << std::endl; // Print each line to console
      }
      inputFile.close(); // Explicitly close the file (RAII also closes it when inputFile goes out of scope)
    } else {
      std::cerr << "Error opening file for reading: " << filename << std::endl;
    }
  } // inputFile automatically closed here due to RAII

  return 0;
}
```

Step-by-step explanation:

1. **#include <fstream>**: Includes the header for file streams.
2. **std::ofstream outputFile(filename);**: Creates an ofstream object named outputFile and attempts to open the file specified by filename ("example.txt") in write mode. If the file does not exist, it will be created. If it exists, its content will be truncated (overwritten by default).
3. **if (outputFile.is_open()) { ... }**: Checks if the file was opened successfully using is_open(). It's good practice to check if file operations were successful before proceeding.
4. **outputFile << "Hello, File I/O!" << std::endl;, outputFile << "This is a second line." << std::endl;**: Uses the stream insertion operator << to write data to the outputFile. std::endl inserts a newline character and flushes the output buffer.
5. **outputFile.close();**: Explicitly closes the output file stream. While ofstream objects will automatically close the file when they go out of scope (due to RAII), explicitly closing it is good practice to ensure that all data is flushed to the file and resources are released promptly.

6. The code is enclosed in a scope { ... } so that outputFile goes out of scope at the end of the block, and its destructor is called, automatically closing the file (RAII).
7. **std::ifstream inputFile(filename);**: Creates an ifstream object inputFile and opens the same file "example.txt" in read mode.
8. **while (std::getline(inputFile, line)) { ... }**: Reads the file line by line using std::getline.
   - **std::getline(inputFile, line)**: Reads a line of text from inputFile and stores it in the std::string variable line. It reads until a newline character is encountered or the end of the file is reached. std::getline returns the input stream object itself, which evaluates to true as long as lines are successfully read and false when the end of file is reached or an error occurs.
   - The while loop continues as long as std::getline successfully reads lines from the file.
9. **std::cout << "Line: " << line << std::endl;**: Prints each line read from the file to the console.
10. **inputFile.close();**: Explicitly closes the input file stream. Similar to ofstream, ifstream objects will also automatically close the file when they go out of scope due to RAII.
11. The input file reading part is also enclosed in a scope { ... } for automatic file closure via RAII.

Real-world scenario: File handling is essential for almost all applications that need to store and retrieve data persistently. This includes saving user preferences, storing game states, reading configuration files, processing data from external files (e.g., CSV, text files), logging application events, and interacting with file-based databases.

By mastering these key components of the STL—containers, iterators, algorithms, functional programming tools, regular expressions, multi-threading, and file handling—Computer Technology students and educators can significantly enhance their C++ programming skills, enabling them to develop robust, efficient, and maintainable software solutions for a wide range of applications. The STL provides a powerful and versatile foundation for modern C++ development, promoting code reusability, efficiency, and best practices in software engineering.

Chapter 7

Modern C++ Features (C++11 to C++23)

Modern C++, encompassing standards from C++11 onwards, represents a significant evolution of the language, introducing features that enhance expressiveness, safety, and performance. These advancements address long-standing challenges in software development, enabling programmers to write more robust, efficient, and maintainable code. For Computer Technology students and educators, understanding these modern features is paramount, as they form the foundation of contemporary C++ programming practices. This section will delve into key modern C++ features, including type inference, smart pointers, move semantics, range-based loops, compile-time evaluation, lambda functions, sum types, type erasure, concepts, and coroutines, providing detailed explanations, practical examples, and insights into their real-world applications and academic significance.

7.1 Type Inference: Simplifying Type Declarations

Type inference, introduced with the auto and decltype keywords, significantly simplifies C++ code by allowing the compiler to deduce the types of variables and expressions automatically. This reduces boilerplate code, improves readability, and enhances code maintainability without sacrificing type safety. As Stroustrup notes in "A Tour of C++," type inference makes C++ code cleaner and more focused on logic rather than verbose type declarations (Stroustrup, 2018).

7.1.1 auto: Automatic Type Deduction

The auto keyword instructs the compiler to deduce the type of a variable from its initializer. This is particularly useful for complex types, iterators, and lambda expressions, where explicitly writing out the type can be cumbersome and error-prone.

Example: Using auto for Type Inference

```
C++
#include <iostream>
#include <vector>

int main() {
    // Type is automatically deduced as int
    auto number = 10;

    // Type is automatically deduced as double
    auto pi = 3.14159;

    // Type is automatically deduced as std::string
    auto message = "Hello, Modern C++";

    // Type is automatically deduced as std::vector<int>::iterator
    std::vector<int> numbers = {1, 2, 3, 4, 5};
    auto iterator = numbers.begin();

    std::cout << "Number: " << number << std::endl;
    std::cout << "Pi: " << pi << std::endl;
    std::cout << "Message: " << message << std::endl;
    std::cout << "First element of numbers: " << *iterator << std::endl;

    return 0;
```

```
}
```

Step-by-step explanation:

1. **auto number = 10;**: The compiler infers the type of number to be int because the initializer 10 is an integer literal.
2. **auto pi = 3.14159;**: The compiler infers the type of pi to be double because 3.14159 is a floating-point literal.
3. **auto message = "Hello, Modern C++";**: The compiler infers the type of message to be const char* (or std::string if you are initializing with a std::string object, depending on context and compiler version). In modern C++, it's often better to use std::string for string literals for safety and flexibility.
4. **std::vector<int> numbers = {1, 2, 3, 4, 5}; auto iterator = numbers.begin();**: The type of iterator is automatically deduced to be std::vector<int>::iterator, which is the return type of numbers.begin(). Without auto, you would have to write std::vector<int>::iterator iterator = numbers.begin();, which is more verbose.

Real-world scenario: auto is extensively used to simplify code when dealing with complex template types, iterators, and return types of functions, especially in generic programming and modern C++ algorithms. It enhances readability by reducing visual clutter from lengthy type names and focuses attention on the logic of the code.

7.1.2 decltype: Declaring Type of an Expression

The decltype keyword allows you to obtain the declared type of an expression. Unlike auto, which deduces the type from the initializer, decltype examines an expression and yields its type without actually evaluating the expression. This is particularly useful in generic programming and template metaprogramming when you need to determine the type of an expression at compile time.

Example: Using decltype to Determine Expression Type

```
C++
#include <iostream>

int add(int a, int b) {
    return a + b;
```

```
}

int main() {
    int x = 5;
    double y = 2.5;

    // Deduce the type of x using decltype
    decltype(x) var1 = x; // var1 is of type int

    // Deduce the type of x + y using decltype
    decltype(x + y) var2 = x + y; // var2 is of type double (due to type promotion)

    // Deduce the return type of the add function
    decltype(add(x, x)) var3 = add(x, x); // var3 is of type int

    std::cout << "Type of var1: " << typeid(var1).name() << std::endl;
    std::cout << "Type of var2: " << typeid(var2).name() << std::endl;
    std::cout << "Type of var3: " << typeid(var3).name() << std::endl;

    return 0;
}
```

Step-by-step explanation:

1. **decltype(x) var1 = x;:** decltype(x) yields the declared type of x, which is int. So, var1 is declared as an int and initialized with the value of x.
2. **decltype(x + y) var2 = x + y;:** decltype(x + y) yields the type of the expression x + y. Since x is int and y is double, due to type promotion rules in C++, the result of x + y is double. Thus, var2 is declared as a double and initialized with the result of x + y.
3. **decltype(add(x, x)) var3 = add(x, x);:** decltype(add(x, x)) yields the return type of the function call add(x, x). The function add is declared to return int, so var3 is declared as an int and initialized with the result of calling add(x, x).
4. **typeid(var1).name(), typeid(var2).name(), typeid(var3).name():** typeid operator (from <typeinfo>) is used to get runtime type information. .name() returns a string representing the type's name (compiler-dependent and may be mangled). This is used here to demonstrate the types deduced by decltype.

Real-world scenario: decltype is essential in template metaprogramming and generic libraries where the exact types involved in expressions are not known until compile time. It allows developers to write code that adapts to different types and expressions, ensuring type correctness and flexibility in generic contexts. For example, decltype can be used to determine the return type of a function template based on its arguments without actually calling the function.

7.2 Smart Pointers: Managing Memory Safely

Smart pointers are RAII (Resource Acquisition Is Initialization) wrappers around raw pointers that automate memory management, preventing memory leaks and dangling pointers. Modern C++ primarily uses unique_ptr and shared_ptr to manage dynamically allocated memory, promoting safer and more exception-safe code. As Sutter and Alexandrescu advocate in "C++ Coding Standards," using smart pointers for resource management is a fundamental best practice in modern C++ (Sutter & Alexandrescu, 2005).

7.2.1 unique_ptr: Exclusive Ownership

std::unique_ptr provides exclusive ownership of dynamically allocated memory. Only one unique_ptr can point to a given object at any time. When the unique_ptr goes out of scope, the object it manages is automatically deleted. unique_ptr is move-only, meaning ownership can be transferred but not copied, enforcing exclusive ownership.

Example: Using unique_ptr for Exclusive Ownership

```
C++
#include <iostream>
#include <memory> // For std::unique_ptr

class MyClass {
public:
    MyClass(int value) : data(value) {
        std::cout << "MyClass constructed with value: " << data << std::endl;
    }
    ~MyClass() {
        std::cout << "MyClass destroyed with value: " << data << std::endl;
    }
    void printData() const {
```

```
        std::cout << "Data: " << data << std::endl;
    }
private:
    int data;
};

int main() {
    { // Scope to demonstrate unique_ptr's lifetime
        // Create a unique_ptr owning a MyClass object
        std::unique_ptr<MyClass> ptr1(new MyClass(100)); // ptr1 takes
ownership of dynamically allocated MyClass object

        ptr1->printData(); // Access object through unique_ptr using -> operator

        // Ownership can be moved
        std::unique_ptr<MyClass> ptr2 = std::move(ptr1); // Ownership
transferred from ptr1 to ptr2, ptr1 becomes null

        if (ptr1 == nullptr) {
            std::cout << "ptr1 is now null after move" << std::endl;
        }
        ptr2->printData();

        // ptr1 = ptr2; // Error: Copying unique_ptr is not allowed (deleted copy
constructor)
        // ptr1 = std::make_unique<MyClass>(200); // OK: Move assignment (if
ptr1 was not null before, the old object would be deleted)
    } // ptr2 goes out of scope here, and the MyClass object it owns is
automatically deleted

    std::cout << "End of main function" << std::endl;
    return 0;
}
```

Step-by-step explanation:

1. **#include <memory>**: Includes the header for smart pointers, including std::unique_ptr.
2. **std::unique_ptr<MyClass> ptr1(new MyClass(100));**: Creates a std::unique_ptr named ptr1 that manages a dynamically allocated MyClass object created using new MyClass(100). ptr1 now exclusively owns the memory.
3. **ptr1->printData();**: Accesses the members of the managed MyClass object using the -> operator, just like with raw pointers.
4. **std::unique_ptr<MyClass> ptr2 = std::move(ptr1);**: Moves ownership from ptr1 to ptr2 using std::move. After the move, ptr1

becomes null (it no longer owns the MyClass object), and ptr2 now owns it.

5. **if (ptr1 == nullptr) { ... }**: Checks if ptr1 is null after the move, demonstrating that ownership has been transferred.
6. **// ptr1 = ptr2; // Error: Copying unique_ptr is not allowed**: Demonstrates that copying unique_ptr is disallowed. unique_ptr's copy constructor and copy assignment operator are deleted to enforce exclusive ownership.
7. **// ptr1 = std::make_unique<MyClass>(200); // OK: Move assignment**: Shows that move assignment is allowed. If ptr1 was owning another object before this assignment, that object would be automatically deleted.
8. **{ ... } scope**: The unique_ptr ptr2 is defined within a scope. When the scope ends, ptr2 goes out of scope, and its destructor is called. The destructor of unique_ptr automatically deletes the MyClass object it manages, as indicated by the "MyClass destroyed..." output.

Real-world scenario: unique_ptr is used whenever you want to ensure exclusive ownership of a resource, such as dynamically allocated objects, file handles, or network connections. It is ideal for representing ownership relationships where only one part of the program should manage a particular resource's lifetime. For example, in factory patterns, a factory function might return a unique_ptr to indicate that the caller now owns the created object.

7.2.2 shared_ptr: Shared Ownership

std::shared_ptr provides shared ownership of dynamically allocated memory. Multiple shared_ptr objects can point to the same object. The object is deleted only when the last shared_ptr pointing to it goes out of scope. shared_ptr uses reference counting to track the number of owners.

Example: Using shared_ptr for Shared Ownership

```cpp
C++
#include <iostream>
#include <memory> // For std::shared_ptr

class SharedClass {
```

```
public:
   SharedClass(int value) : data(value) {
      std::cout << "SharedClass constructed with value: " << data << std::endl;
   }
   ~SharedClass() {
      std::cout << "SharedClass destroyed with value: " << data << std::endl;
   }
   void printData() const {
      std::cout << "Data: " << data << std::endl;
   }
private:
   int data;
};

void useSharedPtr(std::shared_ptr<SharedClass> ptr) { // Pass shared_ptr by
value - reference count will increment
   std::cout << "Shared pointer count inside function: " << ptr.use_count() <<
std::endl;
   ptr->printData();
} // ptr goes out of scope here, reference count decrements

int main() {
   // Create a shared_ptr owning a SharedClass object
   std::shared_ptr<SharedClass> sharedPtr1 =
std::make_shared<SharedClass>(200); // Recommended way to create
shared_ptr

   std::cout << "Initial shared pointer count: " << sharedPtr1.use_count() <<
std::endl; // Reference count is 1

   { // Inner scope
      std::shared_ptr<SharedClass> sharedPtr2 = sharedPtr1; // Copy
shared_ptr - shared ownership, reference count increments

      std::cout << "Shared pointer count inside inner scope: " <<
sharedPtr1.use_count() << std::endl; // Reference count is 2 (sharedPtr1 and
sharedPtr2)
      useSharedPtr(sharedPtr2); // Pass shared_ptr to function - reference
count increments again inside function

      std::cout << "Shared pointer count after function call: " <<
sharedPtr1.use_count() << std::endl; // Reference count back to 2 (ptr in
useSharedPtr went out of scope)
   } // sharedPtr2 goes out of scope here, reference count decrements
```

```
    std::cout << "Shared pointer count after inner scope: " <<
sharedPtr1.use_count() << std::endl; // Reference count back to 1 (only
sharedPtr1 owns the object)

    // sharedPtr1 goes out of scope here, reference count becomes 0, and the
SharedClass object is deleted
    std::cout << "End of main function" << std::endl;
    return 0;
}
```

Step-by-step explanation:

1. **#include <memory>**: Includes the header for smart pointers.
2. **std::shared_ptr<SharedClass> sharedPtr1 = std::make_shared<SharedClass>(200);**: Creates a std::shared_ptr named sharedPtr1 that manages a dynamically allocated SharedClass object. std::make_shared is the recommended way to create shared_ptr as it can be more efficient and exception-safe than using new directly with shared_ptr constructor.
3. **sharedPtr1.use_count()**: use_count() is a member function of shared_ptr that returns the current reference count (number of shared_ptr objects sharing ownership). Initially, it's 1.
4. **std::shared_ptr<SharedClass> sharedPtr2 = sharedPtr1;**: Copying sharedPtr1 to sharedPtr2 creates another shared_ptr that points to the same SharedClass object. This increases the reference count to 2.
5. **useSharedPtr(sharedPtr2);**: Passing sharedPtr2 by value to the function useSharedPtr copies the sharedPtr2. Inside useSharedPtr, the function parameter ptr also shares ownership, increasing the reference count temporarily within the function scope. When ptr goes out of scope at the end of useSharedPtr, the reference count decrements.
6. **{ ... } inner scope**: sharedPtr2 is defined within an inner scope. When this scope ends, sharedPtr2 goes out of scope, and its destructor is called, decrementing the reference count.
7. Finally, when sharedPtr1 goes out of scope at the end of main, the reference count becomes 0. At this point, because no shared_ptr objects are managing the SharedClass object, its destructor is called, and the memory is deallocated.

Real-world scenario: shared_ptr is used when multiple parts of a program need to share ownership of a resource, and the resource should be deallocated only when no part of the program needs it anymore. Examples include shared data structures in concurrent programming, caching systems where multiple caches might hold references to the same data, and complex object relationships where ownership is not strictly hierarchical.

7.3 Move Semantics: Optimizing Resource Transfers

Move semantics, introduced in C++11, optimize resource transfers by moving resources from one object to another instead of copying them. This is particularly beneficial for objects that manage large or expensive resources, such as dynamically allocated memory, file handles, or network connections. Move semantics are implemented through move constructors and move assignment operators, and are triggered by rvalue references and functions like `std::move` and `std::forward`. As Vandevoorde, Josuttis, and Gregor detail in "C++ Templates: The Complete Guide," move semantics are crucial for writing efficient C++ code, especially when dealing with resource-heavy objects (Vandevoorde, Josuttis, & Gregor, 2017).

Example: Demonstrating Move Semantics with `std::vector`

```
C++
#include <iostream>
#include <vector>

class ResourceHolder {
public:
  ResourceHolder() : data(new int[1000000]) { // Allocate a large resource
    std::cout << "ResourceHolder constructed, resource allocated" <<
std::endl;
  }
  ~ResourceHolder() {
    delete[] data; // Deallocate resource
    std::cout << "ResourceHolder destroyed, resource deallocated" <<
std::endl;
  }

  // Copy constructor (demonstrates deep copy - expensive)
  ResourceHolder(const ResourceHolder& other) : data(new int[1000000]) {
    std::cout << "Copy constructor called, deep copy performed" <<
std::endl;
```

```
        std::copy(other.data, other.data + 1000000, data); // Deep copy of data
    }

    // Move constructor (demonstrates move - efficient)
    ResourceHolder(ResourceHolder&& other) noexcept : data(other.data) {
        std::cout << "Move constructor called, resource moved" << std::endl;
        other.data = nullptr; // Important: Set other's pointer to nullptr to
prevent double deletion
    }

    ResourceHolder& operator=(const ResourceHolder& other) {
        std::cout << "Copy assignment operator called, deep copy performed" <<
std::endl;
        if (this != &other) {
            delete[] data;
            data = new int[1000000];
            std::copy(other.data, other.data + 1000000, data);
        }
        return *this;
    }

    ResourceHolder& operator=(ResourceHolder&& other) noexcept {
        std::cout << "Move assignment operator called, resource moved" <<
std::endl;
        if (this != &other) {
            delete[] data;
            data = other.data;
            other.data = nullptr;
        }
        return *this;
    }


private:
    int* data;
};

ResourceHolder createResourceHolder() {
    ResourceHolder holder; // Create ResourceHolder object
    return holder; // Return by value - move constructor will be called (RVO
might optimize this further)
}

int main() {
    std::vector<ResourceHolder> holders;
```

```
    std::cout << "Pushing back a ResourceHolder (move semantics in action):" << std::endl;
    holders.push_back(createResourceHolder()); // Move constructor called when adding to vector

    std::cout << "\nCreating another ResourceHolder and moving it:" << std::endl;
    ResourceHolder holder2;
    holders.push_back(std::move(holder2)); // Explicitly move holder2 - move constructor called

    std::cout << "\nEnd of main function" << std::endl;
    return 0;
}
```

Step-by-step explanation:

1. **class ResourceHolder { ... };**: Defines a class ResourceHolder that manages a large dynamically allocated integer array (data).
2. **Constructor, Destructor, Copy Constructor, Move Constructor, Copy Assignment, Move Assignment**: These special member functions are defined to demonstrate copy and move semantics.
   - **Constructor**: Allocates a large integer array.
   - **Destructor**: Deallocates the array.
   - **Copy Constructor**: Performs a deep copy - allocates new memory and copies the data. This is an expensive operation for large resources.
   - **Move Constructor**: Performs a move - transfers ownership of the resource by simply copying the raw pointer and setting the source object's pointer to nullptr. This is a cheap operation as it avoids deep copying. noexcept is specified because move constructors should ideally not throw exceptions.
   - **Copy Assignment Operator**: Similar to copy constructor, performs deep copy.
   - **Move Assignment Operator**: Similar to move constructor, performs move. noexcept is also specified here.
3. **ResourceHolder createResourceHolder() { ... }**: A function that creates a ResourceHolder object and returns it by value. Returning by value often triggers move semantics (or Return Value Optimization - RVO).

4. **std::vector<ResourceHolder> holders;**: Creates a vector to hold ResourceHolder objects.
5. **holders.push_back(createResourceHolder());**: When createResourceHolder() returns a ResourceHolder object, and push_back adds it to the vector, the move constructor of ResourceHolder is called (or RVO might occur, further optimizing it). This avoids a deep copy and efficiently transfers the resource into the vector.
6. **ResourceHolder holder2; holders.push_back(std::move(holder2));**: std::move(holder2) explicitly casts holder2 to an rvalue reference. This forces the move constructor to be called when holder2 is added to the vector, even though holder2 is an lvalue. Without std::move, the copy constructor would be called (if available and vector requires resizing), resulting in a deep copy.

Real-world scenario: Move semantics are crucial for performance optimization in C++, especially when working with containers, smart pointers, and other resource-managing objects. They are heavily used in STL containers (like std::vector, std::string) to efficiently handle operations like resizing, sorting, and element insertion/deletion. Move semantics are essential for writing high-performance C++ code that avoids unnecessary copying of large data structures.

7.4 Range-based Loops: Simplifying Iteration

Range-based for loops, introduced in C++11, provide a more concise and readable way to iterate over elements in containers and ranges. They simplify iteration by abstracting away iterator management and making the code cleaner and less error-prone.

Example: Using Range-based Loops for Simplified Iteration

```
C++
#include <iostream>
#include <vector>
#include <string>

int main() {
    std::vector<int> numbers = {10, 20, 30, 40, 50};
```

```
    std::string message = "Modern C++";

    // Iterate over vector using range-based for loop
    std::cout << "Vector elements: ";
    for (int number : numbers) { // 'number' takes on the value of each element
in 'numbers'
        std::cout << number << " ";
    }
    std::cout << std::endl;

    // Iterate over string using range-based for loop
    std::cout << "String characters: ";
    for (char character : message) { // 'character' takes on the value of each
character in 'message'
        std::cout << character << " ";
    }
    std::cout << std::endl;

    // Range-based loop with auto and modification (using reference)
    std::cout << "Vector elements doubled: ";
    for (auto& number : numbers) { // Use auto& to modify elements in place
        number *= 2; // Double each element
        std::cout << number << " ";
    }
    std::cout << std::endl;

    return 0;
}
```

Step-by-step explanation:

1. **for (int number : numbers) { ... }**: This is a range-based for loop iterating over the numbers vector. For each iteration, the variable number takes on the value of the current element in numbers. The loop automatically handles iteration from the beginning to the end of the container.
2. **for (char character : message) { ... }**: Iterates over the characters in the message string. For each iteration, character takes on the value of the current character. Range-based loops work not only with STL containers but also with C-style arrays, strings, and any type that supports begin() and end() iterators or has a begin() and end() member function.
3. **for (auto& number : numbers) { ... }**: This range-based loop uses auto& for the loop variable number. auto& declares number as a reference to the elements in numbers. This is important if you

want to *modify* the elements of the container within the loop. Without &, number would be a copy of each element, and modifications would not affect the original vector.

Real-world scenario: Range-based for loops are used extensively in modern C++ code to iterate over collections of data whenever you need to process each element in a container or range. They improve code readability and reduce the chance of iterator-related errors, making iteration logic more straightforward and less verbose.

7.5 constexpr and consteval: Compile-Time Computation

constexpr (C++11) and consteval (C++20) are keywords that enable compile-time computation in C++. They allow you to declare functions and variables that can be evaluated at compile time, leading to performance improvements by shifting computations from runtime to compile time. constexpr functions can be evaluated at both compile time and runtime, while consteval functions are guaranteed to be evaluated only at compile time. As Dos Reis, D'Angelo, and Vandevoorde explain in "C++ Templates: The Definitive Guide," compile-time programming with constexpr and consteval is a powerful technique for optimizing performance and enforcing compile-time constraints (Dos Reis, D'Angelo, & Vandevoorde, 2017).

7.5.1 constexpr: Possible Compile-Time Evaluation

constexpr functions and variables can be evaluated at compile time if the inputs are compile-time constants. If the inputs are not compile-time constants, constexpr functions can still be evaluated at runtime like regular functions.

Example: Using constexpr for Compile-Time and Runtime Evaluation

```
C++
#include <iostream>

constexpr int square(int n) { // constexpr function - can be evaluated at
compile time or runtime
    return n * n;
```

```
}

int main() {
  // Compile-time evaluation: argument is a compile-time constant
  constexpr int compileTimeSquare = square(5); // Evaluated at compile time

  // Runtime evaluation: argument is not a compile-time constant
  int runtimeValue = 10;
  int runtimeSquare = square(runtimeValue); // Evaluated at runtime

  std::cout << "Compile-time square: " << compileTimeSquare << std::endl;
  std::cout << "Runtime square: " << runtimeSquare << std::endl;

  return 0;
}
```

Step-by-step explanation:

1. **constexpr int square(int n) { ... }**: Declares a constexpr function square. This function calculates the square of an integer. Because it's constexpr, the compiler will attempt to evaluate it at compile time if possible.
2. **constexpr int compileTimeSquare = square(5);**: The call square(5) is evaluated at compile time because the argument 5 is a compile-time constant. The result 25 is also a compile-time constant, and compileTimeSquare is declared constexpr, ensuring compile-time initialization.
3. **int runtimeValue = 10; int runtimeSquare = square(runtimeValue);**: The call square(runtimeValue) is evaluated at runtime because runtimeValue is not a compile-time constant (its value is determined at runtime). Even though square is a constexpr function, it can still be called with runtime values and behave like a regular function.

Real-world scenario: constexpr is used for defining constants, compile-time calculations, and template metaprogramming. It can be used to perform calculations at compile time that would otherwise be done at runtime, improving performance, especially in performance-critical applications or embedded systems where runtime resources are limited.

7.5.2 consteval: Guaranteed Compile-Time Evaluation

consteval functions, introduced in C++20, are guaranteed to be evaluated at compile time. If a consteval function cannot be evaluated at compile time (e.g., if its arguments are not compile-time constants), the program will fail to compile. consteval provides a stronger guarantee of compile-time evaluation than constexpr.

Example: Using consteval for Guaranteed Compile-Time Evaluation

```
C++
#include <iostream>

consteval int factorial(int n) { // consteval function - must be evaluated at
compile time
   if (n <= 1) {
      return 1;
   } else {
      return n * factorial(n - 1);
   }
}

int main() {
   // Compile-time evaluation: argument is a compile-time constant
   constexpr int compileTimeFactorial = factorial(5); // Evaluated at compile
time - OK

   std::cout << "Compile-time factorial: " << compileTimeFactorial <<
std::endl;

   // int runtimeValue = 5;
   // int runtimeFactorial = factorial(runtimeValue); // Compile error:
consteval function must be compile-time evaluated

   return 0;
}
```

Step-by-step explanation:

1. **consteval int factorial(int n) { ... }**: Declares a consteval function factorial. This function calculates the factorial of a non-negative integer recursively. Because it's consteval, it *must* be evaluated at compile time.

2. **constexpr int compileTimeFactorial = factorial(5);**: The call factorial(5) is evaluated at compile time because factorial is consteval and the argument 5 is a compile-time constant. The result is assigned to compileTimeFactorial, which is also declared constexpr.
3. **// int runtimeValue = 5; // int runtimeFactorial = factorial(runtimeValue); // Compile error**: This commented-out code demonstrates what happens if you try to call a consteval function with a runtime value. If you uncomment these lines, the code will fail to compile because consteval functions are required to be evaluated at compile time. The compiler will issue an error indicating that factorial must be called in a compile-time context.

Real-world scenario: consteval is used when you absolutely need to ensure that a function or computation is performed at compile time, for example, in template metaprogramming, compile-time assertions, or when generating code or data at compile time. It provides a stricter guarantee than constexpr and can be used to enforce compile-time constraints in critical parts of the code.

7.6 Lambda Functions and std::function: Enhancing Functional Programming

Lambda functions, often simply called lambdas, and std::function are key features that enhance functional programming capabilities in C++. Lambda functions provide a concise way to create anonymous function objects inline, while std::function is a polymorphic function wrapper that can store, copy, and invoke any callable target (like lambdas, function pointers, or function objects). These features enable more flexible and expressive code, especially when working with algorithms and callbacks. As Koeninger, Muskalla, and Petrović describe in "Modern C++ Design: Generic Programming and Design Patterns Applied," lambda functions and std::function are essential tools for modern C++ developers embracing functional programming paradigms (Koeninger, Muskalla, & Petrović, 2013).

7.6.1 Lambda Functions: Anonymous Inline Functions

Lambda functions are unnamed functions defined directly in the code where they are needed. They are particularly useful for creating short, self-contained function objects for use with algorithms or as callbacks. Lambda functions can capture variables from their surrounding scope, making them very flexible.

Example: Using Lambda Functions with std::sort **and** std::for_each

```
C++
#include <iostream>
#include <vector>
#include <algorithm> // For std::sort, std::for_each

int main() {
    std::vector<int> numbers = {3, 1, 4, 1, 5, 9, 2, 6};

    std::cout << "Unsorted vector: ";
    for (int n : numbers) std::cout << n << " ";
    std::cout << std::endl;

    // Sort vector in descending order using a lambda function as comparator
    std::sort(numbers.begin(), numbers.end(), [](int a, int b) { // Lambda
function as comparator
        return a > b; // Sort in descending order
    });

    std::cout << "Sorted vector (descending): ";
    for (int n : numbers) std::cout << n << " ";
    std::cout << std::endl;

    int factor = 10; // Variable to be captured by lambda

    // Multiply each element by factor using std::for_each and a lambda function
with capture
    std::cout << "Vector elements multiplied by " << factor << ": ";
    std::for_each(numbers.begin(), numbers.end(), [factor](int& n) { // Lambda
function with capture by value
        n *= factor; // Modify element in place
        std::cout << n << " ";
    });
    std::cout << std::endl;

    return 0;
```

}

Step-by-step explanation:

1. **std::sort(numbers.begin(), numbers.end(), [](int a, int b) { return a > b; });**: Uses std::sort with a lambda function as the comparator to sort in descending order.
    - **[](int a, int b) { return a > b; }**: This is a lambda expression.
        - **[]**: Capture clause (empty in this case, meaning no external variables are captured).
        - **(int a, int b)**: Parameter list (takes two integers a and b).
        - **{ return a > b; }**: Lambda function body, which returns true if a is greater than b (for descending order).
    - std::sort uses this lambda function to compare elements during sorting.
2. **int factor = 10;**: Declares an integer variable factor in the surrounding scope.
3. **std::for_each(numbers.begin(), numbers.end(), [factor](int& n) { ... });**: Uses std::for_each with a lambda function that captures the factor variable.
    - **[factor]**: Capture clause. factor is captured *by value.* This means the lambda function gets a copy of the current value of factor.
    - **(int& n)**: Parameter list. n is taken as a reference (int&) because we want to modify the elements of the numbers vector in place.
    - **{ n *= factor; std::cout << n << " "; }**: Lambda function body, which multiplies the element n by the captured factor and prints the result.

Real-world scenario: Lambda functions are used extensively in modern C++ for writing concise and expressive code, especially when working with STL algorithms, event handlers, callbacks, and asynchronous programming. They simplify the creation of function objects, making code more readable and maintainable by defining function logic directly where it is used.

7.6.2 std::function: Polymorphic Function Wrappers

std::function is a template class that provides a general-purpose, polymorphic function wrapper. It can store, copy, and invoke any callable target, including function pointers, function objects (functors), lambda functions, and member functions. std::function is useful when you need to store or pass callable entities as objects, especially when the exact type of the callable is not known at compile time or when you need type erasure for function objects.

Example: Using std::function to Store and Invoke Different Callable Types

```
C++
#include <iostream>
#include <functional> // For std::function

// Regular function
int add(int a, int b) {
   return a + b;
}

// Function object (functor)
struct Multiply {
   int operator()(int a, int b) const {
      return a * b;
   }
};

int main() {
   std::function<int(int, int)> operation; // Declare a std::function that can
store any callable taking two ints and returning an int

   // Store a lambda function in std::function
   operation = [](int a, int b) { return a - b; };
   std::cout << "Lambda function result: " << operation(10, 5) << std::endl;

   // Store a regular function in std::function
   operation = add;
   std::cout << "Regular function result: " << operation(10, 5) << std::endl;

   // Store a function object in std::function
   Multiply multiplyFunctor;
   operation = multiplyFunctor;
   std::cout << "Function object result: " << operation(10, 5) << std::endl;
```

```
    return 0;
}
```

Step-by-step explanation:

1. **#include <functional>**: Includes the header for <functional>, which contains std::function.
2. **std::function<int(int, int)> operation;**: Declares a std::function object named operation.
    - **std::function<int(int, int)>**: Specifies the signature of the callable that operation can store. int(int, int) means it can store any callable that takes two int arguments and returns an int.
3. **operation = [](int a, int b) { return a - b; };**: Assigns a lambda function to operation. The lambda function subtracts two integers. std::function can store this lambda because it matches the specified signature.
4. **operation = add;**: Assigns the regular function add to operation. std::function can also store regular functions that match the signature.
5. **Multiply multiplyFunctor; operation = multiplyFunctor;**: Creates an instance of the Multiply functor and assigns it to operation. std::function can store function objects as well.
6. **operation(10, 5)**: Calls the callable object stored in operation. The actual function that gets called depends on what was last assigned to operation (lambda, add, or multiplyFunctor). std::function provides a uniform way to invoke different types of callable entities.

Real-world scenario: std::function is used when you need to work with callable entities of different types in a generic way, such as in callback mechanisms, event handling systems, or when implementing strategies or policies that can be configured with different function objects at runtime. It enables type erasure, allowing you to work with functions without needing to know their exact types at compile time, enhancing flexibility and decoupling in code.

7.7 std::optional, std::variant, std::any: Handling Uncertainty and Flexibility

std::optional, std::variant, and std::any are modern C++ features that provide safer and more expressive ways to handle situations where a value might be absent (std::optional), can be one of several possible types (std::variant), or needs to be of an unknown type (std::any). These features enhance type safety and flexibility compared to traditional C++ approaches like using null pointers or void pointers. As Gurtovoy and Alexandrescu discuss in "Modern C++ Design: Generic Programming and Design Patterns Applied," these types are valuable additions for robust and flexible software design (Gurtovoy & Alexandrescu, 2001).

7.7.1 std::optional: Representing Optional Values

std::optional is a template class that represents an optional value, which may or may not contain a value. It is a type-safe way to represent the concept of a value that might be missing, avoiding the need to use sentinel values like null pointers or special error codes.

Example: Using std::optional to Represent a Potentially Missing Value

```
C++
#include <iostream>
#include <optional> // For std::optional
#include <string>

std::optional<int> tryParseInt(const std::string& str) {
    try {
        return std::stoi(str); // Try to convert string to int
    } catch (const std::invalid_argument&) {
        return std::nullopt; // Return empty optional if conversion fails
    }
}

int main() {
    std::string input1 = "123";
    std::string input2 = "abc";

    std::optional<int> result1 = tryParseInt(input1);
```

```
    std::optional<int> result2 = tryParseInt(input2);

    std::cout << "Parsing '" << input1 << "': ";
    if (result1.has_value()) {
        std::cout << "Value = " << result1.value() << std::endl; // Access value
using value()
    } else {
        std::cout << "Failed to parse as integer" << std::endl;
    }

    std::cout << "Parsing '" << input2 << "': ";
    if (result2.has_value()) {
        std::cout << "Value = " << result2.value() << std::endl;
    } else {
        std::cout << "Failed to parse as integer" << std::endl;
    }

    return 0;
}
```

Step-by-step explanation:

1. **#include <optional>**: Includes the header for std::optional.
2. **std::optional<int> tryParseInt(const std::string& str) { ... }**: Defines a function tryParseInt that attempts to parse a string as an integer and returns an std::optional<int>.
   - **std::optional<int>**: Specifies that the function returns an optional integer.
   - **try { ... } catch (const std::invalid_argument&)**: Uses a try-catch block to handle potential exceptions during string-to-integer conversion using std::stoi.
   - **return std::stoi(str);**: If std::stoi is successful, it returns the converted integer, which is implicitly converted to std::optional<int> containing the value.
   - **return std::nullopt;**: If std::stoi throws std::invalid_argument (meaning the string cannot be converted to an integer), it returns std::nullopt. std::nullopt is a special object that represents an empty std::optional.
3. **std::optional<int> result1 = tryParseInt(input1);**, **std::optional<int> result2 = tryParseInt(input2);**: Calls tryParseInt with two different input strings and stores the results in std::optional<int> variables.

4. **result1.has_value(), result2.has_value():** has_value() is a member function of std::optional that returns true if the std::optional object contains a value, and false otherwise.
5. **result1.value():** value() is a member function that returns the contained value. It should only be called if has_value() is true. If value() is called on an empty std::optional, it throws a std::bad_optional_access exception.

Real-world scenario: std::optional is used to represent function return values that might not always produce a valid result (like parsing functions, lookups in maps that might not find the key), to represent optional parameters in function signatures, and in any situation where you need to explicitly indicate that a value might be absent in a type-safe manner. It is a safer alternative to using null pointers to indicate missing values, as it prevents null pointer dereferencing errors and clearly communicates the optional nature of a value in the type system.

7.7.2 std::variant: Type-Safe Union

std::variant is a type-safe union that can hold a value of one of several specified types. Unlike traditional C-style unions, std::variant keeps track of the type of value it currently holds and enforces type safety, preventing accidental access to a value as the wrong type.

Example: Using std::variant to Store Values of Different Types

```
C++
#include <iostream>
#include <variant> // For std::variant, std::get
#include <string>

int main() {
   // variant can hold int, float, or std::string
   std::variant<int, float, std::string> data;

   data = 10; // Store an int
   std::cout << "Value: " << std::get<int>(data) << ", Type index: " <<
data.index() << std::endl; // Access int value using std::get<int>

   data = 3.14f; // Store a float
   std::cout << "Value: " << std::get<float>(data) << ", Type index: " <<
data.index() << std::endl; // Access float value using std::get<float>
```

```
    data = "hello"; // Store a string
    std::cout << "Value: " << std::get<std::string>(data) << ", Type index: "
<< data.index() << std::endl; // Access string value using std::get<std::string>

    // std::cout << std::get<int>(data) << std::endl; // Error:
std::bad_variant_access - trying to get int when variant holds string

    // Safely access variant value using std::get_if (pointer-based access)
    if (const std::string* strPtr = std::get_if<std::string>(&data)) { // Get
pointer to string if variant holds string
        std::cout << "String value (via pointer): " << *strPtr << std::endl;
    }

    return 0;
}
```

Step-by-step explanation:

1. **#include <variant>**: Includes the header for std::variant.
2. **std::variant<int, float, std::string> data;**: Declares a std::variant named data. <int, float, std::string> specifies that data can hold a value of type int, float, or std::string.
3. **data = 10;, data = 3.14f;, data = "hello";**: Assigns values of different types to data. At any given time, data holds a value of only one of the specified types.
4. **std::get<int>(data), std::get<float>(data), std::get<std::string>(data)**: std::get<T>(variant) is used to access the value of type T stored in the variant. It performs a type check at runtime. If the variant does not currently hold a value of type T, std::get<T> throws a std::bad_variant_access exception.
5. **data.index()**: index() is a member function of std::variant that returns the zero-based index of the type currently held by the variant within the list of possible types (0 for int, 1 for float, 2 for std::string in this example).
6. **// std::cout << std::get<int>(data) << std::endl; // Error: std::bad_variant_access**: Demonstrates that trying to access the wrong type using std::get<T> results in a std::bad_variant_access exception.
7. **std::get_if<std::string>(&data)**: std::get_if<T>(variant_pointer) is a safer way to access variant values. It returns a pointer to the value of type T if the variant holds that type, or nullptr otherwise. It does not throw exceptions.
8. **if (const std::string* strPtr = std::get_if<std::string>(&data)) { ... }**: Uses std::get_if to safely check if data holds a std::string. If it

does, strPtr will point to the string value, and *strPtr dereferences it to access the string.

Real-world scenario: std::variant is used when you need to represent data that can be one of a fixed set of types, but only one type at a time, such as representing different states of a system, messages of different types in a messaging system, or data that can be parsed in different formats. It provides a type-safe alternative to C-style unions, enhancing code safety and clarity when dealing with heterogeneous data.

7.7.3 std::any: Type Erasure for Dynamically Typed Values

std::any is a class that can hold a value of any type. It provides type erasure, allowing you to store objects of different types in the same variable, but you must know the actual type to retrieve the value safely. std::any is useful when you need to handle values of unknown types at compile time or when implementing dynamically typed behavior in C++.

Example: Using std::any to Store Values of Unknown Types

```
C++
#include <iostream>
#include <any>     // For std::any, std::any_cast
#include <string>

int main() {
   std::any value; // std::any can hold any type

   value = 100; // Store an int
   std::cout << "Value (int): " << std::any_cast<int>(value) << std::endl; //
Retrieve as int using std::any_cast<int>

   value = std::string("Hello, Any"); // Store a string
   std::cout << "Value (string): " << std::any_cast<std::string>(value) <<
std::endl; // Retrieve as string using std::any_cast<std::string>

   value = 3.14159; // Store a double
   std::cout << "Value (double): " << std::any_cast<double>(value) <<
std::endl; // Retrieve as double using std::any_cast<double>
```

```
    // std::cout << std::any_cast<int>(value) << std::endl; // Error:
std::bad_any_cast - wrong type cast

    // Safely cast using std::any_cast with pointer (returns nullptr if wrong type)
    if (int* intPtr = std::any_cast<int>(&value)) { // Try to cast to int
        std::cout << "Value as int (via pointer): " << *intPtr << std::endl;
    } else {
        std::cout << "Value is not an int" << std::endl;
    }

    return 0;
}
```

Step-by-step explanation:

1. **#include <any>**: Includes the header for std::any.
2. **std::any value;**: Declares an std::any object named value. std::any can hold a value of any type.
3. **value = 100;, value = std::string("Hello, Any");, value = 3.14159;**: Assigns values of different types (int, string, double) to value. std::any can store values of different types dynamically.
4. **std::any_cast<int>(value), std::any_cast<std::string>(value), std::any_cast<double>(value)**: std::any_cast<T>(any_object) is used to retrieve the value from std::any as type T. It performs a type check at runtime. If the std::any object does not actually hold a value of type T, std::any_cast<T> throws a std::bad_any_cast exception.
5. **// std::cout << std::any_cast<int>(value) << std::endl; // Error: std::bad_any_cast**: Demonstrates that trying to cast to the wrong type using std::any_cast<T> results in a std::bad_any_cast exception.
6. **std::any_cast<int>(&value)**: std::any_cast<T>(any_pointer) is a safer version of std::any_cast. It takes a pointer to an std::any object and returns a pointer to the contained value if it is of type T, or nullptr otherwise. It does not throw exceptions.
7. **if (int* intPtr = std::any_cast<int>(&value)) { ... }**: Uses std::any_cast with a pointer to safely check if value holds an int. If it does, intPtr will point to the integer value, and *intPtr dereferences it.

Real-world scenario: std::any is used in situations where you need to handle values of dynamically determined types, such as in scripting languages, serialization libraries, or when interacting with external systems or data sources where the type of data is not known at compile time. It provides a way to achieve type erasure and work with values of unknown types in a more controlled manner than using `void*`, but it requires careful type management and runtime type checking to avoid errors.

7.8 Concepts and Constraints: Enhancing Generic Programming

Concepts and constraints, introduced in C++20, provide a way to specify requirements on template arguments, making template code easier to write, understand, and debug. Concepts define sets of requirements that types must satisfy to be used with a template, and constraints use concepts to enforce these requirements, leading to more meaningful compiler error messages and improved type safety in generic code. As Garcia, Gregor, and Dos Reis explain in "Effective C++ in an Embedded Environment," concepts and constraints are a significant step forward in making C++ templates more user-friendly and robust (Garcia, Gregor, & Dos Reis, 2017).

7.8.1 `requires` Clauses: Specifying Constraints

`requires` clauses are used to specify constraints on template parameters. They can be used to define requirements directly within template declarations or in `concept` definitions. `requires` clauses can express complex constraints using boolean expressions involving concepts, type traits, and other compile-time predicates.

Example: Using `requires` Clause to Constrain a Template Function

```
C++
#include <iostream>
#include <concepts> // For std::integral

// Constrained template function - works only with integral types
template<typename T>
   requires std::integral<T> // requires clause - T must satisfy the Integral
concept
T add(T a, T b) {
   return a + b;
```

```
}

int main() {
  std::cout << "Adding integers: " << add(5, 3) << std::endl; // OK: int is an
integral type
  std::cout << "Adding chars: " << add('a', 'b') << std::endl; // OK: char is an
integral type
  // std::cout << "Adding doubles: " << add(3.14, 2.71) << std::endl; //
Compile error: double is not an integral type

  return 0;
}
```

Step-by-step explanation:

1. **#include <concepts>**: Includes the header for concepts, including standard concepts like std::integral.
2. **template<typename T> requires std::integral<T> T add(T a, T b) { ... }**: Declares a template function add that is constrained using a requires clause.
   - **template<typename T> requires std::integral<T>**: This is the constrained template declaration.
     - **requires std::integral<T>**: The requires clause specifies a constraint. std::integral<T> is a standard concept (defined in <concepts>) that checks if T is an integral type (like int, char, long, etc.). This constraint means that the add template function will only be valid (instantiated) if the type T satisfies the std::integral concept.
3. **std::cout << "Adding integers: " << add(5, 3) << std::endl;, std::cout << "Adding chars: " << add('a', 'b') << std::endl;**: These calls to add are valid because int and char are integral types, so the template can be instantiated.
4. **// std::cout << "Adding doubles: " << add(3.14, 2.71) << std::endl; // Compile error**: This commented-out line would cause a compile error if uncommented. double is not an integral type, so it does not satisfy the std::integral concept. The compiler will issue an error because the template instantiation add<double> is not valid due to the constraint.

Real-world scenario: requires clauses are used to enforce type constraints in generic code, ensuring that templates are used with types that satisfy specific requirements. This leads to more robust and maintainable generic libraries and code, as compile-time errors are generated when templates are misused, rather than cryptic runtime errors or unexpected behavior.

7.8.2 concept Definitions: Naming and Reusing Constraints

concept definitions allow you to name and reuse sets of requirements, making constraints more modular and readable. A concept is essentially a named set of requires clauses. You can define your own concepts to express domain-specific requirements and use them to constrain templates.

Example: Defining and Using a Custom Sortable Concept

```
C++
#include <iostream>
#include <concepts> // For std::totally_ordered

// Define a custom concept 'Sortable' - requires type to be totally ordered
template<typename T>
concept Sortable = std::totally_ordered<T>; // Sortable concept - T must be
totally ordered

// Constrained template function using the Sortable concept
template<Sortable T> // Using the Sortable concept as a constraint
void sort_array(T arr[], int size) {
   // ... sorting logic (implementation omitted for brevity) ...
   std::cout << "Sorting array of Sortable type" << std::endl; // Placeholder
for sorting logic
}

int main() {
   int intArray[] = {3, 1, 4, 1, 5};
   sort_array(intArray, 5); // OK: int satisfies Sortable concept

   double doubleArray[] = {3.14, 1.0, 2.71};
   sort_array(doubleArray, 3); // OK: double satisfies Sortable concept

   // struct NotSortable {}; // Does not satisfy Sortable concept (no ordering
operators)
   // NotSortable notSortableArray[2];
```

```
    // sort_array(notSortableArray, 2); // Compile error: NotSortable does not satisfy Sortable concept

    return 0;
}
```

Step-by-step explanation:

1. **template<typename T> concept Sortable = std::totally_ordered<T>;**: Defines a custom concept named Sortable.
   - **template<typename T> concept Sortable = ...**: Declares a concept named Sortable that is parameterized by a type T.
   - **std::totally_ordered<T>**: The body of the concept is a requires clause that uses the standard concept std::totally_ordered<T> (from <concepts>). std::totally_ordered<T> checks if type T is totally ordered, meaning it supports all comparison operators (<, >, <=, >=, ==, !=).
   - Effectively, the Sortable concept means "type T must be totally ordered".
2. **template<Sortable T> void sort_array(T arr[], int size) { ... }**: Declares a template function sort_array that is constrained using the Sortable concept.
   - **template<Sortable T>**: This is a shorthand syntax for applying the Sortable concept as a constraint. It is equivalent to template<typename T> requires Sortable<T>. It means that the sort_array template function will only be valid for types T that satisfy the Sortable concept.
3. **sort_array(intArray, 5);, sort_array(doubleArray, 3);**: These calls to sort_array are valid because int and double are totally ordered types, so they satisfy the Sortable concept.
4. **// struct NotSortable {}; // NotSortable notSortableArray[2]; // sort_array(notSortableArray, 2); // Compile error**: This commented-out code demonstrates what happens if you try to use sort_array with a type that does not satisfy the Sortable concept. If you uncomment these lines, the code will fail to compile because NotSortable (as defined) does not have ordering operators, and thus does not satisfy the std::totally_ordered concept, and consequently, not the Sortable

concept. The compiler will issue an error indicating that the constraint is not satisfied.

Real-world scenario: Concepts and constraints are used in modern C++ to build more robust and user-friendly generic libraries. They allow library authors to express clear requirements on template parameters, leading to better error messages when users misuse templates and improving the overall usability and maintainability of generic code. Concepts are particularly valuable in large, complex generic codebases where type constraints are crucial for correctness and performance.

7.9 Coroutines: Asynchronous and Resumable Functions

Coroutines, introduced in C++20, provide a way to write asynchronous and resumable functions in a sequential, synchronous-looking style. Coroutines are functions that can be suspended and resumed at certain points, allowing for non-blocking operations and more efficient handling of asynchronous tasks, such as I/O operations, event handling, and generators. Coroutines are built upon three new keywords: co_await, co_yield, and co_return. As McKinnell details in "Asynchronous C++20," coroutines are a game-changer for asynchronous programming in C++, making asynchronous code easier to write, read, and maintain (McKinnell, 2020).

Example: Basic Coroutine Example using co_await and co_return

```
C++
#include <iostream>
#include <coroutine> // For std::coroutine_traits, std::suspend_never,
std::suspend_always
#include <future>    // For std::future, std::promise
#include <thread>    // For std::thread

// Promise type for our coroutine
struct Task {
    struct promise_type {
        Task get_return_object() { return
{std::coroutine_handle<promise_type>::from_promise(*this)}; }
        std::suspend_never initial_suspend() noexcept { return {}; }
```

```
        std::suspend_never final_suspend() noexcept = default;
        void return_void() {}
        void unhandled_exception() {}
    };
    using handle_type = std::coroutine_handle<promise_type>;
    handle_type coroutine_handle;

    Task(handle_type handle) : coroutine_handle(handle) {}
    ~Task() { if (coroutine_handle) coroutine_handle.destroy(); }

    void resume() { coroutine_handle.resume(); }
};

Task MyCoroutine() {
    std::cout << "Coroutine started" << std::endl;
    co_await std::suspend_always{}; // Suspend coroutine
    std::cout << "Coroutine resumed after first suspend" << std::endl;
    co_await std::suspend_always{}; // Suspend again
    std::cout << "Coroutine resumed after second suspend" << std::endl;
    co_return; // Coroutine completes
}

int main() {
    std::cout << "Main function started" << std::endl;

    Task task = MyCoroutine(); // Start the coroutine, but it doesn't run fully yet

    std::cout << "Coroutine started, about to resume first time" << std::endl;
    task.resume(); // Resume coroutine execution - runs until first co_await

    std::cout << "Coroutine resumed first time, about to resume second time"
<< std::endl;
    task.resume(); // Resume again - runs until second co_await

    std::cout << "Coroutine resumed second time, coroutine should complete"
<< std::endl;
    task.resume(); // Resume again - coroutine completes

    std::cout << "Main function finished" << std::endl;
    return 0;
}
```

Step-by-step explanation:

1. #include <coroutine>, #include <future>, #include <thread>: Includes necessary headers for coroutines, futures, and threads.
2. struct Task { ... };: Defines a custom *promise type* named Task. Coroutines in C++ are based on promises and handles. The promise type defines the behavior of the coroutine. This example provides a basic Task promise type that can be suspended and resumed.
    - struct promise_type { ... };: Nested struct defining the promise.
        - Task get_return_object() { ... }: Returns the *coroutine handle* wrapped in a Task object. This is what MyCoroutine() will return.
        - std::suspend_never initial_suspend() noexcept { return {}; }: Specifies that the coroutine should *not* suspend immediately upon initial invocation.
        - std::suspend_never final_suspend() noexcept = default;: Specifies that the coroutine should *not* suspend upon final return (completion).
        - void return_void() {}: Handles co_return; in the coroutine (for void-returning coroutines).
        - void unhandled_exception() {}: Handles exceptions within the coroutine (basic handling in this example).
    - using handle_type = std::coroutine_handle<promise_type>;: Defines a type alias for the coroutine handle.
    - handle_type coroutine_handle;: Stores the coroutine handle.
    - Task(handle_type handle) : coroutine_handle(handle) {}: Constructor to initialize the Task with a handle.
    - ~Task() { ... }: Destructor to destroy the coroutine handle and clean up resources.
    - void resume() { coroutine_handle.resume(); }: resume() function to resume the coroutine's execution from a suspended point.
3. Task MyCoroutine() { ... }: Defines a coroutine function MyCoroutine that returns a Task.
    - co_await std::suspend_always{};: co_await operator suspends the coroutine at this point.

std::suspend_always{} is a *awaitable* object that always causes suspension. When co_await is encountered, the coroutine suspends, and control returns to the caller (in main function).

- **co_return;**: co_return is used to complete the coroutine. In this case, it's a void returning coroutine, so co_return; simply signifies completion.

4. **Task task = MyCoroutine();**: Calls MyCoroutine(). This *starts* the coroutine, but because of initial_suspend being std::suspend_never, it runs immediately until it hits the first co_await std::suspend_always{};. At this point, it suspends, and MyCoroutine() returns a Task object (the coroutine handle wrapped in Task).
5. **task.resume();**: Calls task.resume(), which resumes the execution of the coroutine from the point where it was suspended (after the first co_await). The coroutine runs until it hits the next co_await std::suspend_always{}; and suspends again.
6. The main function calls task.resume() multiple times to step through the coroutine's execution and demonstrate suspension and resumption.

Real-world scenario: Coroutines are used for asynchronous programming, especially in scenarios involving I/O operations, UI event handling, and game development. They allow you to write asynchronous code that looks like synchronous code, making it easier to reason about and maintain. Coroutines are essential for building responsive and efficient applications that need to perform non-blocking operations and handle concurrency in a more structured and manageable way compared to traditional thread-based concurrency or callback-heavy asynchronous patterns.

By integrating these modern C++ features into their skillset, Computer Technology students and educators can develop software that is not only more efficient and robust but also more expressive and easier to maintain. These features represent a significant advancement in C++ programming, enabling developers to tackle complex challenges with greater elegance and effectiveness.

Chapter 8

Advanced Topics in C++

Beyond the modern features that have reshaped the landscape of C++, certain advanced topics remain crucial for mastering the language and leveraging its full potential. These advanced areas, including templates and generic programming, variadic templates, SFINAE, metaprogramming, exception handling, custom memory allocators, and debugging/profiling techniques, are essential for Computer Technology students and educators seeking to develop sophisticated, high-performance, and reliable software systems. This section will explore these advanced topics in depth, providing theoretical foundations, practical examples, and insights into their application in real-world scenarios, thereby equipping readers with the knowledge and skills necessary to tackle complex programming challenges.

8.1 Templates and Generic Programming: Writing Type-Independent Code

Templates are a cornerstone of C++ and enable generic programming, a paradigm that focuses on writing code that is independent of specific data types. Templates allow the creation of functions and classes that can operate on a variety of types without the need to rewrite the code for each type. This significantly enhances code reusability, reduces redundancy, and promotes the development of flexible and efficient algorithms and data structures. As Meyers emphasizes in "Effective C++," understanding and utilizing templates effectively is crucial for writing modern C++ (Meyers, 2005).

8.1.1 Function Templates: Generic Functions

Function templates define a family of functions where the type parameters are specified later when the template is instantiated. This allows a single function template to work with different data types, as long as those types support the operations used within the function.

Example: A Function Template for Swapping Values

```
C++
#include <iostream>

// Function template to swap values of any type T
template <typename T>
void swapValues(T& a, T& b) {
   T temp = a;
   a = b;
   b = temp;
}

int main() {
   int x = 10, y = 20;
   std::cout << "Before swap: x = " << x << ", y = " << y << std::endl;
   swapValues(x, y); // Instantiation with int
   std::cout << "After swap: x = " << x << ", y = " << y << std::endl;

   double pi = 3.14, e = 2.71;
   std::cout << "Before swap: pi = " << pi << ", e = " << e << std::endl;
   swapValues(pi, e); // Instantiation with double
```

```
    std::cout << "After swap: pi = " << pi << ", e = " << e << std::endl;

    return 0;
}
```

Step-by-step explanation:

1. **template <typename T>**: This line declares a function template. typename T introduces T as a template type parameter, which will be replaced by a concrete type when the template is instantiated.
2. **void swapValues(T& a, T& b)**: This is the function signature of the template function swapValues. It takes two arguments a and b of type T by reference and swaps their values. The type T is a placeholder that will be determined during template instantiation.
3. **T temp = a; a = b; b = temp;**: This is the function body that performs the swapping logic. It uses a temporary variable temp of type T to facilitate the swap. This code works for any type T that supports assignment and copy construction.
4. **swapValues(x, y);**: In main, swapValues(x, y) is called with int variables x and y. The compiler *instantiates* the swapValues template with T replaced by int, effectively creating a function void swapValues<int>(int& a, int& b).
5. **swapValues(pi, e);**: Similarly, swapValues(pi, e) is called with double variables pi and e. The compiler instantiates swapValues again, this time with T replaced by double, creating void swapValues<double>(double& a, double& b).

Real-world scenario: Function templates are widely used in standard libraries like the Standard Template Library (STL). Algorithms like std::sort, std::find, and std::copy are implemented as function templates, allowing them to work with various container types and element types. In custom software, function templates are valuable for creating generic utility functions that can operate on different data types without code duplication.

8.1.2 Class Templates: Generic Classes

Class templates define a blueprint for creating classes that can operate on different data types. Similar to function templates, class templates are instantiated with specific types to create concrete classes. This is particularly useful for creating generic containers, data structures, and algorithms that need to work with various types while maintaining type safety.

Example: A Class Template for a Generic Pair

```
C++
#include <iostream>
#include <string>

// Class template for a generic Pair
template <typename T1, typename T2>
class Pair {
public:
    Pair(T1 first, T2 second) : firstValue(first), secondValue(second) {}

    T1 getFirst() const { return firstValue; }
    T2 getSecond() const { return secondValue; }

private:
    T1 firstValue;
    T2 secondValue;
};

int main() {
    // Instantiate Pair with int and double
    Pair<int, double> intDoublePair(10, 3.14);
    std::cout << "Pair (int, double): First = " << intDoublePair.getFirst() << ",
Second = " << intDoublePair.getSecond() << std::endl;

    // Instantiate Pair with string and int
    Pair<std::string, int> stringIntPair("Age", 30);
    std::cout << "Pair (string, int): First = " << stringIntPair.getFirst() << ",
Second = " << stringIntPair.getSecond() << std::endl;

    return 0;
}
```

Step-by-step explanation:

1. **template <typename T1, typename T2>**: This line declares a class template. typename T1 and typename T2 introduce T1 and T2 as template type parameters. Class templates can have multiple type parameters.
2. **class Pair { ... };**: This defines the class template Pair.
3. **Pair(T1 first, T2 second) : firstValue(first), secondValue(second) {}**: This is the constructor of the Pair class template. It takes two arguments of types T1 and T2 and initializes the member variables firstValue and secondValue.
4. **T1 getFirst() const { return firstValue; }, T2 getSecond() const { return secondValue; }**: These are member functions to access the first and second values of the pair. They return values of types T1 and T2 respectively.
5. **Pair<int, double> intDoublePair(10, 3.14);**: In main, Pair<int, double> instantiates the Pair class template with T1 replaced by int and T2 replaced by double. This creates a concrete class Pair<int, double>. An object intDoublePair of this class is then created and initialized.
6. **Pair<std::string, int> stringIntPair("Age", 30);**: Similarly, Pair<std::string, int> instantiates the Pair class template with T1 replaced by std::string and T2 replaced by int, creating a concrete class Pair<std::string, int>. An object stringIntPair of this class is created.

Real-world scenario: Class templates are fundamental to the STL, with containers like std::vector, std::list, std::map, and std::set being class templates. They are essential for building reusable data structures and components that can work with different data types. In custom applications, class templates are used to create generic data structures, algorithms, and components that need to be type-agnostic, promoting code reuse and flexibility.

8.2 Variadic Templates: Templates with Variable Number of Arguments

Variadic templates, introduced in C++11, extend the power of templates by allowing them to accept a variable number of template arguments. This feature is particularly useful for functions and classes that need to work with a flexible number of types or values, such as in tuple implementations, function wrappers, and print functions. As Abrahams and Gurtovoy explain in "C++ Template Metaprogramming," variadic templates are a powerful tool for creating highly flexible and expressive generic code (Abrahams & Gurtovoy, 2004).

Example: A Variadic Template Function for Printing Values

```
C++
#include <iostream>

// Variadic template function to print multiple arguments
template <typename... Args>
void printValues(Args... args) {
  // Recursive base case: no arguments left
  if constexpr (sizeof...(args) == 0) {
    std::cout << std::endl; // End line when no more arguments
    return;
  }

  // Print the first argument
  std::cout << ... << args << " "; // Fold expression to print arguments

  // Recursively call printValues with remaining arguments (not directly
recursive, fold expression handles it)
  // printValues(args...); // This would be infinite recursion without proper
handling - fold expression is the correct approach
}

int main() {
  printValues(10, 3.14, "Hello", 'C++'); // Call with multiple arguments of
different types
  printValues("Only one argument");
  printValues(); // Call with no arguments

  return 0;
```

```
}
```

Step-by-step explanation:

1. **template <typename... Args>**: This line declares a variadic template. typename... Args introduces a *template parameter pack* named Args. Args can represent zero or more type arguments.
2. **void printValues(Args... args)**: This is the function signature of the variadic template function printValues. Args... args declares a *function parameter pack* named args. args can represent zero or more function arguments, with their types corresponding to the types in Args.
3. **if constexpr (sizeof...(args) == 0) { ... }**: This is a base case for the recursion using a compile-time if constexpr. sizeof...(args) gives the number of arguments in the parameter pack args. If it's 0, it means no arguments were passed, so the function prints a newline and returns.
4. **std::cout << ... << args << " ";**: This is a *fold expression.* ... << args expands the parameter pack args and applies the << operator to each argument. Effectively, if args contains arguments a1, a2, a3, this fold expression expands to std::cout << a1 << " " << a2 << " " << a3 << " ". This is how all arguments in the pack are printed.
5. **printValues(10, 3.14, "Hello", 'C++');, printValues("Only one argument");, printValues();**: These are calls to printValues with different numbers and types of arguments. The compiler instantiates printValues for each call, creating function overloads that handle the specific number and types of arguments passed.

Real-world scenario: Variadic templates are used in many advanced C++ libraries and frameworks. std::tuple is a prime example, allowing you to create tuples of arbitrary size and types. Variadic templates are also used in implementing perfect forwarding, which is crucial for move semantics and efficient function wrappers. In custom code, they are useful for creating flexible interfaces that can accept a variable number of arguments, such as logging functions, data serialization routines, and generic factory functions.

8.3 SFINAE and std::enable_if: Compile-Time Conditionals for Templates

SFINAE (Substitution Failure Is Not An Error) is a principle in C++ template instantiation that allows the compiler to discard template instantiations that are ill-formed (substitution failures) without causing a compilation error. std::enable_if, a template from <type_traits>, is commonly used to leverage SFINAE to conditionally enable or disable template overloads or specializations based on type traits or compile-time conditions. SFINAE and std::enable_if are powerful tools for advanced template metaprogramming, enabling conditional compilation and type-based dispatch at compile time. As Vandevoorde, Josuttis, and Gregor explain in "C++ Templates: The Complete Guide," SFINAE is a complex but essential aspect of C++ template behavior, crucial for advanced generic programming techniques (Vandevoorde, Josuttis, & Gregor, 2017).

Example: Using std::enable_if to Conditionally Enable Template Overloads

```
C++
#include <iostream>
#include <type_traits> // For std::enable_if, std::is_integral,
std::is_floating_point

// Overload for integral types (enabled if T is integral)
template <typename T>
std::enable_if_t<std::is_integral_v<T>, void> printTypeCategory(T value) {
   std::cout << "Value is an integer: " << value << std::endl;
}

// Overload for floating-point types (enabled if T is floating-point)
template <typename T>
std::enable_if_t<std::is_floating_point_v<T>, void> printTypeCategory(T
value) {
   std::cout << "Value is a floating-point number: " << value << std::endl;
}

// Fallback overload (enabled if neither integral nor floating-point - using
negation)
template <typename T>
std::enable_if_t<(!std::is_integral_v<T> && !std::is_floating_point_v<T>),
void> printTypeCategory(T value) {
```

```
    std::cout << "Value is of another type" << std::endl;
}


int main() {
    printTypeCategory(10);      // Calls integral overload
    printTypeCategory(3.14);    // Calls floating-point overload
    printTypeCategory("hello"); // Calls fallback overload

    return 0;
}
```

Step-by-step explanation:

1. **#include <type_traits>**: Includes the header for type traits, including std::enable_if, std::is_integral, and std::is_floating_point.
2. **template <typename T> std::enable_if_t<std::is_integral_v<T>, void> printTypeCategory(T value) { ... }**: This is the first overload of the printTypeCategory function template, enabled for integral types.
    - **std::enable_if_t<std::is_integral_v<T>, void>**: This is the *return type* of the function. std::enable_if_t<Condition, T> is a type alias that is equivalent to T if Condition is true, and it results in a substitution failure (making the template instantiation ill-formed) if Condition is false.
    - **std::is_integral_v<T>**: This is a *type trait* that is a compile-time boolean constant. It is true if T is an integral type (like int, char, bool, etc.), and false otherwise. The _v suffix is a C++17 feature that provides a convenient way to get the boolean value of a type trait.
    - So, this overload is enabled (participates in overload resolution) *only if* std::is_integral_v<T> is true. If T is not an integral type, this template instantiation is discarded due to SFINAE.
3. **template <typename T> std::enable_if_t<std::is_floating_point_v<T>, void> printTypeCategory(T value) { ... }**: This is the second overload, enabled for floating-point types. It's similar to the first overload, but it uses std::is_floating_point_v<T> as the condition.
4. **template <typename T> std::enable_if_t<(!std::is_integral_v<T> && !std::is_floating_point_v<T>), void> printTypeCategory(T**

value) { ... }: This is a fallback overload, enabled for types that are *neither* integral nor floating-point. It uses a more complex condition (!std::is_integral_v<T> && !std::is_floating_point_v<T>).

5. **printTypeCategory(10);, printTypeCategory(3.14);, printTypeCategory("hello");**: These calls demonstrate overload resolution based on SFINAE.
   - printTypeCategory(10): int is integral, so the first overload is enabled and chosen.
   - printTypeCategory(3.14): double is floating-point, so the second overload is enabled and chosen.
   - printTypeCategory("hello"): const char* (string literal) is neither integral nor floating-point, so the first two overloads are disabled due to SFINAE. The fallback overload is enabled, and thus chosen.

Real-world scenario: SFINAE and std::enable_if are used in advanced template libraries to create highly specialized and optimized code paths based on the properties of types. They are used for conditional compilation of template code, enabling different implementations or optimizations based on type traits. For example, a generic algorithm might have different implementations for integral types versus floating-point types, or for types with specific properties. SFINAE is also crucial for implementing type detection and introspection mechanisms at compile time.

8.4 Metaprogramming: Compile-Time Computation and Type Manipulation

Metaprogramming is a programming technique where programs manipulate or generate other programs, or themselves, at compile time. C++ template metaprogramming leverages templates to perform computations and type manipulations during compilation, rather than at runtime. This can lead to significant performance improvements by shifting computations to compile time and enabling compile-time optimizations. Key tools for C++ metaprogramming include type traits, std::conditional, and template recursion. As Czarnecki and Eisenecker detail in "Generative Programming: Methods, Tools, and Applications," metaprogramming is a powerful paradigm for creating highly adaptable and efficient software systems (Czarnecki & Eisenecker, 2000).

8.4.1 Type Traits: Compile-Time Type Information

Type traits are a set of templates in <type_traits> that provide compile-time information about types. They can be used to query properties of types, such as whether a type is integral, floating-point, a pointer, or has certain constructors or operators. Type traits are fundamental building blocks for metaprogramming, allowing you to write code that adapts its behavior based on type properties at compile time.

Example: Using Type Traits to Check if a Type is Integral

```
C++
#include <iostream>
#include <type_traits> // For std::is_integral_v, std::is_floating_point_v

template <typename T>
void checkType(T value) {
   if constexpr (std::is_integral_v<T>) { // Compile-time check for integral
type
      std::cout << "Type is integral" << std::endl;
   } else if constexpr (std::is_floating_point_v<T>) { // Compile-time check
for floating-point type
      std::cout << "Type is floating-point" << std::endl;
   } else {
      std::cout << "Type is neither integral nor floating-point" << std::endl;
   }
}

int main() {
   checkType(10);      // int is integral
   checkType(3.14);    // double is floating-point
   checkType("hello"); // const char* is neither

   return 0;
}
```

Step-by-step explanation:

1. **#include <type_traits>**: Includes the header for type traits.
2. **template <typename T> void checkType(T value) { ... }**: Defines a function template checkType that takes an argument of type T.
3. **if constexpr (std::is_integral_v<T>) { ... }**: Uses a compile-time if constexpr statement to check if T is an integral type using std::is_integral_v<T>.

   - **std::is_integral_v<T>**: This type trait is evaluated at compile time. If T is an integral type, the condition is true, and the code inside the if constexpr block is compiled; otherwise, it is discarded.
4. **else if constexpr (std::is_floating_point_v<T>) { ... }**: Another if constexpr to check if T is a floating-point type using std::is_floating_point_v<T>.
5. **else { ... }**: Fallback case if T is neither integral nor floating-point.
6. **checkType(10);, checkType(3.14);, checkType("hello");**: Calls to checkType with different types. The if constexpr conditions are evaluated at compile time based on the type T in each call, and only the corresponding code block is compiled into the executable.

Real-world scenario: Type traits are used extensively in generic libraries and frameworks to adapt code behavior based on type properties at compile time. They are used in implementing conditional template logic, optimizing algorithms for specific types, and enforcing type constraints in generic code. Type traits are essential for creating highly flexible and efficient C++ libraries that can work seamlessly with a wide range of types.

8.4.2 std::conditional: Compile-Time Type Selection

std::conditional, a template from <type_traits>, allows you to choose between two types at compile time based on a boolean condition. It is a fundamental tool for metaprogramming, enabling you to create type-level conditional logic and select types based on compile-time predicates.

Example: Using std::conditional to Choose a Type at Compile Time

```
C++
#include <iostream>
#include <type_traits> // For std::conditional, std::is_integral_v

template <typename T>
using ConditionalType = std::conditional_t<std::is_integral_v<T>, int,
double>; // Type alias using std::conditional
```

```
template <typename T>
void printValueWithType(T value) {
   ConditionalType<T> convertedValue; // Use ConditionalType to declare a
variable
   if constexpr (std::is_integral_v<T>) {
      convertedValue = static_cast<int>(value); // Convert to int if integral
      std::cout << "Original value (integral): " << convertedValue << ", Type:
int" << std::endl;
   } else {
      convertedValue = static_cast<double>(value); // Convert to double
otherwise
      std::cout << "Original value (non-integral): " << convertedValue << ",
Type: double" << std::endl;
   }
}

int main() {
   printValueWithType(5);      // int - ConditionalType<int> resolves to int
   printValueWithType(3.14f);  // float - ConditionalType<float> resolves to
double
   printValueWithType('a');    // char - ConditionalType<char> resolves to int

   return 0;
}
```

Step-by-step explanation:

1. **#include <type_traits>**: Includes the header for type traits.
2. **template <typename T> using ConditionalType = std::conditional_t<std::is_integral_v<T>, int, double>;**: Defines a type alias ConditionalType using std::conditional_t.
   - **std::conditional_t<std::is_integral_v<T>, int, double>**: std::conditional_t<Condition, TypeIfTrue, TypeIfFalse> is a type alias. It evaluates Condition at compile time. If Condition is true, it resolves to TypeIfTrue; otherwise, it resolves to TypeIfFalse.
   - In this case, if std::is_integral_v<T> is true (i.e., T is integral), ConditionalType<T> becomes int; otherwise, it becomes double.
3. **template <typename T> void printValueWithType(T value) { ... }**: Defines a function template printValueWithType.
4. **ConditionalType<T> convertedValue;**: Declares a variable convertedValue of type ConditionalType<T>. The actual type of

convertedValue (either int or double) is determined at compile time based on whether T is integral or not.

5. **if constexpr (std::is_integral_v<T>) { ... } else { ... }**: Uses if constexpr to conditionally perform type conversion and print output. If T is integral, it converts value to int; otherwise, it converts to double.
6. **printValueWithType(5);, printValueWithType(3.14f);, printValueWithType('a');**: Calls to printValueWithType with different types. The ConditionalType<T> type alias and the if constexpr statement together ensure that the code behaves differently at compile time based on the type T.

Real-world scenario: std::conditional is used in metaprogramming to perform type-level branching and select different types or code paths based on compile-time conditions. It is used in implementing policy-based design, creating type-dependent algorithms, and customizing template behavior based on type properties. std::conditional is a fundamental tool for building highly configurable and adaptable C++ templates.

8.5 Exception Handling: Managing Errors Gracefully

Exception handling is a crucial mechanism in C++ for managing runtime errors and exceptional situations in a structured and robust manner. C++ exception handling uses try, catch, and throw keywords to handle errors, allowing programs to recover from unexpected conditions and prevent crashes. The noexcept specifier is used to indicate whether a function is guaranteed not to throw exceptions, which can be important for performance and exception safety. As Sutter and Alexandrescu advocate in "C++ Coding Standards," effective exception handling is a cornerstone of robust and reliable C++ software (Sutter & Alexandrescu, 2005).

Example: Basic Exception Handling with try, catch, and throw

```
C++
#include <iostream>
#include <stdexcept> // For std::runtime_error, std::out_of_range
```

```
int divide(int numerator, int denominator) {
    if (denominator == 0) {
        throw std::runtime_error("Division by zero!"); // Throw an exception if
denominator is zero
    }
    return numerator / denominator;
}

int accessVectorElement(const std::vector<int>& vec, int index) {
    if (index < 0 || index >= vec.size()) {
        throw std::out_of_range("Index out of range!"); // Throw exception if
index is invalid
    }
    return vec[index];
}

int main() {
    try {
        int result1 = divide(10, 2);
        std::cout << "10 / 2 = " << result1 << std::endl;

        int result2 = divide(10, 0); // This will throw an exception
        std::cout << "10 / 0 = " << result2 << std::endl; // This line will not be
reached

    } catch (const std::runtime_error& error) { // Catch runtime_error
exceptions
        std::cerr << "Runtime error caught: " << error.what() << std::endl;
    }

    std::vector<int> numbers = {1, 2, 3};
    try {
        int element = accessVectorElement(numbers, 5); // This will throw an
exception
        std::cout << "Element at index 5: " << element << std::endl; // Not
reached
    } catch (const std::out_of_range& error) { // Catch out_of_range
exceptions
        std::cerr << "Out of range error caught: " << error.what() << std::endl;
    }

    std::cout << "Program continues after exception handling" << std::endl;
    return 0;
}
```

Step-by-step explanation:

1. **#include <stdexcept>**: Includes the header for standard exception classes like std::runtime_error and std::out_of_range.
2. **int divide(int numerator, int denominator) { ... }**: Defines a function divide that performs integer division.
   - **if (denominator == 0) { throw std::runtime_error("Division by zero!"); }**: Checks for division by zero. If the denominator is 0, it throws a std::runtime_error exception with a descriptive message.
3. **int accessVectorElement(const std::vector<int>& vec, int index) { ... }**: Defines a function accessVectorElement that accesses an element in a vector.
   - **if (index < 0 || index >= vec.size()) { throw std::out_of_range("Index out of range!"); }**: Checks if the index is valid. If the index is out of range, it throws a std::out_of_range exception.
4. **try { ... } catch (const std::runtime_error& error) { ... }**: This is a try-catch block.
   - **try { ... }**: Code within the try block is monitored for exceptions.
   - **int result2 = divide(10, 0);**: This line inside the try block will throw a std::runtime_error exception because the denominator is 0.
   - **catch (const std::runtime_error& error) { ... }**: This catch block is designed to catch exceptions of type std::runtime_error (or any derived class). If a std::runtime_error exception is thrown within the try block, the execution jumps to this catch block.
   - **std::cerr << "Runtime error caught: " << error.what() << std::endl;**: Inside the catch block, the error message associated with the caught exception is printed using error.what().
5. Another try-catch block is used to handle std::out_of_range exceptions that might be thrown by accessVectorElement.
6. **std::cout << "Program continues after exception handling" << std::endl;**: Demonstrates that after an exception is caught and handled, the program execution continues normally from after the try-catch block.

Real-world scenario: Exception handling is crucial for writing robust and fault-tolerant software. It is used in almost all non-trivial C++

applications to handle errors such as file I/O errors, network errors, invalid user input, and resource allocation failures. Effective exception handling prevents program crashes, allows for graceful error recovery, and improves the overall reliability and maintainability of software systems.

8.6 Custom Memory Allocators: Fine-Grained Memory Management

Custom memory allocators allow developers to override the default memory allocation behavior in C++ and implement specialized allocation strategies tailored to specific application needs. Custom allocators can be used to improve performance, reduce memory fragmentation, or implement specific memory management policies, especially in performance-critical applications or systems with unique memory requirements. As Bulka and Mayhew discuss in "Efficient C++: Performance Programming Techniques," custom memory allocation is an advanced technique for optimizing memory usage and performance in C++ applications (Bulka & Mayhew, 2000).

Example: A Simple Custom Allocator for std::vector

```
C++
#include <iostream>
#include <vector>
#include <memory> // For std::allocator_traits

// Simple custom allocator
template <typename T>
class MyAllocator {
public:
    using value_type = T;
    using pointer = T*;
    using const_pointer = const T*;
    using reference = T&;
    using const_reference = const T&;
    using size_type = std::size_t;
    using difference_type = std::ptrdiff_t;

    MyAllocator() noexcept = default;
    template <typename U> MyAllocator(const MyAllocator<U>&) noexcept
{} // Allow conversion from other allocators
```

```
    pointer allocate(size_type n, std::allocator<void>::pointer hint = 0) {
        std::cout << "Allocating " << n * sizeof(T) << " bytes with MyAllocator"
<< std::endl;
        return static_cast<pointer>(::operator new(n * sizeof(T))); // Use
::operator new for allocation
    }

    void deallocate(pointer p, size_type n) {
        std::cout << "Deallocating " << n * sizeof(T) << " bytes with
MyAllocator" << std::endl;
        ::operator delete(p); // Use ::operator delete for deallocation
    }

    template <typename U, typename... Args>
    void construct(U* p, Args&&... args) {
        std::cout << "Constructing object with MyAllocator" << std::endl;
        ::new (p) U(std::forward<Args>(args)...); // Use placement new for
construction
    }

    void destroy(pointer p) {
        std::cout << "Destroying object with MyAllocator" << std::endl;
        p->~T(); // Explicitly call destructor
    }

    size_type max_size() const noexcept {
        return std::numeric_limits<size_type>::max() / sizeof(T);
    }

    bool operator==(const MyAllocator&) const noexcept { return true; }
    bool operator!=(const MyAllocator&) const noexcept { return false; }
};

template <typename T, typename U>
bool operator==(const MyAllocator<T>&, const MyAllocator<U>&)
noexcept { return true; }
template <typename T, typename U>
bool operator!=(const MyAllocator<T>&, const MyAllocator<U>&) noexcept
{ return false; }


int main() {
    // Use std::vector with custom allocator
    std::vector<int, MyAllocator<int>> myVector({1, 2, 3, 4, 5}); // Vector
using MyAllocator
```

```
    for (int val : myVector) {
        std::cout << val << " ";
    }
    std::cout << std::endl;

    return 0;
}
```

Step-by-step explanation:

1. **#include <memory>**: Includes the header for <memory>, which contains allocator-related templates and traits.
2. **template <typename T> class MyAllocator { ... };**: Defines a class template MyAllocator that will serve as a custom allocator for type T.
3. **Allocator Requirements**: Inside MyAllocator, several type aliases and member functions are defined to meet the requirements of a C++ allocator. These include:
    - value_type, pointer, const_pointer, reference, const_reference, size_type, difference_type: Standard allocator type aliases.
    - MyAllocator() noexcept = default;: Default constructor.
    - template <typename U> MyAllocator(const MyAllocator<U>&) noexcept {}: Converting copy constructor to allow allocators for different types to be compatible (often required for stateful allocators, but in this stateless example, it's mostly boilerplate).
    - **allocate(size_type n, ...)**: This is the core allocation function.
        - std::cout << "Allocating " << n * sizeof(T) << " bytes with MyAllocator" << std::endl;: Prints a message indicating allocation is happening via the custom allocator.
        - return static_cast<pointer>(::operator new(n * sizeof(T)));: Uses the global ::operator new to allocate raw memory. The global ::operator new is used to bypass any overloaded operator new at class scope and use the default global allocation mechanism.
    - **deallocate(pointer p, size_type n)**: This is the deallocation function.

        - std::cout << "Deallocating " << n * sizeof(T) << " bytes with MyAllocator" << std::endl;: Prints a deallocation message.
        - ::operator delete(p);: Uses the global ::operator delete to deallocate memory allocated by ::operator new.
    - **construct(U* p, Args&&... args)**: Constructs an object of type U at the memory location pointed to by p using placement new.
        - std::cout << "Constructing object with MyAllocator" << std::endl;: Print construction message.
        - ::new (p) U(std::forward<Args>(args)...);: Uses *placement new* (::new (p) U(...)) to construct an object of type U at the pre-allocated memory location p. std::forward<Args>(args)... perfect forwards the constructor arguments.
    - **destroy(pointer p)**: Destroys the object at the memory location p by explicitly calling its destructor (p->~T()).
        - std::cout << "Destroying object with MyAllocator" << std::endl;: Print destruction message.
        - p->~T();: Explicitly calls the destructor of the object pointed to by p.
    - max_size(), operator==, operator!=: Other required allocator members (often default implementations are sufficient for simple allocators).
4. **std::vector<int, MyAllocator<int>> myVector({1, 2, 3, 4, 5});**: Declares a std::vector named myVector that stores int elements and uses MyAllocator<int> as its allocator. By providing MyAllocator<int> as the second template argument to std::vector, we instruct the vector to use our custom allocator for all its memory management operations.
5. When myVector is constructed and elements are added, and when myVector goes out of scope and is destroyed, you will see the output messages from MyAllocator's allocate, deallocate, construct, and destroy functions, demonstrating that the custom allocator is being used by the std::vector.

Real-world scenario: Custom memory allocators are used in specialized applications where the default memory allocation behavior is not optimal. Examples include:

1. **Real-time systems:** To ensure deterministic memory allocation and deallocation times.
2. **Embedded systems:** To manage memory in constrained environments or use specific memory regions.
3. **High-performance** computing: To reduce memory fragmentation, improve cache locality, or implement pool allocators for frequently allocated objects.
4. **Game development**: To optimize memory management for game objects and resources.

8.7 Debugging and Profiling: Ensuring Correctness and Performance

Debugging and profiling are essential practices in software development to ensure both the correctness and performance of code. Debugging involves identifying and fixing errors in the code, while profiling involves analyzing the performance characteristics of the code to identify bottlenecks and areas for optimization. Tools like GDB (GNU Debugger) and Visual Studio Debugger are powerful debuggers, and profiling tools help in performance analysis. As McConnell highlights in "Code Complete," effective debugging and performance tuning are critical skills for software engineers (McConnell, 2004).

8.7.1 Debugging with GDB and Visual Studio Debugger

Debuggers like GDB and Visual Studio Debugger provide a range of features to help developers understand and fix errors in their code. These features include:

- **Breakpoints**: Allow pausing program execution at specific lines of code.
- **Stepping**: Step through code line by line (step over, step into, step out).
- **Variable Inspection**: Examine the values of variables at runtime.
- **Call Stack Examination**: Inspect the function call stack to trace program flow.
- **Memory Inspection**: Examine memory contents.

- **Conditional Breakpoints**: Break only when certain conditions are met.

Example: Debugging a Simple Program with GDB (Conceptual Steps)

Let's consider a simple C++ program with a bug:

```
C++
#include <iostream>

int sumArray(int arr[], int size) {
  int sum = 0;
  for (int i = 1; i <= size; ++i) { // Bug: loop should start from 0 and go up
to size-1
    sum += arr[i]; // Potential out-of-bounds access
  }
  return sum;
}

int main() {
  int numbers[] = {1, 2, 3, 4, 5};
  int size = sizeof(numbers) / sizeof(numbers[0]);
  int total = sumArray(numbers, size);
  std::cout << "Sum of array: " << total << std::endl;
  return 0;
}
```

Conceptual Debugging Steps with GDB:

1. **Compile with Debugging Symbols**: Compile the program with the -g flag to include debugging information: g++ -g program.cpp -o program.
2. **Start GDB**: Run GDB on the executable: gdb program.
3. **Set a Breakpoint**: Set a breakpoint at the beginning of the sumArray function: break sumArray.
4. **Run the Program**: Run the program under GDB: run. Program execution will pause at the breakpoint in sumArray.
5. **Step Through Code**: Use next (or n) to step over lines and step (or s) to step into function calls. Observe the program flow and variable values.
6. **Inspect Variables**: Use print sum to examine the value of the sum variable, and print i to check the loop counter. Examine the array arr using print arr.

7. **Identify the Bug**: Notice that the loop in `sumArray` starts from `i = 1` instead of `i = 0`, and goes up to `i <= size`, causing an out-of-bounds access (`arr[size]` is accessed, which is beyond the valid range of the array).
8. **Fix the Bug**: Correct the loop condition in `sumArray` to `for (int i = 0; i < size; ++i)`.
9. **Recompile and Re-run**: Recompile the corrected code and run it again, verifying that the bug is fixed.

Visual Studio Debugger: Visual Studio Debugger provides a GUI-based debugging environment with similar capabilities: setting breakpoints, stepping, variable inspection, call stack examination, and memory debugging. Visual Studio simplifies the debugging process with its integrated environment and visual tools.

Real-world scenario: Debugging is an integral part of software development. Debuggers are used daily by developers to identify and fix bugs, understand program behavior, and ensure code correctness. Mastering debugging tools and techniques is essential for any Computer Technology professional.

8.7.2 Profiling: Performance Analysis

Profiling involves analyzing the runtime performance of a program to identify performance bottlenecks and areas for optimization. Profiling tools can measure various aspects of program execution, such as:

- **CPU Usage**: Time spent in different functions or code sections.
- **Memory Allocation**: Memory usage patterns, allocation and deallocation hotspots.
- **Cache Misses**: Cache performance metrics.
- **I/O Operations**: Time spent in I/O operations.

Example: Basic Profiling Concepts (Conceptual)

1. **Choose a Profiling Tool**: Select a suitable profiling tool for your platform and needs (e.g., `gprof`, `perf`, Visual Studio Profiler, Intel VTune).
2. **Compile for Profiling**: Compile the program with profiling enabled (e.g., `-pg` flag for `gprof`).

3. **Run the Program Under Profiler**: Run the program under the profiling tool. The profiler will collect performance data during execution.
4. **Analyze Profiling Data**: Use the profiling tool to analyze the collected data. Profiling tools typically generate reports or visualizations showing function call counts, execution times, CPU usage per function, memory allocation statistics, etc.
5. **Identify Bottlenecks**: Analyze the profiling report to identify functions or code sections that consume the most execution time or resources (performance bottlenecks).
6. **Optimize Bottlenecks**: Focus on optimizing the identified bottleneck areas. This might involve algorithm optimization, data structure changes, code restructuring, or using more efficient libraries or techniques.
7. **Re-profile and Verify**: After optimization, re-profile the program to measure the performance improvement and verify that the bottlenecks have been addressed.

Real-world scenario: Profiling is essential for optimizing performance-critical applications. It is used in game development, high-frequency trading, scientific computing, and any application where performance is a primary concern. Profiling helps developers make data-driven optimization decisions, focusing their efforts on the areas that will yield the most significant performance gains.

By mastering these advanced C++ topics, Computer Technology students and educators can significantly enhance their programming capabilities, enabling them to develop more sophisticated, efficient, and reliable software solutions. These topics represent the deeper aspects of C++ programming, essential for tackling complex software engineering challenges and building high-performance systems.

Chapter 9

Parallel and Concurrent Programming: Harnessing Multi-Core Architectures

Modern computer architectures are increasingly multi-core, emphasizing the importance of parallel and concurrent programming. These paradigms enable software to perform multiple tasks simultaneously, significantly improving application responsiveness and throughput, especially for computationally intensive tasks. For Computer Technology students and educators, understanding and applying parallel and concurrent programming techniques is vital for developing efficient and scalable software in today's computing landscape. This section delves into the core concepts of parallel and concurrent programming in C++, covering thread management, synchronization, atomic operations, parallel algorithms, and asynchronous programming, providing a robust foundation for building high-performance applications.

9.1 Thread Management with <thread>: The Foundation of Concurrency

The <thread> library in C++ provides the fundamental tools for thread management, allowing developers to create and control threads of execution within a program. Threads are lightweight processes that can run concurrently, sharing the same memory space but executing independently. Effective thread management is crucial for leveraging multi-core processors and achieving parallelism. As Williams notes in "C++ Concurrency in Action," understanding thread management is the first step towards mastering concurrent programming (Williams, 2019).

9.1.1 Creating and Joining Threads: Basic Thread Operations

Creating a thread in C++ is straightforward using the std::thread class. You pass a callable object (function, lambda, or function object) to the std::thread constructor, which then begins executing in a new thread. To ensure the main thread waits for the completion of a newly created thread, the join() method is used.

Example: Creating and Joining Threads

```
C++
#include <iostream>
#include <thread> // For std::thread
#include <chrono> // For std::chrono::seconds
#include <string> // For std::string

void taskFunction(const std::string& message) {
   std::cout << "Thread started: " << message << std::endl;
   std::this_thread::sleep_for(std::chrono::seconds(2)); // Simulate work
   std::cout << "Thread finished: " << message << std::endl;
}

int main() {
   std::thread thread1(taskFunction, "Task 1"); // Create thread 1, passing a
string argument
   std::thread thread2(taskFunction, "Task 2"); // Create thread 2, passing a
string argument
```

```
    std::cout << "Main thread continues execution..." << std::endl;

    thread1.join(); // Wait for thread1 to finish
    thread2.join(); // Wait for thread2 to finish

    std::cout << "Both threads have completed." << std::endl;
    return 0;
}
```

Step-by-step explanation:

1. **#include <thread>**: Includes the <thread> header, which is necessary for using the std::thread class and related functionalities.
2. **#include <chrono>**: Includes the <chrono> header, used here for simulating work with std::this_thread::sleep_for.
3. **void taskFunction(const std::string& message)**: Defines a function taskFunction that will be executed by each thread. It takes a std::string argument and prints messages to the console, simulating some work by sleeping for 2 seconds.
4. **std::thread thread1(taskFunction, "Task 1");**: Creates a new thread named thread1.
    - std::thread: Constructs a thread object.
    - taskFunction: The function to be executed in the new thread.
    - "Task 1": An argument passed to taskFunction. The arguments after the function name in the std::thread constructor are forwarded to the function when the new thread starts executing.
5. **std::thread thread2(taskFunction, "Task 2");**: Creates a second thread thread2, similar to thread1, but with a different message.
6. **std::cout << "Main thread continues execution..." << std::endl;**: The main thread continues to execute concurrently with thread1 and thread2.
7. **thread1.join();**: The join() method is called on thread1. This makes the main thread *wait* for thread1 to complete its execution before proceeding further. The main thread will block until taskFunction in thread1 finishes.
8. **thread2.join();**: Similarly, thread2.join() makes the main thread wait for thread2 to finish.

9. **std::cout << "Both threads have completed." << std::endl;**: This line is executed only after both thread1 and thread2 have finished and been joined by the main thread.

Real-world scenario: Thread management is fundamental in applications requiring parallel processing. For example, in a video editing software, different threads can be used to handle video decoding, audio processing, and user interface updates concurrently, improving responsiveness and performance. In web servers, each incoming request can be handled by a separate thread, allowing the server to serve multiple clients simultaneously.

9.2 Synchronization (mutex, condition_variable): Coordinating Concurrent Access

When multiple threads access shared resources, synchronization mechanisms are essential to prevent race conditions and ensure data integrity. C++ provides tools like mutex (mutual exclusion) and condition_variable to coordinate thread execution and protect shared data. As McKenney details in "Is Parallel Programming Hard, And, If So, What Can You Do About It?", proper synchronization is crucial for writing correct and efficient concurrent programs (McKenney, 2011).

9.2.1 Mutex: Ensuring Mutual Exclusion

A mutex (mutual exclusion) is a synchronization primitive that protects shared data by allowing only one thread to access it at a time. Threads must acquire a lock on the mutex before accessing the shared resource and release the lock after they are done. This ensures that concurrent access to the shared resource is serialized, preventing data corruption and race conditions.

Example: Using std::mutex for Mutual Exclusion

```
C++
#include <iostream>
#include <thread>
#include <mutex> // For std::mutex
#include <string>

int sharedCounter = 0;
std::mutex counterMutex; // Mutex to protect sharedCounter

void incrementCounter(const std::string& threadName) {
   for (int i = 0; i < 100000; ++i) {
      std::lock_guard<std::mutex> lock(counterMutex); // RAII-style mutex
locking
      sharedCounter++; // Increment shared counter under mutex protection
      // Mutex is automatically unlocked when lock goes out of scope
   }
   std::cout << threadName << " finished incrementing." << std::endl;
}

int main() {
   std::thread thread1(incrementCounter, "Thread 1");
   std::thread thread2(incrementCounter, "Thread 2");

   thread1.join();
   thread2.join();

   std::cout << "Final counter value: " << sharedCounter << std::endl;
   return 0;
}
```

Step-by-step explanation:

1. **#include <mutex>**: Includes the <mutex> header for using std::mutex and related classes.
2. **int sharedCounter = 0;**: Declares a shared integer variable sharedCounter that will be incremented by multiple threads. This is the shared resource that needs protection.
3. **std::mutex counterMutex;**: Declares a mutex object counterMutex. This mutex will be used to protect access to sharedCounter.
4. **void incrementCounter(const std::string& threadName)**: Defines a function incrementCounter that increments sharedCounter multiple times.

5. **std::lock_guard<std::mutex> lock(counterMutex);**: This line is crucial for mutual exclusion.
   - std::lock_guard<std::mutex> lock(...): std::lock_guard is a RAII (Resource Acquisition Is Initialization) wrapper for mutexes. It automatically locks the mutex when it is constructed and automatically unlocks it when it goes out of scope (when the function or block exits). This ensures that the mutex is always unlocked, even if exceptions occur.
   - (counterMutex): The constructor of std::lock_guard takes the mutex counterMutex as an argument and locks it. If another thread already holds the lock, the current thread will block until the lock becomes available.
6. **sharedCounter++;**: sharedCounter is incremented *inside* the critical section protected by the mutex. Only one thread can execute this line of code at any given time because of the mutex lock.
7. **Mutex Unlocking**: When the lock object goes out of scope at the end of the for loop iteration (or if the function exits), the destructor of std::lock_guard is automatically called, which unlocks counterMutex, allowing other threads to acquire the lock and access sharedCounter.
8. **Thread Creation and Joining**: main creates two threads, thread1 and thread2, both executing incrementCounter. The join() calls ensure the main thread waits for both incrementing threads to finish before printing the final counter value.

Real-world scenario: Mutexes are essential for protecting shared data in concurrent applications. In database systems, mutexes are used to protect database records during transactions, ensuring that concurrent transactions do not corrupt data. In file systems, mutexes can protect file metadata when multiple processes access the same file concurrently.

9.2.2 Condition Variables: Signaling and Waiting for Conditions

Condition variables are synchronization primitives that allow threads to wait for specific conditions to become true. They are typically used in conjunction with mutexes. A thread can wait on a condition variable, which atomically releases the mutex and puts the thread to sleep. When another thread changes the condition, it can notify the waiting thread, which then re-acquires the mutex and checks the condition again.

Condition variables are crucial for implementing complex synchronization patterns, such as producer-consumer queues and thread pools.

Example: Using std::condition_variable for Condition Synchronization

```
C++
#include <iostream>
#include <thread>
#include <mutex>
#include <condition_variable> // For std::condition_variable
#include <queue> // For std::queue
#include <string>

std::mutex queueMutex;
std::condition_variable dataCondition;
std::queue<int> dataQueue;
bool producerFinished = false; // Flag to signal producer completion

void producerFunction() {
   for (int i = 1; i <= 10; ++i) {
      { // Scope for lock_guard
         std::lock_guard<std::mutex> lock(queueMutex);
         dataQueue.push(i);
         std::cout << "Produced: " << i << std::endl;
      }
      dataCondition.notify_one(); // Notify one waiting consumer
      std::this_thread::sleep_for(std::chrono::milliseconds(500)); // Simulate
production time
   }
   { // Scope for lock_guard to set producerFinished
      std::lock_guard<std::mutex> lock(queueMutex);
      producerFinished = true; // Signal producer is done
   }
   dataCondition.notify_all(); // Notify all consumers that producer is finished
}

void consumerFunction(const std::string& consumerName) {
   while (true) {
      int dataItem;
      { // Scope for unique_lock
         std::unique_lock<std::mutex> lock(queueMutex); // unique_lock
needed for wait()
         dataCondition.wait(lock, []{ return !dataQueue.empty() ||
producerFinished; }); // Wait until condition is met
```

```
        if (dataQueue.empty() && producerFinished) { // Exit condition:
queue empty and producer finished
            std::cout << consumerName << " exiting, producer finished." <<
std::endl;
            break;
        }
        dataItem = dataQueue.front();
        dataQueue.pop();
        std::cout << consumerName << " consumed: " << dataItem <<
std::endl;
      } // lock is released here
      std::this_thread::sleep_for(std::chrono::milliseconds(200)); // Simulate
consumption time
   }
}

int main() {
   std::thread producer(producerFunction);
   std::thread consumer1(consumerFunction, "Consumer 1");
   std::thread consumer2(consumerFunction, "Consumer 2");

   producer.join();
   consumer1.join();
   consumer2.join();

   std::cout << "Producer and consumers finished." << std::endl;
   return 0;
}
```

Step-by-step explanation:

1. **#include <condition_variable>**: Includes the <condition_variable> header for using std::condition_variable.
2. **#include <queue>**: Includes the <queue> header for using std::queue to implement a producer-consumer queue.
3. **std::mutex queueMutex;, std::condition_variable dataCondition;, std::queue<int> dataQueue;**: Declares a mutex queueMutex to protect the shared queue dataQueue, a condition variable dataCondition for signaling, and the queue itself dataQueue. producerFinished is a boolean flag to signal when the producer is done.
4. **void producerFunction() { ... }**: Defines the producer function.
   - **Producer Loop**: The producer produces integers from 1 to 10 and pushes them into dataQueue.

- **std::lock_guard<std::mutex> lock(queueMutex);**: A lock_guard is used to protect access to dataQueue.
- **dataQueue.push(i);**: Pushes data into the queue.
- **dataCondition.notify_one();**: After pushing data, notify_one() is called on dataCondition. This wakes up *one* of the threads that are waiting on dataCondition.
- **std::this_thread::sleep_for(std::chrono::milliseconds(500));**: Simulates production time.
- **Signaling Producer Completion**: After the loop, the producer sets producerFinished = true under mutex protection and calls dataCondition.notify_all() to wake up all waiting consumers, signaling that no more data will be produced.

5. **void consumerFunction(const std::string& consumerName) { ... }**: Defines the consumer function.
    - **Consumer Loop**: Consumers continuously try to consume data from dataQueue.
    - **std::unique_lock<std::mutex> lock(queueMutex);**: A std::unique_lock is used here instead of std::lock_guard because std::unique_lock provides more flexibility, including the ability to unlock and relock the mutex, which is required for wait() on a condition variable.
    - **dataCondition.wait(lock, []{ return !dataQueue.empty() || producerFinished; });**: This is the core of condition synchronization.
        - dataCondition.wait(lock, ...): The consumer thread *waits* on dataCondition. This atomically unlocks queueMutex and puts the consumer thread to sleep.
        - []{ return !dataQueue.empty() || producerFinished; }: This is a *predicate* (a lambda function) that wait() uses. wait() will keep the thread blocked (sleeping) as long as this predicate returns false. When notify_one() or notify_all() is called on dataCondition by another thread, the waiting thread wakes up, re-acquires queueMutex, and *re-evaluates* the predicate. If the predicate is now true, wait() returns, and the consumer thread proceeds; otherwise, it goes back to sleep.
        - In this example, the consumer waits until either dataQueue is not empty (meaning there is data

to consume) or producerFinished is true (meaning the producer is done and will not produce more data).

- **Exit Condition:** if (dataQueue.empty() && producerFinished) { break; } checks if the queue is empty and the producer is finished. If both are true, the consumer exits the loop because there will be no more data.
- **Data Consumption**: If the wait condition is met and it's not the exit condition, the consumer retrieves data from dataQueue, prints it, and simulates consumption time.

6. **Thread Creation and Joining**: main creates one producer thread and two consumer threads. join() ensures the main thread waits for all of them to complete.

Real-world scenario: Condition variables are used in scenarios involving producer-consumer patterns, thread pools, and event-driven systems. In a multi-threaded image processing application, producer threads might load images from disk and place them in a queue, while consumer threads process images from the queue. Condition variables ensure that consumers wait efficiently until images are available in the queue, and producers can signal consumers when new images are ready.

9.3 Atomic Operations (std::atomic): Lock-Free Concurrency

Atomic operations, provided by the <atomic> library and the std::atomic template class, offer a lower-level mechanism for managing concurrent access to shared variables. Atomic operations are guaranteed to be indivisible, meaning they execute as a single, uninterruptible unit, even when multiple threads are accessing the same atomic variable concurrently. This can provide lock-free concurrency in certain scenarios, potentially improving performance by avoiding the overhead of mutex locks. As Boehm discusses in "Foundations of Multithreaded, Parallel, and Distributed Programming," atomic operations are essential for building efficient and scalable concurrent data structures and algorithms (Boehm, 2018).

Example: Using std::atomic for Atomic Counter

```
C++
#include <iostream>
#include <thread>
#include <atomic> // For std::atomic
#include <string>

std::atomic<int> atomicCounter = 0; // Atomic integer counter

void incrementAtomicCounter(const std::string& threadName) {
   for (int i = 0; i < 100000; ++i) {
      atomicCounter++; // Atomic increment operation
      // No explicit mutex needed - increment is atomic
   }
   std::cout << threadName << " finished incrementing." << std::endl;
}

int main() {
   std::thread thread1(incrementAtomicCounter, "Thread 1");
   std::thread thread2(incrementAtomicCounter, "Thread 2");

   thread1.join();
   thread2.join();

   std::cout << "Final atomic counter value: " << atomicCounter << std::endl;
   return 0;
}
```

Step-by-step explanation:

1. **#include <atomic>**: Includes the <atomic> header for using std::atomic.
2. **std::atomic<int> atomicCounter = 0;**: Declares an atomic integer variable atomicCounter initialized to 0.
    - std::atomic<int>: Specifies that atomicCounter is an atomic integer. Operations on atomicCounter will be atomic.
3. **void incrementAtomicCounter(const std::string& threadName)**: Defines a function incrementAtomicCounter that increments atomicCounter multiple times.
4. **atomicCounter++;**: This is the atomic increment operation. Because atomicCounter is declared as std::atomic<int>, the increment operation ++ is performed atomically. This means that even if multiple threads execute this line concurrently, the

increment operation will be performed as a single, indivisible step. There is no need for explicit mutex locking here.

5. **Thread Creation and Joining**: main creates two threads, thread1 and thread2, both executing incrementAtomicCounter. join() ensures the main thread waits for both threads to finish.

Real-world scenario: Atomic operations are used in scenarios where low-level, lock-free concurrency is needed for performance reasons. They are used in implementing lock-free data structures (e.g., lock-free queues, stacks, counters), in operating system kernels, and in high-performance libraries where minimizing synchronization overhead is critical. Atomic operations are also used in implementing spin locks and other low-level synchronization primitives.

9.4 Parallel Algorithms (std::execution_policy): Data Parallelism

C++17 introduced parallel algorithms in the <algorithm> library, which allow many standard algorithms (like std::for_each, std::transform, std::sort, std::accumulate) to be executed in parallel using execution policies. Execution policies specify how an algorithm should be executed—sequentially, in parallel, or vectorized. This provides a high-level and convenient way to achieve data parallelism, where the same operation is performed on different parts of a data set concurrently. As Reinders discusses in "Intel Threading Building Blocks," parallel algorithms simplify the process of parallelizing common algorithmic tasks (Reinders, 2007).

Example: Using std::for_each with Parallel Execution Policy

```
C++
#include <iostream>
#include <vector>
#include <algorithm> // For std::for_each, std::execution::par
#include <execution> // For std::execution::par
#include <chrono> // For std::chrono
#include <cmath> // For std::sqrt

void processData(double& value) {
  // Simulate some computationally intensive operation
  for (int i = 0; i < 1000000; ++i) {
```

```
        value = std::sqrt(value * value + i);
    }
}

int main() {
    std::vector<double> data(1000);
    for (int i = 0; i < data.size(); ++i) {
        data[i] = i + 1.0; // Initialize data
    }

    // Sequential execution
    auto start_seq = std::chrono::high_resolution_clock::now();
    std::for_each(data.begin(), data.end(), processData);
    auto end_seq = std::chrono::high_resolution_clock::now();
    std::chrono::duration<double> sequential_duration = end_seq - start_seq;
    std::cout << "Sequential execution time: " << sequential_duration.count()
<< " seconds" << std::endl;

    // Parallel execution
    std::vector<double> parallelData = data; // Copy data for parallel execution
    auto start_par = std::chrono::high_resolution_clock::now();
    std::for_each(std::execution::par, parallelData.begin(), parallelData.end(),
processData); // Parallel for_each
    auto end_par = std::chrono::high_resolution_clock::now();
    std::chrono::duration<double> parallel_duration = end_par - start_par;
    std::cout << "Parallel execution time: " << parallel_duration.count() << "
seconds" << std::endl;

    return 0;
}
```

Step-by-step explanation:

1. **#include <algorithm>**: Includes the <algorithm> header for std::for_each and execution policies.
2. **#include <execution>**: Includes the <execution> header for std::execution::par (parallel execution policy).
3. **void processData(double& value)**: Defines a function processData that performs a computationally intensive operation on a double value. This function will be applied to each element of the vector.
4. **std::vector<double> data(1000);**: Creates a vector data of 1000 doubles and initializes it with values.
5. **Sequential Execution**:

- auto start_seq = std::chrono::high_resolution_clock::now();: Records the start time for sequential execution.
- std::for_each(data.begin(), data.end(), processData);: Executes std::for_each sequentially. It iterates through each element of data and applies processData to it.
- auto end_seq = std::chrono::high_resolution_clock::now();: Records the end time.
- Calculates and prints the sequential execution time.

6. **Parallel Execution**:
   - std::vector<double> parallelData = data;: Creates a copy of the original data vector (parallelData). It's important to use a copy if you want to compare sequential and parallel execution on the same initial `data, as std::for_each modifies the data in place.
   - auto start_par = std::chrono::high_resolution_clock::now();: Records the start time for parallel execution.
   - std::for_each(std::execution::par, parallelData.begin(), parallelData.end(), processData);: Executes std::for_each in parallel.
     - std::execution::par: This is the *execution policy* that tells std::for_each to execute in parallel. The algorithm will attempt to divide the work among multiple threads for parallel execution.
   - auto end_par = std::chrono::high_resolution_clock::now();: Records the end time.
   - Calculates and prints the parallel execution time.

Real-world scenario: Parallel algorithms are highly beneficial for data-intensive applications. In scientific computing, parallel algorithms can be used to process large datasets in parallel, significantly reducing computation time. In financial analysis, parallel algorithms can speed up risk calculations and portfolio optimizations. In machine learning, parallel algorithms can accelerate model training and data preprocessing.

9.5 Asynchronous Programming (std::async, std::future): Task-Based Concurrency

Asynchronous programming in C++ is facilitated by std::async and std::future. std::async launches an asynchronous task, which can run concurrently, and returns a std::future object that represents the result of the asynchronous operation. std::future allows you to retrieve the result of the asynchronous task when it becomes available, or check if the task has completed. Asynchronous programming is useful for tasks that can be performed independently and for improving application responsiveness by offloading long-running operations to background threads. As Duffy explains in "Concurrent Programming in C++20," asynchronous programming is a key paradigm for modern concurrent applications (Duffy, 2021).

Example: Using std::async and std::future for Asynchronous Task

```
C++
#include <iostream>
#include <future> // For std::async, std::future
#include <chrono> // For std::chrono::seconds
#include <string>

int longComputation(int input) {
   std::cout << "Starting long computation for input: " << input << std::endl;
   std::this_thread::sleep_for(std::chrono::seconds(3)); // Simulate long
computation
   std::cout << "Long computation finished for input: " << input << std::endl;
   return input * 2; // Return result
}

int main() {
   std::future<int> futureResult = std::async(std::launch::async,
longComputation, 10); // Launch async task

   std::cout << "Main thread continues, waiting for result..." << std::endl;

   std::chrono::seconds timeout(5);
   std::future_status status = futureResult.wait_for(timeout); // Wait with
timeout

   if (status == std::future_status::ready) {
```

```
        int result = futureResult.get(); // Get the result (will block if not ready yet, but it is ready here)
        std::cout << "Asynchronous result is ready: " << result << std::endl;
    } else if (status == std::future_status::timeout) {
        std::cout << "Asynchronous computation timed out!" << std::endl;
    } else if (status == std::future_status::deferred) {
        std::cout << "Asynchronous computation was deferred (not started asynchronously)." << std::endl; // std::launch::deferred was not used here, so this won't happen in this example
    }

    std::cout << "Main thread finished." << std::endl;
    return 0;
}
```

Step-by-step explanation:

1. **#include <future>**: Includes the <future> header for std::async and std::future.
2. **int longComputation(int input)**: Defines a function longComputation that simulates a long-running computation.
3. **std::future<int> futureResult = std::async(std::launch::async, longComputation, 10);**: Launches an asynchronous task using std::async.
    - std::async(std::launch::async, ...): std::async is used to start an asynchronous operation.
        - std::launch::async: This is the *launch policy*. std::launch::async *forces* the task to run in a new thread (if the system can create a new thread). The other option is std::launch::deferred, which would defer execution until get() or wait() is called on the future, and might run it on the calling thread. std::launch::async is used here to ensure true asynchrony.
        - longComputation: The function to be executed asynchronously.
        - 10: An argument passed to longComputation.
    - std::future<int> futureResult = ...: std::async returns a std::future<int> object. std::future<int> represents a future result of type int that will be available when the asynchronous task completes.
4. **std::cout << "Main thread continues, waiting for result..." << std::endl;**: The main thread continues execution while

longComputation is running asynchronously in another thread (if std::launch::async is successful).

5. **std::future_status status = futureResult.wait_for(timeout);**: The main thread waits for the result of the asynchronous computation with a timeout.
   - futureResult.wait_for(timeout): Waits for the future to become ready (i.e., for the asynchronous task to complete) for a maximum duration of timeout (5 seconds in this case).
   - std::future_status status = ...: wait_for() returns a std::future_status enum value indicating the status of the future after waiting.
6. **Status Check**: The code checks the status to determine what happened after waiting.
   - **std::future_status::ready**: If the status is ready, it means the asynchronous task has completed within the timeout.
     - int result = futureResult.get();: futureResult.get() retrieves the result of the asynchronous computation. If the result is ready, get() will return immediately. If it were not ready yet, get() would block until the result becomes available. In this if (status == std::future_status::ready) block, we know it's ready, so get() will not block.
     - std::cout << "Asynchronous result is ready: " << result << std::endl;: Prints the result.
   - **std::future_status::timeout**: If the status is timeout, it means the timeout expired before the asynchronous task completed.
     - std::cout << "Asynchronous computation timed out!" << std::endl;: Prints a timeout message.
   - **std::future_status::deferred**: This status would occur if std::launch::deferred was used as the launch policy. In this example, std::launch::async is used, so this case will not be reached.
7. **std::cout << "Main thread finished." << std::endl;**: The main thread continues after handling the asynchronous result (or timeout).

Real-world scenario: Asynchronous programming is crucial for building responsive user interfaces and applications that perform background tasks without blocking the main thread. In GUI applications, asynchronous tasks can be used to perform long-running operations (e.g., network requests, file I/O, complex calculations) in the background, keeping the UI responsive. In game development, asynchronous loading of game assets can improve startup time and reduce loading screens. In network programming, asynchronous I/O operations can handle multiple connections concurrently without blocking threads.

By understanding and applying these parallel and concurrent programming techniques in C++, Computer Technology students and educators can develop software that effectively utilizes modern multi-core processors, leading to significant performance and responsiveness improvements in their applications. These advanced topics are essential for building the next generation of high-performance, scalable, and reliable software systems.

Chapter 10

Building and Managing C++ Projects: From Source Code to Executable

Effectively building and managing C++ projects is paramount for software development success, particularly in complex, real-world applications. Moving beyond single-file programs requires robust tools and methodologies to handle compilation, linking, dependency management, and build configurations. For Computer Technology students and educators, mastering these aspects is crucial for transitioning from learning the language fundamentals to developing and maintaining substantial software systems. This section will explore essential tools and techniques for building and managing C++ projects, including build systems like Makefiles and CMake, dependency managers such as vcpkg and Conan, library types, build configurations, and continuous integration practices, providing a comprehensive guide to modern C++ project management.

10.1 Build Systems: Automating the Build Process with Makefiles and CMake

Build systems automate the process of compiling source code, linking object files, and creating executables or libraries. They are indispensable for managing projects of any significant size, ensuring consistent and reproducible builds. Two prominent build systems in the C++ ecosystem are Makefiles and CMake, each offering different levels of complexity and flexibility. As Lakos notes in "Large-Scale C++ Software Design," a well-defined build process is essential for managing the complexity of large C++ projects (Lakos, 1996).

10.1.1 Makefiles: Simplicity for Smaller Projects

Makefiles are a traditional build system that uses a text file named Makefile to define build rules. These rules specify dependencies between files and the commands needed to build targets, such as executables or object files. Makefiles are relatively simple and effective for smaller projects, particularly in Unix-like environments.

Example: A Simple Makefile for a C++ Project
Let's consider a project with two source files, main.cpp and hello.cpp, and a header file hello.h.

Project Structure:

```
project/
├── main.cpp
├── hello.cpp
└── hello.h
```

hello.h:

```
C++

#ifndef HELLO_H
#define HELLO_H

void sayHello(const char* name);

#endif // HELLO_H
```

hello.cpp:
C++

```
#include <iostream>
#include "hello.h"

void sayHello(const char* name) {
    std::cout << "Hello, " << name << "!" << std::endl;
}
```
main.cpp:
C++

```
#include "hello.h"

int main() {
    sayHello("C++ User");
    return 0;
}
```

Makefile:
Makefile

```
CXX = g++
CXXFLAGS = -std=c++17 -Wall -g # C++ compiler and flags
TARGET = hello_program # Name of the executable

SOURCES = main.cpp hello.cpp # Source files
OBJECTS = $(SOURCES:.cpp=.o) # Object files (replace .cpp with .o)

all: $(TARGET) # Default target is the executable

$(TARGET): $(OBJECTS) # Rule to build the executable
		$(CXX) $(CXXFLAGS) -o $@ $^ # Link object files to create
executable

%.o: %.cpp hello.h # Rule to compile .cpp files to .o files, depends on hello.h
		$(CXX) $(CXXFLAGS) -c $< -o $@ # Compile a single .cpp file

clean: # Rule to clean up build artifacts
		rm -f $(TARGET) $(OBJECTS) # Remove executable and object
files
```

Step-by-step explanation:

1. **CXX = g++, CXXFLAGS = -std=c++17 -Wall -g, TARGET = hello_program:** These lines define variables. CXX sets the C++ compiler to g++, CXXFLAGS sets compiler flags (C++17 standard,

warnings, debug symbols), and TARGET defines the name of the executable.

2. **SOURCES = main.cpp hello.cpp, OBJECTS = $(SOURCES:.cpp=.o)**: SOURCES lists the source files. OBJECTS uses a substitution to create a list of object files (.o) from the source files (.cpp).
3. **all: $(TARGET)**: all is the default target. When you run make without specifying a target, it builds the all target, which depends on $(TARGET) (the executable).
4. **$(TARGET): $(OBJECTS)**: This is a rule for building the executable $(TARGET). It depends on $(OBJECTS) (the object files).
    - $(CXX) $(CXXFLAGS) -o $@ $^: This is the command to link the object files.
        - $(CXX) $(CXXFLAGS): Uses the compiler and flags defined earlier.
        - -o $@: -o specifies the output file name. $@ is an automatic variable that expands to the target name ($(TARGET) in this case, i.e., hello_program).
        - $^: $^ is an automatic variable that expands to the list of dependencies ($(OBJECTS) in this case).
5. **%.o: %.cpp hello.h**: This is a pattern rule for compiling .cpp files to .o files.
    - %.o: Matches any file ending in .o.
    - %.cpp hello.h: Specifies that a .o file depends on the corresponding .cpp file and hello.h.
    - $(CXX) $(CXXFLAGS) -c $< -o $@: This is the compile command.
        - -c: Tells the compiler to compile and assemble, but not link (creating an object file).
        - $<: $< is an automatic variable that expands to the first dependency (%.cpp in this case).
        - -o $@: -o specifies the output file name. $@ expands to the target name (%.o in this case).
6. **clean:**: This is a rule for cleaning up the build.
    - rm -f $(TARGET) $(OBJECTS): Removes the executable and object files.

To build and run:

1. **Save:** Save the Makefile, hello.h, hello.cpp, and main.cpp in the project/ directory.
2. **Open Terminal:** Navigate to the project/ directory in your terminal.
3. **Build:** Run make. This will compile and link the project, creating the hello_program executable.
4. **Run:** Execute the program using ./hello_program.

5. **Clean:** Run make clean to remove the build artifacts (executable and object files).

Real-world scenario: Makefiles are still used in many open-source projects and for simpler C++ applications, especially in Unix-like environments. They are suitable for projects with a relatively straightforward build process and where cross-platform compatibility is not a primary concern. However, for larger, more complex, and cross-platform projects, CMake is generally preferred.

10.1.2 CMake: Cross-Platform Build System for Complex Projects

CMake is a more advanced, cross-platform build system generator. Unlike Makefiles, CMake does not directly perform the build process. Instead, it generates build files (like Makefiles, Ninja build files, or Visual Studio project files) that are then used by native build tools to compile and link the project. CMake excels in managing complex projects, handling dependencies, and ensuring cross-platform compatibility. As Martin and Hoffman highlight in "Mastering CMake," CMake is the de facto standard for building modern C++ projects (Martin & Hoffman, 2023).

Example: Using CMake for a C++ Project
Using the same project structure as the Makefile example:

Project Structure:

```
project_cmake/
├── main.cpp
├── hello.cpp
└── hello.h
└── CMakeLists.txt
```

CMakeLists.txt:

```
CMake

cmake_minimum_required(VERSION 3.10) # Minimum CMake version
required
project(hello_cmake_project) # Project name

set(CMAKE_CXX_STANDARD 17) # Set C++ standard
set(CMAKE_CXX_STANDARD_REQUIRED TRUE) # Require C++
standard
```

```
add_executable(hello_program main.cpp hello.cpp) # Create executable target
```

Step-by-step explanation:

1. **cmake_minimum_required(VERSION 3.10)**: Specifies the minimum CMake version required to build the project.
2. **project(hello_cmake_project)**: Sets the name of the project to hello_cmake_project.
3. **set(CMAKE_CXX_STANDARD 17), set(CMAKE_CXX_STANDARD_REQUIRED TRUE)**: Sets the C++ standard to C++17 and requires it. This ensures that the compiler uses C++17 features.
4. **add_executable(hello_program main.cpp hello.cpp)**: Defines an executable target named hello_program. It specifies that the executable should be built from the source files main.cpp and hello.cpp. CMake automatically detects dependencies and handles linking.

To build and run:

1. **Save:** Save CMakeLists.txt, hello.h, hello.cpp, and main.cpp in the project_cmake/ directory.
2. **Create Build Directory:** In the project_cmake/ directory, create a build directory: mkdir build.
3. **Navigate to Build Directory:** Change directory to the build directory: cd build.
4. **Configure:** Run CMake to generate build files (e.g., Makefiles): cmake .. (the .. points to the parent directory where CMakeLists.txt is located). You can also specify a generator, e.g., cmake -G "Unix Makefiles" .. or cmake -G "Visual Studio 17 2022" ...
5. **Build:** Run the native build tool (e.g., make if you used "Unix Makefiles" generator, or build from Visual Studio if you used "Visual Studio" generator). For Makefiles, run make.
6. **Run:** Execute the program from the build directory: ./hello_program.
7. **Clean (using Makefiles generator):** Run make clean from the build directory. For other generators, use the appropriate clean command or IDE functionality.

Real-world scenario: CMake is widely adopted in the C++ community for projects of all sizes, from small libraries to large-scale applications. It is used by major open-source projects like LLVM, Qt, and OpenCV. CMake's cross-platform nature and ability to handle complex build configurations make it indispensable for modern C++ development. It supports generating build files for various IDEs and build tools, ensuring projects can be built on different platforms with minimal changes to the build configuration.

10.2 Dependency Management: Integrating External Libraries with vcpkg and Conan

Modern C++ projects often rely on external libraries to provide functionalities ranging from networking and graphics to data processing and testing. Managing these dependencies—including downloading, building, and linking them—can be complex and error-prone. Dependency managers like vcpkg and Conan simplify this process, automating dependency acquisition and integration. As Westfall emphasizes in "Effective CMake," dependency management is a critical aspect of modern CMake-based C++ projects (Westfall, 2022).

10.2.1 vcpkg: Microsoft's Cross-Platform Package Manager

vcpkg is a free, open-source package manager for C++ libraries developed by Microsoft. It simplifies the process of acquiring and managing C++ dependencies across Windows, Linux, and macOS. vcpkg integrates seamlessly with CMake, making it easy to add external libraries to CMake-based projects.

Example: Using vcpkg to Add the `fmt` Library to a CMake Project
Let's assume you want to use the `fmt` library for formatted output in your CMake project.

Prerequisites:

- vcpkg needs to be installed and bootstrapped on your system. Instructions can be found on the vcpkg GitHub repository.
-

Modified `CMakeLists.txt`:
CMake

```
cmake_minimum_required(VERSION 3.10)
project(hello_cmake_vcpkg_project)

set(CMAKE_CXX_STANDARD 17)
set(CMAKE_CXX_STANDARD_REQUIRED TRUE)
```

```
find_package(fmt CONFIG REQUIRED) # Find fmt using CMake's
find_package

add_executable(hello_program main.cpp)
target_link_libraries(hello_program PRIVATE fmt::fmt) # Link fmt library to
the executable
```

Modified main.cpp (using fmt library):

C++

```cpp
#include <fmt/core.h> // Include fmt header

int main() {
  fmt::print("Hello, {}!\n", "fmt User"); // Use fmt::print for formatted
output
  return 0;
}
```

Step-by-step explanation:

1. **Install fmt using vcpkg:** Open a terminal and navigate to your vcpkg directory. Run the command to install fmt for your desired triplet (e.g., x64-linux, x64-windows, x64-osx). For example, for 64-bit Linux:
   Bash

   ```bash
   ./vcpkg install fmt
   ```
2. **Integrate vcpkg with CMake:** CMake needs to know where to find the vcpkg toolchain file. This can be done by setting the CMAKE_TOOLCHAIN_FILE variable when configuring CMake.
3. **Modified CMakeLists.txt:**
   - **find_package(fmt CONFIG REQUIRED)**: This CMake command searches for the fmt library using CMake's find_package mechanism. When vcpkg is properly integrated, it provides CMake configuration files for the libraries it manages. CONFIG mode is used to find package configuration files provided by vcpkg. REQUIRED means CMake will fail with an error if fmt is not found.
   - **target_link_libraries(hello_program PRIVATE fmt::fmt)**: This command links the fmt library to the hello_program executable target. fmt::fmt is the CMake target name provided by the fmt library's vcpkg integration. PRIVATE indicates that fmt is a private dependency of hello_program (only needed for linking hello_program, not for projects that link against hello_program as a library).

4. **Modified** main.cpp: Includes the fmt/core.h header and uses fmt::print for formatted output.
5. **Build and Run (similar to CMake example):**
    - Create a build directory, navigate to it, and run CMake configuration, but now you need to specify the vcpkg toolchain file. Assuming vcpkg is in ~/vcpkg, the configuration command would be:
      Bash
      ```
      cmake -DCMAKE_TOOLCHAIN_FILE=~/vcpkg/scripts/buildsystems/vcpkg.cmake ..
      ```
      Adjust the path to vcpkg.cmake according to your vcpkg installation location.
    - Build using make (or your chosen generator's build command).
    - Run the executable.

Real-world scenario: vcpkg is widely used in C++ projects, especially those targeting Windows, Linux, and macOS. It simplifies dependency management for projects using CMake, making it easier to include popular libraries like Boost, Qt, and many others. vcpkg is particularly valuable in CI/CD environments, ensuring consistent and reproducible builds across different platforms and development environments.

10.2.2 Conan: Decentralized and Flexible Package Manager

Conan is another popular, open-source C++ package manager. Conan is designed to be decentralized and highly flexible, supporting a wide range of build systems (including CMake, Makefiles, Meson, etc.) and platforms. Conan focuses on binary package management and allows for fine-grained control over package versions, configurations, and dependencies. As Gonzalez and Seijo explain in "Conan C++ Package Manager," Conan provides advanced features for managing complex C++ dependencies in diverse environments (Gonzalez & Seijo, 2019).

Example: Using Conan to Add the fmt Library to a CMake Project

Prerequisites:

- Conan needs to be installed on your system. Instructions can be found on the Conan website.

conanfile.txt:

Create a conanfile.txt in the project root directory to define project dependencies.

Code snippet

```
[requires]
fmt/10.2.1 # Specify fmt library and version

[generators]
CMakeDeps # Generates CMake dependency files
CMakeToolchain # Generates CMake toolchain file

[options]
fmt:header_only=True # Example option, fmt can be header-only

[conf]
tools.cmake.cmaketoolchain:generator=Ninja # Example: Use Ninja generator
```

Modified CMakeLists.txt:

CMake

```
cmake_minimum_required(VERSION 3.15) # Conan CMakeToolchain
requires CMake >= 3.15
project(hello_cmake_conan_project)

set(CMAKE_CXX_STANDARD 17)
set(CMAKE_CXX_STANDARD_REQUIRED TRUE)

include(${CMAKE_BINARY_DIR}/conan_toolchain.cmake) # Include
Conan CMakeToolchain

find_package(fmt REQUIRED CONFIG) # Find fmt using CMakeDeps
generator

add_executable(hello_program main.cpp)
target_link_libraries(hello_program PRIVATE fmt::fmt) # Link fmt library
```

Modified main.cpp (same as vcpkg example):

```
C++

#include <fmt/core.h>

int main() {
    fmt::print("Hello, {}!\n", "Conan User");
    return 0;
}
```

Step-by-step explanation:

1. **Create conanfile.txt:** This file defines the project's dependencies and build requirements.
    - [requires]: Lists project dependencies. fmt/10.2.1 specifies the fmt library and version.
    - [generators]: Specifies Conan generators to create files for build system integration. CMakeDeps generates find_package() compatible files for CMake. CMakeToolchain generates a CMake toolchain file to configure the build environment.
    - [options]: Specifies options for dependencies. fmt:header_only=True is an example option for the fmt library (if applicable).
    - [conf]: Configuration settings. tools.cmake.cmaketoolchain:generator=Ninja is an example to use the Ninja build system (optional).
2. **Modified CMakeLists.txt:**
    - **cmake_minimum_required(VERSION 3.15):** CMakeToolchain generator requires CMake 3.15 or higher.
    - **include(${CMAKE_BINARY_DIR}/conan_toolchain.cmake):** Includes the CMake toolchain file generated by Conan. This configures CMake with the necessary settings to find and use Conan-managed dependencies.
    - **find_package(fmt REQUIRED CONFIG):** Uses find_package to find the fmt library. CMakeDeps generator creates the necessary CMake files for find_package to work.
    - **target_link_libraries(...):** Links the fmt::fmt target to the executable, similar to the vcpkg example.
3. **Modified main.cpp:** Same as vcpkg example, using fmt/core.h and fmt::print.
4. **Build and Run:**
    - Create a build directory and navigate to it.
    - Run Conan install to fetch and prepare dependencies: conan install .. --build=missing. The .. points to the directory containing conanfile.txt. --build=missing tells Conan to build packages from source if binaries are not available.

- Run CMake configuration: `cmake ..` (Conan's CMakeToolchain already configured CMake).
- Build using `make` or your chosen generator's build command.
- Run the executable.

Real-world scenario: Conan is favored in larger, more complex projects and organizations that require fine-grained control over dependency versions, configurations, and binary management. It is suitable for projects with diverse dependency requirements, cross-platform builds, and a need for reproducible builds in different environments. Conan's decentralized nature also makes it suitable for projects with dependencies from various sources and repositories.

10.3 Static vs. Dynamic Libraries: Choosing the Right Library Type

Libraries are collections of pre-compiled code that provide reusable functionalities. In C++, libraries can be either static or dynamic (shared), each with distinct characteristics and use cases. Understanding the differences between static and dynamic libraries is crucial for making informed decisions about project architecture and deployment. As Libeskind-Hadas and Zobel explain in "Programming with Libraries," the choice between static and dynamic libraries impacts application size, runtime behavior, and update mechanisms (Libeskind-Hadas & Zobel, 1998).

10.3.1 Static Libraries (`.a` on Linux, `.lib` on Windows): Archive of Object Code

Static libraries are archives of object code that are linked directly into the executable during the linking phase of the build process. When a program uses a static library, the necessary code from the library is copied into the executable, making the executable self-contained.

Pros of Static Libraries:

- **Self-contained executables:** Executables built with static libraries do not depend on external library files at runtime. Everything is included in the executable.
- **Performance:** Static linking can sometimes offer slightly better performance because function calls to library code are direct, without the overhead of dynamic linking at runtime.
- **Simpler deployment:** Deployment can be simpler as you only need to distribute the executable, without worrying about separate library files.

Cons of Static Libraries:

- **Larger executable size:** Static libraries increase the size of the executable because the library code is duplicated in every executable that uses it.
- **Code duplication:** If multiple executables use the same static library, the library code is duplicated in each executable, wasting disk space and memory.
- **Updates and maintenance:** Updating a static library requires recompiling and relinking all executables that use it. If a security vulnerability or bug fix is released in a static library, all applications using it need to be rebuilt and redistributed.

Example: Creating and Using a Static Library with CMake Project Structure:

```
static_library_example/
├── lib/
│   ├── hello.h
│   └── hello.cpp
└── app/
  └── main.cpp
└── CMakeLists.txt
```

lib/hello.h and lib/hello.cpp (same as previous examples):

app/main.cpp:

```
C++

#include "hello.h"

int main() {
  sayHello("Static Library User");
  return 0;
}
```

CMakeLists.txt:

```
CMake

cmake_minimum_required(VERSION 3.10)
project(static_library_project)

set(CMAKE_CXX_STANDARD 17)
set(CMAKE_CXX_STANDARD_REQUIRED TRUE)

add_library(hello_lib STATIC # Create static library target
  lib/hello.cpp
  lib/hello.h
)

add_executable(hello_app app/main.cpp) # Create executable target
target_link_libraries(hello_app PRIVATE hello_lib) # Link static library to the
executable
target_include_directories(hello_app PRIVATE
${CMAKE_CURRENT_SOURCE_DIR}/lib) # Add include directory for
hello.h
```

Step-by-step explanation:

1. **add_library(hello_lib STATIC ...)**: Creates a static library target named hello_lib.
    - STATIC: Specifies that a static library should be created.
    - lib/hello.cpp lib/hello.h: Lists the source files for the library.
2. **add_executable(hello_app app/main.cpp)**: Creates an executable target hello_app.
3. **target_link_libraries(hello_app PRIVATE hello_lib)**: Links the static library hello_lib to the executable hello_app.
4. **target_include_directories(hello_app PRIVATE ${CMAKE_CURRENT_SOURCE_DIR}/lib)**: Adds the lib directory as an include directory for the hello_app target, so the compiler can find hello.h.

Build and run: Follow the standard CMake build process (create build directory, configure, build, run from the build directory).

10.3.2 Dynamic Libraries (.so on Linux, .dll on Windows, .dylib on macOS): Shared Code at Runtime

Dynamic libraries (also known as shared libraries) are libraries that are loaded at runtime when an executable that depends on them is launched. Instead of being copied into the executable, the executable only contains references to the dynamic library. Multiple executables can share the same dynamic library file, saving disk space and memory.

Pros of Dynamic Libraries:

- **Smaller executable size:** Executables are smaller because they don't contain the library code.
- **Code sharing:** Multiple programs can share the same dynamic library in memory and on disk, saving resources.
- **Easier updates:** Updating a dynamic library can benefit all applications that use it without recompiling the applications themselves. If a dynamic library is updated (e.g., for bug fixes or security patches), applications using it will automatically use the updated library the next time they are run (assuming binary compatibility is maintained).
- **Plugin architectures:** Dynamic libraries are essential for plugin architectures, where applications can load and unload modules (plugins) at runtime.

Cons of Dynamic Libraries:

- **Dependency on external files:** Executables depend on external dynamic library files at runtime. These library files must be present in the system's library path or in a location where the executable can find them.
- **Dynamic linking overhead:** There is a small runtime overhead associated with dynamic linking, as the operating system needs to load and link the library at program startup.
- **Dependency management complexity:** Managing dynamic library dependencies and ensuring that the correct versions are available at runtime can be more complex than with static libraries. "DLL hell" (on Windows) and similar issues on other platforms can arise if incompatible versions of dynamic libraries are present.

Example: Creating and Using a Dynamic Library with CMake

Project Structure: Same as the static library example.

CMakeLists.txt:

CMake

```
cmake_minimum_required(VERSION 3.10)
project(dynamic_library_project)

set(CMAKE_CXX_STANDARD 17)
set(CMAKE_CXX_STANDARD_REQUIRED TRUE)

add_library(hello_lib SHARED # Create dynamic library target
   lib/hello.cpp
   lib/hello.h
)

add_executable(hello_app app/main.cpp)
```

```
target_link_libraries(hello_app PRIVATE hello_lib) # Link dynamic library
target_include_directories(hello_app PRIVATE
${CMAKE_CURRENT_SOURCE_DIR}/lib)
```

lib/hello.h, lib/hello.cpp, app/main.cpp: Same as static library example.

Step-by-step explanation:

The CMakeLists.txt is almost identical to the static library example, except for one key change:

1. **add_library(hello_lib SHARED ...):** Creates a *dynamic* library target by specifying SHARED instead of STATIC. All other CMake commands remain the same.

Build and run: Follow the standard CMake build process. After building the dynamic library, when you run hello_app, the operating system will need to find the dynamic library (hello_lib.so on Linux, hello_lib.dll on Windows, hello_lib.dylib on macOS) at runtime. The library will typically be placed in the same directory as the executable, or in a system library path.

Real-world scenario: Dynamic libraries are essential for operating systems, shared system libraries, plugin architectures, and applications where code sharing, updatability, and smaller executable sizes are important. Most desktop applications and operating system components rely heavily on dynamic libraries. For example, on Windows, DLLs (Dynamic Link Libraries) are the standard for shared libraries, and on Linux, shared objects (.so files) serve the same purpose.

10.4 Debug vs. Release Builds: Optimizing for Development and Deployment

Software projects are typically built in two main configurations: Debug and Release. These build configurations differ significantly in terms of compiler optimizations, debugging symbols, and overall performance characteristics. Understanding and utilizing both build types is crucial for the software development lifecycle. As Maguire emphasizes in "Writing Solid Code," using debug and release builds effectively is a key practice for producing high-quality software (Maguire, 1993).

10.4.1 Debug Builds: For Development and Debugging

Debug builds are optimized for development and debugging. They are compiled with:

- **Debugging symbols:** Debugging symbols are included in the executable, which allows debuggers (like GDB or Visual Studio Debugger) to map machine code instructions back to the original source code lines and variable names. This is essential for setting breakpoints, stepping through code, and inspecting variables during debugging.
- **Minimal or no optimizations:** Compiler optimizations are typically disabled or minimized in debug builds. Optimizations can sometimes make debugging harder because they can reorder or eliminate code, making the execution flow less predictable and variable values harder to inspect in a debugger.
- **Assertions and error checks:** Debug builds often include assertions and extra runtime error checks to detect programming errors early in development.

Characteristics of Debug Builds:

- **Slower execution:** Due to the lack of optimizations and inclusion of debugging overhead, debug builds are typically slower than release builds.
- **Larger executable size:** Debugging symbols and extra error-checking code increase the size of debug executables.
- **Easier debugging:** Debug builds are designed to be easily debuggable with tools like debuggers.

10.4.2 Release Builds: For Deployment and Performance

Release builds are optimized for deployment and performance. They are compiled with:

- **No debugging symbols:** Debugging symbols are typically excluded from release builds to reduce executable size and improve performance.
- **Full optimizations:** Compiler optimizations are enabled to maximize performance. Optimizations can include inlining functions, loop unrolling, register allocation, and other techniques to make the code run faster and more efficiently.
- **Assertions and error checks often disabled:** Assertions and runtime error checks are often disabled in release builds to eliminate

their runtime overhead and improve performance. Error handling in release builds typically relies on more robust error reporting and recovery mechanisms rather than assertions.

Characteristics of Release Builds:

- **Faster execution:** Release builds are significantly faster than debug builds due to compiler optimizations.
- **Smaller executable size:** Without debugging symbols and with optimizations, release executables are smaller.
- **Harder debugging:** Debugging release builds is more challenging because debugging symbols are absent, and optimizations can make the execution flow less straightforward to follow.

Example: Configuring Debug and Release Builds in CMake

CMake provides built-in support for build types, with common types being Debug, Release, RelWithDebInfo, and MinSizeRel. The build type can be specified during CMake configuration using the CMAKE_BUILD_TYPE variable.

Modified CMakeLists.txt (no changes needed for build type configuration):

```
CMake

cmake_minimum_required(VERSION 3.10)
project(build_type_example)

set(CMAKE_CXX_STANDARD 17)
set(CMAKE_CXX_STANDARD_REQUIRED TRUE)

add_executable(build_type_program main.cpp)
```

Building in Debug and Release Modes:

1. **Create separate build directories (recommended):**
   ```
   Bash

   mkdir build_debug
   mkdir build_release
   ```
2. **Configure Debug Build:**
   ```
   Bash

   cd build_debug
   cmake -DCMAKE_BUILD_TYPE=Debug .. # Specify Debug build
   type
   ```

3. **Build Debug Build:**
   Bash

   ```
   make # Or your chosen generator's build command
   ```
   The executable in build_debug/ will be a debug build.

4. **Configure Release Build:**
   Bash

   ```
   cd ../build_release # Go to release build directory
   cmake -DCMAKE_BUILD_TYPE=Release .. # Specify Release build type
   ```
5. **Build Release Build:**
   Bash

   ```
   make # Or your chosen generator's build command
   ```
   The executable in build_release/ will be a release build.

Real-world scenario: Debug builds are used during development and testing to find and fix bugs. Release builds are used for deploying the final software to users. Developers typically work with debug builds during active development and switch to release builds for performance testing, benchmarking, and final deployment. It's essential to thoroughly test both debug and release builds to ensure correctness and performance in both development and production environments.

10.5 Continuous Integration (CI) with GitHub Actions: Automating Build, Test, and Integration

Continuous Integration (CI) is a software development practice where code changes are frequently integrated into a shared repository, and automated builds and tests are run on each integration. CI helps to detect integration issues early, improve code quality, and automate the build and testing process. GitHub Actions is a CI/CD (Continuous Integration and Continuous Delivery) service directly integrated with GitHub, making it easy to set up CI pipelines for projects hosted on GitHub. As Fowler and Foemmel describe in "Continuous Integration," CI is a cornerstone of modern agile software development practices (Fowler & Foemmel, 2006).

Example: Setting up CI for a C++ Project with GitHub Actions

Let's create a simple GitHub Actions workflow to build a C++ project using CMake and run tests on every push and pull request.

Project Structure (assuming a simple CMake project):

```
ci_example/
├── main.cpp
├── CMakeLists.txt
└── .github/workflows/
    └── cmake-ci.yml # GitHub Actions workflow file
```

.github/workflows/cmake-ci.yml:

YAML

```
name: CMake CI # Workflow name

on: # Trigger events for the workflow
  push: # Trigger on push events
    branches: [ "main" ] # Trigger only for pushes to the "main" branch
  pull_request: # Trigger on pull requests
    branches: [ "main" ]

jobs: # Define jobs to be executed
  build: # Build job
    runs-on: ubuntu-latest # Run on Ubuntu latest

    steps: # Steps within the build job
    - uses: actions/checkout@v4 # Checkout repository code

    - name: Install dependencies # Install necessary dependencies
      run: sudo apt-get update && sudo apt-get install -y cmake g++

    - name: Create Build Directory # Create build directory
      run: mkdir build

    - name: Configure CMake # Configure CMake
      working-directory: ./build # Run commands in build directory
      run: cmake ..

    - name: Build # Build the project
      working-directory: ./build
      run: make -j2 # -j2 for parallel build (using 2 cores)

    - name: Run Tests (Example - Replace with actual tests) # Example test step
      working-directory: ./build
      run: ./build_type_program # Assuming your executable is named
build_type_program
```

Step-by-step explanation:

1. **Create .github/workflows/cmake-ci.yml**: Create this YAML file in your project's .github/workflows/ directory. This file defines the CI workflow.
2. **name: CMake CI**: Sets the name of the workflow, which will be displayed in GitHub Actions.
3. **on:**: Defines the events that trigger the workflow.
    - push:: Triggers the workflow on every push to the repository.
        - branches: ["main"]: Specifies that the workflow should only run for pushes to the main branch.
    - pull_request:: Triggers the workflow on every pull request to the main branch.
4. **jobs:**: Defines the jobs to be executed in the workflow. In this case, there is a single job named build.
    - **build:**: Defines the build job.
        - runs-on: ubuntu-latest: Specifies that the job should run on the latest version of Ubuntu Linux, provided by GitHub Actions.
        - **steps:**: Defines the steps to be executed within the build job, executed sequentially.
            - - uses: actions/checkout@v4: Uses the actions/checkout@v4 action to checkout the repository's code to the GitHub Actions runner environment. This makes your project's code available in the workflow.
            - - name: Install dependencies: Installs necessary dependencies.
                - run: sudo apt-get update && sudo apt-get install -y cmake g++: Runs shell commands to update the package list and install cmake and g++ (essential for building C++ projects) on the Ubuntu runner.
            - - name: Create Build Directory: Creates a build directory.
                - run: mkdir build: Creates a directory named build in the workflow's workspace.
            - - name: Configure CMake: Configures CMake.
                - working-directory: ./build: Sets the working directory for the

following `run` step to be the `build` directory.

- `run: cmake ..`: Runs the CMake configuration command, with `..` pointing to the project root directory where `CMakeLists.txt` is located.

- `- name: Build`: Builds the project.
  - `working-directory: ./build`: Sets the working directory to `build`.
  - `run: make -j2`: Runs the `make` command to build the project. `-j2` enables parallel build using 2 cores, which can speed up the build process.
- `- name: Run Tests (Example - Replace with actual tests)`: Example step to run tests.
  - `working-directory: ./build`: Sets working directory to `build`.
  - `run: ./build_type_program`: Runs the executable `build_type_program` (replace with your actual test execution command). This is a placeholder; you would typically replace this with a proper test suite execution command (e.g., using a testing framework like Google Test).

To set up CI:

1. **Create GitHub Repository:** Create a GitHub repository for your C++ project.
2. **Push Project Code:** Push your project code (including `.github/workflows/cmake-ci.yml`, `CMakeLists.txt`, source files, etc.) to the GitHub repository.
3. **GitHub Actions will automatically run:** Once you push the workflow file to `.github/workflows/`, GitHub Actions will automatically detect it and start running the workflow on every push to the `main` branch and on every pull request targeting the `main` branch.
4. **View Workflow Status:** You can view the status of your workflows in the "Actions" tab of your GitHub repository. You can see the logs, check for build failures, and monitor the CI process.

Real-world scenario: CI with GitHub Actions (or similar CI systems like Jenkins, GitLab CI, Azure DevOps Pipelines) is a standard practice in modern software development. CI automates the build and test process, ensuring that code changes are continuously validated and integrated. This helps to catch integration issues early, maintain code quality, and streamline the development workflow. CI is particularly crucial for team-based projects and for ensuring the stability and reliability of software releases.

By mastering these tools and techniques for building and managing C++ projects, Computer Technology students and educators will be well-equipped to handle the complexities of real-world software development. From automating the build process with Makefiles and CMake to managing dependencies with vcpkg and Conan, choosing the right library type, utilizing build configurations, and implementing continuous integration, these skills are essential for creating robust, efficient, and maintainable C++ software systems.

Chapter 11

C++ for Systems and Embedded Programming: Bridging the Gap Between Hardware and Software

C++ stands as a powerful and versatile language that extends its reach beyond high-level application development into the realms of systems and embedded programming. Its unique blend of performance, control, and abstraction capabilities makes it an ideal choice for developing software that directly interacts with hardware, manages system resources, and operates in resource-constrained environments. For Computer Technology students and educators, understanding C++ in this context is crucial as embedded systems become increasingly pervasive in everyday life, from automotive systems and industrial controllers to IoT devices and medical equipment. This section explores the key aspects of using C++ for systems and embedded programming, including low-level memory manipulation, hardware interfacing, embedded C++ best practices, and techniques for writing performant code, equipping developers with the necessary skills to tackle the challenges of this demanding field.

11.1 Low-Level Memory Manipulation: Direct Access and Control

In systems and embedded programming, direct memory manipulation is often necessary to interact with hardware, manage memory efficiently, and optimize performance. C++ provides powerful features for low-level memory access, including pointers, memory allocation control, bit manipulation, and memory-mapped I/O. These capabilities allow developers to operate at a level close to the hardware, which is essential for tasks such as device driver development, real-time systems, and memory-constrained applications. As Patterson and Hennessy emphasize in "Computer Organization and Design," understanding memory hierarchy and manipulation is fundamental to computer systems engineering (Patterson & Hennessy, 2021).

11.1.1 Pointers and Memory Addresses: The Foundation of Low-Level Access

Pointers in C++ are variables that store memory addresses. They provide a direct way to access and manipulate data stored at specific memory locations. Understanding pointer arithmetic, dereferencing, and pointer types is crucial for low-level programming.

Example: Direct Memory Access using Pointers

```
C++
#include <iostream>

int main() {
   int value = 10;
   int *ptr = &value; // ptr stores the memory address of 'value'

   std::cout << "Value: " << value << std::endl;        // Output: Value: 10
   std::cout << "Address of value: " << &value << std::endl; // Output:
Address of value: 0x... (memory address)
   std::cout << "Pointer ptr: " << ptr << std::endl;       // Output: Pointer ptr:
0x... (same memory address)
   std::cout << "Value pointed to by ptr: " << *ptr << std::endl; // Output:
Value pointed to by ptr: 10 (dereferencing)

   *ptr = 20; // Modify the value at the memory address pointed to by ptr
```

```
    std::cout << "Modified Value: " << value << std::endl;  // Output:
Modified Value: 20 (value is changed through ptr)

    return 0;
}
```

Step-by-step explanation:

1. **int value = 10;**: Declares an integer variable value and initializes it to 10. This variable is stored at a specific memory address.
2. **int *ptr = &value;**: Declares a pointer variable ptr of type int* (pointer to integer) and initializes it with the memory address of value using the address-of operator &.
3. **std::cout << "Address of value: " << &value << std::endl;**: Prints the memory address of the variable value.
4. **std::cout << "Pointer ptr: " << ptr << std::endl;**: Prints the value of the pointer ptr, which is the memory address of value.
5. **std::cout << "Value pointed to by ptr: " << *ptr << std::endl;**: Dereferences the pointer ptr using the dereference operator *. *ptr accesses the value stored at the memory address held by ptr, which is the value of value.
6. ***ptr = 20;**: Modifies the value at the memory location pointed to by ptr. Since ptr points to the memory location of value, this line changes the value of value to 20.
7. **std::cout << "Modified Value: " << value << std::endl;**: Prints the value of value after it has been modified through the pointer ptr.

Real-world scenario: Pointers are fundamental in systems programming for tasks like dynamic memory allocation, implementing data structures, and directly accessing hardware registers in memory-mapped I/O. For instance, in operating system kernels, pointers are extensively used to manage memory, handle process contexts, and interact with hardware devices. In embedded systems, pointers are crucial for accessing and controlling hardware peripherals at specific memory addresses.

11.1.2 Memory Allocation and Deallocation: Managing Memory Resources

C++ offers control over memory allocation through `new` and `delete` operators, as well as lower-level functions like `malloc` and `free` inherited from C. In systems and embedded programming, efficient memory management is critical, especially in resource-constrained environments. Understanding dynamic memory allocation, deallocation, and avoiding memory leaks is essential.

Example: Dynamic Memory Allocation and Deallocation

```
C++
#include <iostream>

int main() {
    int *dynamicArray = new int[10]; // Allocate an array of 10 integers
dynamically

    if (dynamicArray == nullptr) {
        std::cerr << "Memory allocation failed!" << std::endl;
        return 1;
    }

    for (int i = 0; i < 10; ++i) {
        dynamicArray[i] = i * 2; // Initialize array elements
    }

    std::cout << "Dynamic array elements: ";
    for (int i = 0; i < 10; ++i) {
        std::cout << dynamicArray[i] << " "; // Print array elements
    }
    std::cout << std::endl;

    delete[] dynamicArray; // Deallocate the dynamically allocated array
    dynamicArray = nullptr; // Set pointer to nullptr after deallocation (good
practice)

    return 0;
}
```

Step-by-step explanation:

1. **int *dynamicArray = new int[10];**: Dynamically allocates memory for an array of 10 integers using the `new` operator.

- new int[10]: Allocates enough memory to hold 10 integers from the heap. It returns a pointer to the first element of the allocated memory block.
- int *dynamicArray = ...: The returned pointer is assigned to the pointer variable dynamicArray.

2. **if (dynamicArray == nullptr) { ... }**: Checks if memory allocation was successful. If new fails to allocate memory (e.g., due to insufficient memory), it returns a null pointer (nullptr). It's crucial to check for allocation failures, especially in embedded systems where memory is limited.
3. **Array Initialization and Access**: The code initializes and prints the elements of the dynamically allocated array using a for loop and array indexing (dynamicArray[i]).
4. **delete[] dynamicArray;**: Deallocates the memory that was previously allocated for the array using delete[].
    - delete[] dynamicArray: The delete[] operator is used to deallocate memory that was allocated with new[]. It's important to use delete[] for arrays allocated with new[] to properly release the memory back to the heap.
5. **dynamicArray = nullptr;**: Sets the pointer dynamicArray to nullptr after deallocation. This is a good practice to prevent dangling pointers, which are pointers that point to memory that has been deallocated. Accessing a dangling pointer leads to undefined behavior.

Real-world scenario: Dynamic memory allocation is essential for systems and embedded applications that need to adapt to varying memory requirements at runtime. For example, in a real-time operating system (RTOS), dynamic memory allocation might be used to create task control blocks or message queues as needed. In embedded devices, dynamic allocation can be used to manage buffers for sensor data or network communication. However, in resource-constrained embedded systems, dynamic memory allocation should be used judiciously to avoid fragmentation and ensure deterministic behavior. Static allocation or memory pools are often preferred in critical embedded systems for better predictability and reliability.

11.1.3 Bit Manipulation: Operating at the Bit Level

Bit manipulation involves directly manipulating individual bits within bytes or words. This is often necessary in systems and embedded programming for tasks like controlling hardware registers, packing data efficiently, and implementing low-level protocols. C++ provides bitwise operators (AND &, OR |, XOR ^, NOT ~, left shift <<, right shift >>) for bit manipulation.

Example: Bit Manipulation for Register Control

```
C++
#include <iostream>

int main() {
    unsigned char registerValue = 0b00000000; // 8-bit register, initially all bits 0

    std::cout << "Initial register value: 0b" << std::bitset(registerValue) <<
std::endl;

    // Set bit 3 (0-indexed) to 1
    registerValue |= (1 << 3); // Bitwise OR with (1 shifted left by 3)

    std::cout << "Register value after setting bit 3: 0b" <<
std::bitset(registerValue) << std::endl;

    // Clear bit 5 (set to 0)
    registerValue &= ~(1 << 5); // Bitwise AND with NOT of (1 shifted left
by 5)

    std::cout << "Register value after clearing bit 5: 0b" <<
std::bitset(registerValue) << std::endl;

    // Toggle bit 1
    registerValue ^= (1 << 1); // Bitwise XOR with (1 shifted left by 1)

    std::cout << "Register value after toggling bit 1: 0b" <<
std::bitset(registerValue) << std::endl;

    // Check if bit 3 is set
    if (registerValue & (1 << 3)) {
        std::cout << "Bit 3 is set." << std::endl;
    } else {
        std::cout << "Bit 3 is not set." << std::endl;
    }
```

```
    return 0;
}
```

Step-by-step explanation:

1. **unsigned char registerValue = 0b00000000;**: Declares an unsigned 8-bit character registerValue and initializes it to binary 00000000. unsigned char is often used to represent byte-sized registers.
2. **std::cout << "Initial register value: 0b" << std::bitset(registerValue) << std::endl;**: Prints the initial value of the register in binary format using std::bitset for easy visualization.
3. **registerValue |= (1 << 3);**: Sets bit 3 to 1.
   - (1 << 3): Left-shifts the integer 1 by 3 bits. This creates a bitmask 0b00001000 (binary), where only bit 3 is set to 1.
   - registerValue |= ...: Performs a bitwise OR operation between registerValue and the bitmask. The OR operation sets bit 3 of registerValue to 1, while leaving other bits unchanged.
4. **registerValue &= ~(1 << 5);**: Clears bit 5 (sets it to 0).
   - (1 << 5): Creates a bitmask 0b00100000 with bit 5 set.
   - ~(1 << 5): Performs a bitwise NOT operation on the bitmask. This inverts all the bits, resulting in a mask where all bits are 1 except bit 5, which is 0 (0b11011111).
   - registerValue &= ...: Performs a bitwise AND operation between registerValue and the inverted bitmask. The AND operation clears bit 5 of registerValue to 0, while leaving other bits unchanged.
5. **registerValue ^= (1 << 1);**: Toggles bit 1 (if it's 0, it becomes 1; if it's 1, it becomes 0).
   - (1 << 1): Creates a bitmask 0b00000010 with bit 1 set.
   - registerValue ^= ...: Performs a bitwise XOR (exclusive OR) operation between registerValue and the bitmask. The XOR operation toggles bit 1 of registerValue.
6. **if (registerValue & (1 << 3)) { ... }**: Checks if bit 3 is set.
   - (1 << 3): Creates the bitmask 0b00001000 again.
   - registerValue & ...: Performs a bitwise AND operation between registerValue and the bitmask. If bit 3 of registerValue is set, the result of the AND operation will

be non-zero (specifically, `0b00001000`). If bit 3 is not set, the result will be zero.

- The `if` condition checks if the result of the AND operation is non-zero, which indicates whether bit 3 is set.

Real-world scenario: Bit manipulation is extensively used in embedded systems for controlling hardware peripherals. Microcontroller registers are often controlled by setting or clearing specific bits. For example, to enable or disable a peripheral, configure communication protocols, or set output pin states, bit manipulation is used to directly interact with hardware registers at their memory addresses. In network programming, bit manipulation is used for tasks like parsing packet headers and implementing network protocols.

11.2 Interfacing with Hardware: GPIO and Serial Ports

C++ in systems and embedded programming often involves direct interaction with hardware components. Two fundamental interfaces for hardware interaction are General Purpose Input/Output (GPIO) pins and serial ports. GPIO pins allow for digital input and output, while serial ports enable communication with other devices using serial protocols like UART. As Furr and Davies detail in "Embedded Systems Architecture," understanding hardware interfaces is crucial for embedded systems development (Furr & Davies, 2005).

11.2.1 GPIO (General Purpose Input/Output): Digital Interaction

GPIO pins are versatile pins on microcontrollers and embedded processors that can be configured as either inputs or outputs. As outputs, they can control external devices by setting digital signals (high or low). As inputs, they can read digital signals from sensors or other devices.

Conceptual Example: GPIO Control (Platform-Specific Code Required)

```
C++
// Note: This is a conceptual example. GPIO interaction is highly platform-
specific
// and requires hardware-specific libraries and initialization.
// This code will NOT compile and run directly without platform-specific
adaptations.

#include <iostream>
// #include <platform_gpio.h> // Hypothetical platform-specific GPIO
library

int main() {
   int gpioPin = 18; // Example GPIO pin number (platform-dependent)

   // Initialize GPIO pin as output (platform-specific function)
   // gpio_init_output(gpioPin); // Hypothetical function

   std::cout << "Setting GPIO pin " << gpioPin << " HIGH" << std::endl;
   // Set GPIO pin HIGH (platform-specific function)
   // gpio_set_high(gpioPin);   // Hypothetical function

   // Wait for a short period (e.g., 1 second)
   // platform_delay_ms(1000);  // Hypothetical platform-specific delay
function

   std::cout << "Setting GPIO pin " << gpioPin << " LOW" << std::endl;
   // Set GPIO pin LOW (platform-specific function)
   // gpio_set_low(gpioPin);    // Hypothetical function

   return 0;
}
```

Explanation and Challenges:

- **Platform Dependency:** GPIO interaction is *highly platform-specific.* The code to control GPIO pins varies significantly depending on the microcontroller or embedded processor being used. You need to use hardware-specific libraries and APIs provided by the chip vendor or a hardware abstraction layer (HAL).
- **Hypothetical Functions:** The example code uses placeholder functions like `gpio_init_output()`, `gpio_set_high()`, `gpio_set_low()`, and `platform_delay_ms()`. These functions are *not* standard C++ and would need to be replaced with actual functions from a platform-specific GPIO library for your target hardware.
- **Hardware Initialization:** Before using GPIO pins, they usually need to be initialized and configured correctly. This often involves setting pin modes (input or output), pull-up/pull-down resistors, and other hardware-specific settings.
- **Real-time Considerations:** In many embedded systems, GPIO operations need to be performed in real-time or with precise timing. This might require careful programming and consideration of interrupt handling and real-time scheduling.

To make this example runnable, you would need to:

1. **Choose a specific hardware platform:** (e.g., Raspberry Pi, Arduino, STM32 microcontroller).
2. **Identify the GPIO library for that platform:** (e.g., `wiringPi` or `pigpio` for Raspberry Pi, Arduino built-in GPIO functions, STM32 HAL or LL libraries).
3. **Replace the hypothetical functions** in the example code with the actual functions from the chosen platform's GPIO library.
4. **Compile and run the code** on the target hardware.

Real-world scenario: GPIO pins are used in a vast array of embedded applications. Examples include controlling LEDs, reading button inputs, interfacing with sensors (e.g., temperature sensors, motion sensors), controlling actuators (e.g., motors, relays), and implementing simple digital communication protocols. In IoT devices, GPIOs are used to interface with sensors and actuators for data collection and control. In industrial automation, GPIOs are used to control machinery and monitor industrial processes.

11.2.2 Serial Ports (UART): Asynchronous Serial Communication

Serial ports, particularly UART (Universal Asynchronous Receiver/Transmitter), are another fundamental hardware interface for communication in embedded systems. UART enables asynchronous serial communication between devices, where data is transmitted bit by bit over a single wire (or pair of wires for full-duplex communication). UART is commonly used for communication between microcontrollers and computers, sensors, GPS modules, and other serial devices.

Conceptual Example: UART Communication (Platform-Specific Code Required)

```
C++
// Note: This is a conceptual example. UART interaction is highly platform-
specific
// and requires hardware-specific libraries and initialization.
// This code will NOT compile and run directly without platform-specific
adaptations.

#include <iostream>
#include <string>
// #include <platform_uart.h> // Hypothetical platform-specific UART
library

int main() {
   // Initialize UART (platform-specific function)
   // uart_init("/dev/ttyS0", 115200); // Hypothetical: UART device path,
baud rate

   std::string message = "Hello from UART!\n";
   std::cout << "Sending message via UART: " << message;

   // Send message via UART (platform-specific function)
   // uart_send_string(message.c_str()); // Hypothetical function to send a
string

   // Receive data via UART (platform-specific function)
   char buffer[256];
   int bytesRead = 0;
   // bytesRead = uart_receive_bytes(buffer, sizeof(buffer), 1000); //
Hypothetical: buffer, size, timeout (ms)
```

```
  if (bytesRead > 0) {
    buffer[bytesRead] = '\0'; // Null-terminate received data
    std::cout << "Received from UART: " << buffer << std::endl;
  } else {
    std::cout << "No data received from UART." << std::endl;
  }

  // Close UART (platform-specific function)
  // uart_close(); // Hypothetical function

  return 0;
}
```

Explanation and Challenges:

- **Platform Dependency:** Like GPIO, UART communication is also *highly platform-specific.* The code to interact with UART ports varies depending on the hardware. You need to use platform-specific libraries and APIs.
- **Hypothetical Functions:** The example uses placeholder functions like `uart_init()`, `uart_send_string()`, `uart_receive_bytes()`, and `uart_close()`. These are not standard C++ and would need to be replaced with actual functions from a platform-specific UART library.
- **UART Configuration:** UART communication requires configuring parameters like baud rate, data bits, stop bits, and parity. These settings must be matched between communicating devices.
- **Device Path/Port Identification:** You need to identify the correct device path or port name for the UART interface on your system (e.g., `/dev/ttyS0` on Linux, `COM1` on Windows).
- **Error Handling:** Serial communication can be prone to errors (e.g., framing errors, parity errors, overrun errors). Robust UART code needs to handle these errors appropriately.
- **Buffering and Flow Control:** For reliable communication, buffering and flow control mechanisms might be needed to manage data transmission and reception rates.

To make this example runnable, you would need to:

1. **Choose a specific hardware platform** with a UART interface (e.g., a microcontroller development board or a computer with a serial port).

2. **Identify the UART library for that platform:** (e.g., libraries for serial port access on Linux, Windows, or microcontroller-specific UART libraries).
3. **Replace the hypothetical functions** with actual functions from the chosen platform's UART library.
4. **Connect two devices via UART:** (e.g., connect your microcontroller board to your computer's serial port using a UART-to-USB adapter if needed).
5. **Compile and run the code** on the device intended to send or receive UART data. You might need a separate program or terminal emulator on the receiving end to observe the UART communication.

Real-world scenario: UART communication is ubiquitous in embedded systems and systems programming. It is used for:

1. **Debugging and logging:** Sending debug messages from embedded systems to a host computer for monitoring and debugging.
2. **Sensor communication**: Interfacing with various sensors that use serial communication protocols (e.g., GPS receivers, environmental sensors).
3. **Inter-device communication:** Communication between microcontrollers, processors, and other embedded devices.
4. **Console interfaces:** Providing a serial console interface for embedded systems for configuration and control.
5. **Industrial communication:** Many industrial protocols (e.g., Modbus RTU) are based on serial communication standards like UART.

11.3 Embedded C++ Best Practices: Navigating Resource Constraints

Embedded systems often operate under strict resource constraints, including limited memory, processing power, and energy. Embedded C++ development requires adhering to best practices that optimize resource usage, ensure reliability, and maintain code efficiency. As Koopman emphasizes in "Embedded Systems Design with Platform FPGAs," resource-aware programming is a critical skill in embedded systems engineering (Koopman, 2012).

11.3.1 Minimize Dynamic Memory Allocation: Favor Static Allocation

Dynamic memory allocation (using `new` and `delete` or `malloc` and `free`) can be problematic in embedded systems due to:

- **Fragmentation:** Repeated allocation and deallocation can lead to memory fragmentation, reducing the availability of contiguous memory blocks.
- **Non-determinism:** Dynamic allocation times can be unpredictable, which is undesirable in real-time systems.
- **Overhead:** Dynamic allocation and deallocation operations have runtime overhead.
- **Memory leaks:** Memory leaks due to improper deallocation are a common source of bugs.

Best Practice:

- **Favor static allocation:** Whenever possible, use static or stack-based allocation for variables and data structures. Declare variables with fixed sizes at compile time.
- **Use fixed-size buffers:** Instead of dynamically allocating buffers, use fixed-size arrays or buffers allocated statically or on the stack.
- **Memory pools or custom allocators:** If dynamic allocation is unavoidable, consider using memory pools or custom allocators to manage memory more efficiently and predictably. Memory pools pre-allocate a large block of memory and then allocate and deallocate from within this pool, reducing fragmentation and overhead.

Example: Static Allocation vs. Dynamic Allocation
Dynamic Allocation (Avoid in critical embedded code):

```
C++
void processDataDynamically(int size) {
  int *data = new int[size]; // Dynamic allocation

  if (data != nullptr) {
    // ... use data ...
    delete[] data; // Deallocate
  }
}
```

Static Allocation (Preferred in embedded systems when size is known):

```
C++
void processDataStatically() {
  int data[100]; // Static allocation (fixed size)

  // ... use data (up to 100 elements) ...
}
```

Real-world scenario: In safety-critical embedded systems like automotive control units or medical devices, dynamic memory allocation is often strictly avoided in critical code paths to ensure deterministic behavior and prevent memory-related failures. Static allocation is preferred for predictable memory usage and to simplify memory management.

11.3.2 Exception Handling: Use Judiciously or Avoid

Exception handling in C++ (`try`, `catch`, `throw`) can introduce overhead in terms of code size and runtime performance. In resource-constrained embedded systems, exception handling might be disabled or used very sparingly.

Considerations for Exception Handling in Embedded Systems:

- **Code size:** Exception handling mechanisms can increase the code size, which is a concern in memory-limited embedded systems.
- **Performance overhead:** Throwing and catching exceptions can have runtime performance overhead, which might be unacceptable in real-time applications.
- **Non-deterministic behavior:** Exception handling paths can be less predictable than regular code paths, potentially affecting real-time determinism.
- **Alternative error handling:** In embedded systems, alternative error handling mechanisms like return codes, status flags, and assertions are often preferred over exceptions.

Best Practice:

- **Minimize or avoid exceptions:** In critical embedded code, consider avoiding exception handling altogether or using it very judiciously only for truly exceptional error conditions that are unrecoverable.

- **Use return codes and status flags:** For recoverable errors or normal error conditions, use return codes or status flags to indicate the outcome of operations.
- **Assertions for development:** Use assertions (assert()) during development to detect programming errors early, but disable assertions in release builds for performance.

Example: Error Handling with Return Codes vs. Exceptions Exception Handling (Potentially Avoid in Critical Embedded Code):

```
C++
int divide(int a, int b) {
   if (b == 0) {
      throw std::runtime_error("Division by zero"); // Throw exception
   }
   return a / b;
}

void process() {
   try {
      int result = divide(10, 0);
      // ... use result ...
   } catch (const std::runtime_error& e) {
      std::cerr << "Error: " << e.what() << std::endl; // Catch exception
   }
}
```

Return Codes (Often Preferred in Embedded Systems):

```
C++
enum class ErrorCode {
   SUCCESS,
   DIVISION_BY_ZERO,
   // ... other error codes
};

ErrorCode divide(int a, int b, int& result) {
   if (b == 0) {
      return ErrorCode::DIVISION_BY_ZERO; // Return error code
   }
   result = a / b;
   return ErrorCode::SUCCESS; // Return success code
}
```

```
void process() {
    int resultValue;
    ErrorCode error = divide(10, 0, resultValue);
    if (error != ErrorCode::SUCCESS) {
        std::cerr << "Error: Division failed with code: " <<
static_cast<int>(error) << std::endl; // Check error code
    } else {
        // ... use resultValue ...
    }
}
```

Real-world scenario: In hard real-time embedded systems, like flight control systems or engine management systems, exception handling is often completely disabled due to its potential for non-deterministic behavior and runtime overhead. Error handling relies heavily on return codes, status flags, and robust error detection and recovery mechanisms.

11.3.3 RTTI (Runtime Type Information) and Templates: Minimize Usage

RTTI (Runtime Type Information) and excessive use of templates can increase code size and runtime overhead, which can be problematic in embedded systems.

Considerations for RTTI and Templates:

- **RTTI overhead:** RTTI (enabled with `-frtti` compiler flag) adds metadata to objects to support runtime type identification (e.g., using `dynamic_cast` and `typeid`). This increases code size and can have a small runtime performance impact.
- **Template code bloat:** Templates, while powerful for generic programming, can lead to code bloat if used excessively. Each instantiation of a template generates new code, potentially increasing the executable size.

Best Practice:

- **Disable RTTI if not needed:** If runtime type identification is not essential for your embedded application, disable RTTI using compiler flags (e.g., `-fno-rtti` in GCC/Clang) to reduce code size and potentially improve performance.
- **Use templates judiciously:** Use templates where they provide significant benefits for code reusability and type safety. Be mindful of potential code bloat when using templates

extensively. Consider alternatives like compile-time polymorphism (using CRTP - Curiously Recurring Template Pattern) or type erasure techniques if code size is a critical concern.
- **Static polymorphism:** Favor static polymorphism (templates, CRTP) over dynamic polymorphism (virtual functions, RTTI) when possible in performance-critical embedded code. Static polymorphism can often lead to better performance as it resolves function calls at compile time, avoiding virtual function call overhead.

Real-world scenario: In deeply embedded systems with very limited memory, developers often carefully consider the use of RTTI and templates. For example, in bootloaders or very basic firmware, RTTI might be disabled, and templates used sparingly to minimize code footprint and maximize performance. In more complex embedded applications with more resources, a more balanced approach might be taken, using templates where appropriate but still being mindful of code size and performance implications.

11.3.4 Coding Standards and Code Reviews: Ensure Reliability and Maintainability

Adhering to coding standards and conducting regular code reviews are crucial for developing reliable and maintainable embedded C++ code. Coding standards promote consistency, readability, and reduce the likelihood of errors. Code reviews help to catch bugs early, improve code quality, and share knowledge within the development team.

Best Practices:
- **Establish and follow coding standards:** Define and enforce coding standards for your project. Standards should cover aspects like naming conventions, code formatting, commenting, code complexity, and error handling. Consider adopting established coding standards like MISRA C++ or AUTOSAR C++ for safety-critical embedded systems.
- **Conduct regular code reviews:** Implement a code review process where code changes are reviewed by other developers before being integrated into the main codebase. Code reviews

help identify potential bugs, improve code quality, and ensure adherence to coding standards.

- **Static analysis tools:** Use static analysis tools to automatically check code for potential errors, coding standard violations, and security vulnerabilities. Static analysis tools can help catch issues early in the development cycle.
- **Unit testing:** Implement unit tests to verify the functionality of individual code components. Unit tests are essential for ensuring code correctness and for regression testing when code changes are made.

Real-world scenario: In regulated industries like automotive, aerospace, and medical devices, adherence to coding standards and rigorous code review processes are often mandatory for safety and compliance reasons. Standards like MISRA C++ are specifically designed for safety-critical C++ development and are widely used in these industries. Code reviews and static analysis are integral parts of the software development lifecycle to minimize defects and ensure the reliability of embedded systems.

11.4 Writing Performant C++ Code: Optimizing for Speed and Efficiency

Performance is often a primary concern in systems and embedded programming. Writing performant C++ code in this context involves careful consideration of memory usage, algorithm choices, and compiler optimizations. As Butenhof highlights in "Programming in C++," writing efficient C++ code is not just about language features but also about understanding the underlying hardware and compiler behavior (Butenhof, 2004).

11.4.1 Algorithm and Data Structure Selection: Choosing Wisely for Performance

The choice of algorithms and data structures significantly impacts the performance of C++ code, especially in resource-constrained embedded systems. Selecting algorithms and data structures that are efficient in terms of both time and memory complexity is crucial for achieving optimal performance.

Best Practices:

- **Analyze algorithm complexity:** Carefully analyze the time and space complexity of algorithms. Choose algorithms that are appropriate for the expected input sizes and performance requirements. For example, for searching in a sorted array, binary search (O(log n)) is much more efficient than linear search (O(n)) for large datasets.
- **Select appropriate data structures:** Choose data structures that are well-suited for the operations you need to perform. For example, if you need frequent insertions and deletions in the middle of a sequence, a std::list or std::deque might be more efficient than a std::vector, despite the latter's contiguous memory layout often being beneficial for cache locality in other scenarios. Consider the trade-offs between different data structures in terms of memory usage, insertion/deletion speed, search speed, and iteration speed.
- **Avoid unnecessary copying:** Minimize unnecessary copying of objects, especially large objects. Use references or pointers when possible to avoid copying. Consider move semantics (introduced in C++11) to efficiently transfer resources when copying is conceptually necessary but can be optimized.
- **Use standard library algorithms and data structures:** Leverage the highly optimized algorithms and data structures provided by the C++ Standard Library (std::vector, std::array, std::map, std::algorithm, etc.). These are generally well-implemented and often more efficient than custom implementations, especially for common tasks.

Example: Algorithm Choice - Linear Search vs. Binary Search
Linear Search (O(n) - Less efficient for large sorted data):

```
C++
#include <vector>

int linearSearch(const std::vector<int>& arr, int target) {
  for (size_t i = 0; i < arr.size(); ++i) {
    if (arr[i] == target) {
      return i; // Found at index i
    }
  }
  return -1; // Not found
}
```

Binary Search (O(log n) - More efficient for large sorted data):

```
C++
#include <vector>
#include <algorithm> // For std::binary_search (and std::lower_bound,
std::upper_bound, etc.)

int binarySearch(const std::vector<int>& arr, int target) {
  auto it = std::lower_bound(arr.begin(), arr.end(), target); // Find first
element not less than target
  if (it != arr.end() && *it == target) {
    return std::distance(arr.begin(), it); // Found at index (distance from
beginning)
  }
  return -1; // Not found
}
```

Real-world scenario: In embedded systems, algorithm and data structure choices are often critical for meeting real-time deadlines and minimizing resource consumption. For instance, in control systems, efficient control algorithms are essential for fast response times. In data processing applications within embedded systems (e.g., sensor data processing), choosing appropriate algorithms and data structures ensures timely and efficient data handling within limited memory and processing power.

11.4.2 Compiler Optimizations: Letting the Compiler Work for You

Modern C++ compilers are highly sophisticated and can perform a wide range of optimizations to improve code performance. Enabling compiler optimizations is a fundamental step in writing performant C++ code, especially for release builds.

Best Practices:

- **Enable compiler optimizations:** Use compiler flags to enable optimizations. Common optimization flags include `-O2`, `-O3`, or `-Ofast` (for GCC/Clang) and `/O2` (for MSVC). `-O3` typically provides the highest level of optimization, but `-O2` is often a good balance between performance and compile time. `-Ofast` can enable aggressive optimizations that may violate strict standards compliance but can sometimes provide further performance gains (use with caution).

- **Profile to guide optimization:** Compiler optimizations are effective, but profiling is essential to identify specific performance bottlenecks in your code. Focus your manual optimization efforts on the parts of the code that profiling reveals as performance-critical, rather than blindly optimizing everything.
- **Link-time optimization (LTO):** Enable link-time optimization (LTO) if supported by your compiler and build system. LTO allows the compiler to perform optimizations across the entire program at link time, potentially leading to further performance improvements compared to compiling each source file separately.
- **Profile-guided optimization (PGO):** For maximum performance, consider using profile-guided optimization (PGO). PGO involves compiling the code, running a representative workload to collect profiling data, and then recompiling the code using the profiling data to guide optimizations. PGO can significantly improve performance by optimizing code paths that are frequently executed in real-world usage scenarios.
-

Example: Compiler Optimization Levels (CMake Configuration) Modified CMakeLists.txt **(setting optimization level based on build type):**

```
CMake
cmake_minimum_required(VERSION 3.10)
project(compiler_optimization_example)

set(CMAKE_CXX_STANDARD 17)
set(CMAKE_CXX_STANDARD_REQUIRED TRUE)

if(CMAKE_BUILD_TYPE STREQUAL "Release") # Set optimization level
for Release build
   set(CMAKE_CXX_FLAGS_RELEASE "-O3") # Use -O3 for Release
elseif(CMAKE_BUILD_TYPE STREQUAL "Debug") # Set optimization
level for Debug build
   set(CMAKE_CXX_FLAGS_DEBUG "-O0 -g") # -O0 (no optimization), -g
(debug symbols) for Debug
endif()
```

```
add_executable(optimization_program main.cpp)
```

Step-by-step explanation:

1. **if(CMAKE_BUILD_TYPE STREQUAL "Release") ... elseif(CMAKE_BUILD_TYPE STREQUAL "Debug") ... endif():** Conditional block to set compiler flags based on the CMake build type (CMAKE_BUILD_TYPE).
2. **set(CMAKE_CXX_FLAGS_RELEASE "-O3"):** If the build type is "Release", sets the CMAKE_CXX_FLAGS_RELEASE variable to -O3. This variable will be used by CMake to set compiler flags for Release builds. -O3 enables high-level optimizations in GCC/Clang.
3. **set(CMAKE_CXX_FLAGS_DEBUG "-O0 -g"):** If the build type is "Debug", sets CMAKE_CXX_FLAGS_DEBUG to -O0 -g. -O0 disables optimizations, and -g enables debugging symbols, which are appropriate for Debug builds.

Build in Release mode:

```
Bash
mkdir build_release_optimized
cd build_release_optimized
cmake -DCMAKE_BUILD_TYPE=Release ..
make
```

Build in Debug mode:

```
Bash
mkdir build_debug_no_opt
cd build_debug_no_opt
cmake -DCMAKE_BUILD_TYPE=Debug ..
make
```

The executables built in build_release_optimized/ will be compiled with -O3 optimizations, while those in build_debug_no_opt/ will be compiled with no optimizations (-O0) and debugging symbols.

Real-world scenario: Compiler optimizations are a cornerstone of achieving performance in both systems and embedded programming. In high-performance computing and systems software, compiler optimizations are extensively used to maximize throughput and minimize latency. In embedded systems, compiler optimizations are crucial for reducing code size, improving execution speed, and minimizing power consumption, all of which are often critical constraints.

11.4.3 Inline Functions: Reducing Function Call Overhead

Inline functions are a compiler hint to replace function calls with the actual function body at the call site. Inlining can eliminate function call overhead (function call setup, parameter passing, return), potentially improving performance, especially for small, frequently called functions.

Best Practices:

- **Use inline keyword for small, frequently called functions:** Mark small functions that are called frequently as inline. The compiler may choose to inline these functions, reducing function call overhead.
- **Compiler discretion:** The inline keyword is a hint, not a directive. The compiler ultimately decides whether to inline a function based on factors like function size, complexity, and optimization level. Very large or complex functions might not be inlined even if marked inline.
- **Header file placement:** For inlining to be effective, the function definition (not just declaration) should be visible at the call site. Therefore, inline function definitions are typically placed in header files.
- **Template functions are implicitly inline:** Template functions are implicitly inline because the compiler needs to generate code for each template instantiation at the call site.

Example: Inline Function

```cpp
C++
// hello.h (header file - inline function definition)
#ifndef HELLO_H
#define HELLO_H

inline void inlineSayHello(const char* name) { // Inline function definition in
header
    std::cout << "Hello (inline), " << name << "!" << std::endl;
}

#endif // HELLO_H
```

```
C++
// main.cpp
#include "hello.h"

int main() {
  inlineSayHello("Inline User"); // Call to inline function
  return 0;
}
```

Step-by-step explanation:

1. **inline void inlineSayHello(const char* name) { ... }**: The inline keyword is placed before the function definition of inlineSayHello. This suggests to the compiler that it should consider inlining calls to this function.
2. **Function Definition in Header:** The definition of inlineSayHello is placed directly in the header file hello.h. This is essential for inlining to work effectively because the compiler needs to see the function body at the point where the function is called.
3. **inlineSayHello("Inline User");**: The main function calls inlineSayHello. If the compiler chooses to inline this call, the code for inlineSayHello will be directly inserted at this point in main, avoiding a function call.

Real-world scenario: Inline functions are commonly used in performance-critical code, especially in embedded systems and systems programming. For example, in device drivers or real-time control systems, small, frequently used functions that perform basic operations (e.g., accessing hardware registers, performing simple calculations) are often made inline to minimize function call overhead and improve performance.

11.4.4 Loop Optimization: Enhancing Iteration Performance

Loops are fundamental control structures in programming, and optimizing loops is often crucial for improving performance, especially in computationally intensive tasks. Loop optimization techniques aim to reduce the overhead of loop iterations and improve data access patterns within loops.

Best Practices:

- **Minimize loop overhead:** Reduce the amount of work done within the loop that is not directly related to the loop's core computation. For example, move loop-invariant calculations outside the loop.
- **Loop unrolling:** For small, fixed-size loops, consider loop unrolling. Loop unrolling reduces loop control overhead by replicating the loop body multiple times, reducing the number of loop iterations. Compilers can often perform loop unrolling automatically at higher optimization levels.
- **Cache-friendly data access:** Arrange data access patterns within loops to improve cache locality. Access data in a sequential manner to maximize cache hits and minimize cache misses. For example, when iterating through a 2D array, iterate in row-major order (if the array is stored in row-major order in memory) to access contiguous memory locations.
- **Vectorization (SIMD):** Leverage compiler vectorization capabilities (Single Instruction, Multiple Data) to perform operations on multiple data elements simultaneously within a loop. Compilers can often automatically vectorize loops at higher optimization levels if the loop structure and data access patterns are suitable.
- **Avoid function calls within inner loops (if possible):** Function calls within inner loops can add overhead. If possible, move function calls outside the inner loop or consider inlining the function if it's small and frequently called within the loop.

Example: Loop Unrolling (Manual Unrolling for Illustration)
Original Loop (Potentially less efficient):

```
C++
void processArrayLoop(int* arr, int size) {
  for (int i = 0; i < size; ++i) {
    arr[i] *= 2; // Simple operation in loop
  }
}
```

Loop Unrolled (Manually unrolled - for illustration, compilers often do this automatically):

```
C++

void processArrayUnrolled(int* arr, int size) {
```

```
    for (int i = 0; i < size; i += 4) { // Increment by 4, process 4 elements per
iteration
        arr[i] *= 2;
        if (i + 1 < size) arr[i + 1] *= 2; // Check bounds to avoid out-of-bounds
access
        if (i + 2 < size) arr[i + 2] *= 2;
        if (i + 3 < size) arr[i + 3] *= 2;
    }
}
```

Explanation:

- **Original Loop:** The `processArrayLoop` function has a standard `for` loop that iterates through each element of the array and multiplies it by 2.
- **Loop Unrolled (Manually):** The `processArrayUnrolled` function manually unrolls the loop by processing 4 elements in each iteration. This reduces the loop control overhead (incrementing `i`, comparing `i` with `size`) by a factor of 4. The code includes bounds checks (`if (i + 1 < size)`, etc.) to handle cases where the array size is not a multiple of 4 and to prevent out-of-bounds access.

Note: Manual loop unrolling is often less necessary with modern optimizing compilers. Compilers can automatically unroll loops at higher optimization levels when it is beneficial. The example is mainly for illustration of the concept. In practice, relying on compiler optimizations and focusing on cache-friendly data access and vectorization is often more effective than manual loop unrolling.

Real-world scenario: Loop optimization is critical in many systems and embedded applications. For example, in signal processing algorithms, image processing, and numerical computations, loops are often the performance-critical sections of code. Optimizing loops can significantly improve the overall performance of these applications, enabling faster processing, lower latency, and reduced power consumption. In embedded systems, efficient loops are essential for tasks like real-time data acquisition, control algorithms, and communication protocol processing.

11.4.5 Data Alignment and Packing: Memory Access and Footprint Efficiency

Data alignment and packing are techniques that can impact both memory access performance and memory footprint in C++ programs, particularly in systems and embedded programming.

Data Alignment:

- **Memory access efficiency:** Modern processors access memory most efficiently when data is aligned to natural boundaries (e.g., 4-byte integers aligned at 4-byte boundaries, 8-byte doubles aligned at 8-byte boundaries). Misaligned memory accesses can be significantly slower, especially on some architectures, as they might require multiple memory accesses instead of a single aligned access.
- **Compiler alignment:** Compilers typically align data structures by default to ensure efficient memory access. For example, a `struct` might be padded with extra bytes to ensure that members are properly aligned.
- **`alignas` specifier (C++11):** C++11 introduced the `alignas` specifier to control the alignment of variables and data structures explicitly.

Data Packing:

- **Memory footprint reduction:** Data packing aims to reduce the memory footprint of data structures by eliminating padding bytes inserted for alignment. This is particularly important in memory-constrained embedded systems.
- **`#pragma pack` (compiler-specific):** Compilers often provide `#pragma pack` directives (or similar mechanisms) to control struct packing and disable padding.
- **Trade-off: performance vs. size:** Data packing can reduce memory footprint but might also lead to misaligned memory accesses, potentially degrading performance on some architectures. The trade-off between memory size and access performance needs to be considered.

Example: Data Alignment and Packing
Default Alignment (Compiler-aligned struct):

C++

```
#include <iostream>

struct AlignedStruct {
   char c; // 1 byte
   int i;  // 4 bytes
}; // Compiler might add padding after 'c' to align 'i' to a 4-byte boundary

int main() {
   std::cout << "Size of AlignedStruct: " << sizeof(AlignedStruct) << " bytes"
<< std::endl; // Size might be > 5 due to padding
   std::cout << "Offset of c: " << offsetof(AlignedStruct, c) << std::endl; //
Offset 0
   std::cout << "Offset of i: " << offsetof(AlignedStruct, i) << std::endl; //
Offset might be 4 (due to padding)
   return 0;
}
```

Packed Struct (#pragma pack(1) - Compiler-specific packing):

```
C++
#include <iostream>
#pragma pack(push, 1) // Push current alignment, set alignment to 1 byte
(pack)
struct PackedStruct {
   char c;
   int i;
};
#pragma pack(pop) // Restore previous alignment

int main() {
   std::cout << "Size of PackedStruct: " << sizeof(PackedStruct) << " bytes"
<< std::endl; // Size will be exactly 5 bytes (no padding)
   std::cout << "Offset of c: " << offsetof(PackedStruct, c) << std::endl; //
Offset 0
   std::cout << "Offset of i: " << offsetof(PackedStruct, i) << std::endl; //
Offset 1 (no padding)
   return 0;
}
```

Explanation:

- **AlignedStruct (Default Alignment):** The compiler typically adds padding after the `char c` member to ensure that the `int i` member is aligned to a 4-byte boundary. This can result in `sizeof(AlignedStruct)` being greater than 5 bytes (e.g., 8 bytes on a 64-bit system if the default alignment is 8 bytes).

- **PackedStruct (#pragma pack(1)):** The #pragma pack(push, 1) directive (compiler-specific) instructs the compiler to pack the PackedStruct with 1-byte alignment. This means no padding is added between members. sizeof(PackedStruct) will be exactly 5 bytes. #pragma pack(pop) restores the previous alignment setting.

Caution: #pragma pack is compiler-specific and can affect code portability. Misaligned memory accesses resulting from packing can lead to performance penalties or even crashes on some architectures. Use data packing judiciously and profile your code to evaluate the impact on performance.

Real-world scenario: Data alignment and packing are important considerations in embedded systems where memory is scarce, and efficient memory access is crucial. In communication protocols, data structures are often packed to minimize packet sizes and transmission overhead. In memory-constrained embedded systems, data packing can help reduce overall memory usage. However, in performance-critical sections, the potential performance impact of misaligned accesses should be carefully evaluated.

11.4.6 Profiling and Benchmarking: Measuring and Identifying Bottlenecks

Profiling and benchmarking are essential steps in the performance optimization process. Profiling helps identify performance bottlenecks in your code by measuring the execution time of different code sections. Benchmarking measures the overall performance of your code or specific functions under realistic workloads.

Best Practices:

- **Use profiling tools:** Utilize profiling tools (e.g., gprof, perf (Linux), VTune Amplifier (Intel), Xcode Instruments (macOS), Visual Studio Profiler (Windows)) to identify performance bottlenecks in your C++ code. Profilers can show you which functions or code sections consume the most execution time, allowing you to focus your optimization efforts effectively.
- **Benchmark performance-critical sections:** Create benchmarks to measure the performance of critical code

sections or algorithms. Benchmarks should simulate realistic workloads and measure relevant performance metrics (e.g., execution time, throughput, latency).

- **Iterative optimization and measurement:** Performance optimization is often an iterative process. After making code changes to improve performance, re-profile and re-benchmark to measure the actual performance impact and ensure that your optimizations are effective and have not introduced regressions.
- **Consider different workloads:** Benchmark your code under different workloads and input data sets to understand how performance varies under different conditions and to identify potential performance issues in specific scenarios.
- **Compare different optimization techniques:** When evaluating different optimization techniques, use benchmarks to compare their performance impact objectively and choose the most effective approach for your specific application.

Example: Simple Benchmarking in C++

```
C++
#include <iostream>
#include <chrono> // For time measurement

void functionToBenchmark() {
  // Code to benchmark (e.g., a loop, an algorithm)
  for (int i = 0; i < 1000000; ++i) {
    // Some computation
    volatile int temp = i * i; // Volatile to prevent over-optimization
  }
}

int main() {
  auto start_time = std::chrono::high_resolution_clock::now(); // Start time

  functionToBenchmark(); // Function to benchmark

  auto end_time = std::chrono::high_resolution_clock::now(); // End time
  auto duration =
std::chrono::duration_cast<std::chrono::milliseconds>(end_time - start_time);
// Calculate duration

  std::cout << "functionToBenchmark execution time: " << duration.count()
<< " milliseconds" << std::endl;
```

```
    return 0;
}
```

Explanation:

- **#include <chrono>**: Includes the <chrono> header for time measurement functionalities.
- **std::chrono::high_resolution_clock::now()**: Gets the current time point with high resolution.
- **std::chrono::duration_cast<std::chrono::milliseconds>(end_time - start_time)**: Calculates the duration between the start and end time points and converts it to milliseconds.
- **duration.count()**: Gets the duration in milliseconds as a numerical value.
- **volatile int temp = i * i;**: The volatile keyword is used to prevent the compiler from over-optimizing away the loop computation, ensuring that the benchmark measures the intended code section. In real benchmarks, you would typically benchmark actual application code.

Real-world scenario: Profiling and benchmarking are indispensable in systems and embedded programming for achieving performance targets. In high-frequency trading systems, network servers, or real-time embedded control systems, even small performance improvements can have significant impact. Profiling helps developers pinpoint the most performance-critical parts of the code, and benchmarking provides quantitative data to evaluate the effectiveness of optimization efforts and ensure that performance requirements are met.

By applying these principles and techniques for writing performant C++ code, and by adhering to embedded C++ best practices, Computer Technology students and educators can develop efficient, reliable, and resource-conscious systems and embedded software solutions. The combination of low-level control, hardware interfacing capabilities, and performance optimization techniques makes C++ a powerful and versatile language for bridging the gap between hardware and software in the demanding field of systems and embedded programming.

Chapter 12

GUI Development with C++: Crafting User Interfaces

Graphical User Interfaces (GUIs) are the primary means of interaction for most software applications, providing intuitive and visually engaging ways for users to interact with programs. While C++ is often associated with backend systems and performance-critical applications, it is also a robust language for developing sophisticated GUIs. Its performance capabilities, combined with various GUI frameworks and libraries, make it suitable for a wide range of applications, from resource-intensive desktop software to embedded systems with graphical displays. For Computer Technology students and educators, understanding GUI development in C++ is essential for creating complete, user-friendly applications. This section will explore three prominent approaches to GUI development with C++: Qt for cross-platform applications, Dear ImGui for lightweight interfaces, and WinAPI for native Windows applications, providing insights into their strengths, weaknesses, and practical applications.

12.1 Qt: A Comprehensive Cross-Platform GUI Framework

Qt is a widely acclaimed, cross-platform application development framework, renowned for its comprehensive suite of tools and libraries for creating visually appealing and functional GUIs. Qt is not merely a GUI library; it's a complete framework offering functionalities beyond GUI elements, including networking, database access, multimedia, and more. Its cross-platform nature allows developers to write code once and deploy it across various operating systems, including Windows, macOS, Linux, and mobile platforms, significantly reducing development effort and time. As Blanchette and Summerfield detail in "C++ GUI Programming with Qt 4," Qt provides an elegant and efficient approach to cross-platform GUI development (Blanchette & Summerfield, 2008).

12.1.1 Key Features of Qt for GUI Development

Qt's strength in GUI development stems from several core features:

- **Widgets:** Qt provides a rich set of pre-built GUI widgets (buttons, labels, text boxes, layouts, etc.) that are highly customizable and styleable. These widgets form the building blocks of Qt GUIs.
- **Signals and Slots:** Qt's signals and slots mechanism is a powerful and type-safe way to handle inter-object communication, particularly for GUI event handling. Signals are emitted by widgets when events occur (e.g., button clicks), and slots are functions that can be connected to these signals to respond to events.
- **Cross-Platform Abstraction:** Qt abstracts platform-specific details, allowing developers to write code that is largely platform-independent. Qt handles the complexities of rendering widgets and managing events on different operating systems.
- **Qt Creator IDE:** Qt Creator is a powerful Integrated Development Environment (IDE) specifically designed for Qt development. It provides visual GUI designers, code editors, debuggers, and build tools, streamlining the Qt development workflow.
- **QML and Qt Quick:** For modern, fluid user interfaces, Qt offers QML (Qt Meta-Object Language) and Qt Quick, a declarative framework for creating dynamic UIs with animations and transitions, often used for mobile and touch-centric applications.

12.1.2 Getting Started with Qt: A "Hello World" Example

To illustrate the basics of Qt GUI development, let's create a simple "Hello World" application using Qt widgets.

Step-by-step guide:

1. **Install Qt:** Download and install the Qt framework from the official Qt website. Choose the appropriate installer for your operating system and follow the installation instructions. Ensure you select the Qt modules you need (e.g., Qt Widgets, Qt Core, Qt GUI).
2. **Create a Qt Widgets Application Project:** Open Qt Creator. Go to "File" -> "New File or Project" -> "Qt Widgets Application" -> "Choose...".
    - In the "Project Location" dialog, choose a name for your project (e.g., HelloWorldQt) and a location to save it. Click "Next".
    - In the "Kit Selection" dialog, select the Qt kit you installed (e.g., Desktop Qt ...). Click "Next".
    - In the "Class Information" dialog, leave the default class names or modify them if you wish. Click "Next".
    - In the "Project Management" dialog, leave the defaults and click "Finish".
3. **Modify mainwindow.h:** Open mainwindow.h from the "Projects" pane. Add a QLabel widget to the private section of the MainWindow class and a QPushButton.

C++

```
#ifndef MAINWINDOW_H
#define MAINWINDOW_H

#include <QMainWindow>

QT_BEGIN_NAMESPACE
namespace Ui { class MainWindow; }
QT_END_NAMESPACE

class MainWindow : public QMainWindow
{
```

```
    Q_OBJECT

public:
    MainWindow(QWidget *parent = nullptr);
    ~MainWindow();

private:
    Ui::MainWindow *ui;
    QLabel *helloLabel; // Add QLabel
    QPushButton *helloButton; // Add QPushButton
};
#endif // MAINWINDOW_H
```

4. **Modify mainwindow.cpp:** Open mainwindow.cpp. In the MainWindow constructor, add code to create and configure the QLabel and QPushButton, and connect the button's click signal to a slot.

```
C++

#include "mainwindow.h"
#include "ui_mainwindow.h"
#include <QLabel> // Include QLabel header
#include <QPushButton> // Include QPushButton header
#include <QVBoxLayout> // Include QVBoxLayout for layout
management

MainWindow::MainWindow(QWidget *parent)
    : QMainWindow(parent)
    , ui(new Ui::MainWindow)
{
    ui->setupUi(this);

    // Create QLabel
    helloLabel = new QLabel("Hello World!", this);
    helloLabel->setAlignment(Qt::AlignCenter);

    // Create QPushButton
    helloButton = new QPushButton("Click Me", this);

    // Create layout and add widgets
    QVBoxLayout *layout = new QVBoxLayout;
    layout->addWidget(helloLabel);
    layout->addWidget(helloButton);

    // Set layout for the central widget
```

```
    QWidget *centralWidget = new QWidget(this);
    centralWidget->setLayout(layout);
    setCentralWidget(centralWidget);

    // Connect button click signal to a lambda slot
    connect(helloButton, &QPushButton::clicked, [=]() {
        helloLabel->setText("Button Clicked!");
    });
}

MainWindow::~MainWindow()
{
    delete ui;
}
```

5. **Build and Run:** In Qt Creator, press Ctrl+B (or "Build" -> "Build Project") to build the project. Then, press Ctrl+R (or "Debug" -> "Start Debugging" or "Run" -> "Run") to run the application.

Code Explanation:

- **QLabel *helloLabel = new QLabel("Hello World!", this);**: Creates a QLabel widget with the text "Hello World!" and sets the MainWindow as its parent.
- **helloLabel->setAlignment(Qt::AlignCenter);**: Centers the text within the label.
- **QPushButton *helloButton = new QPushButton("Click Me", this);**: Creates a QPushButton widget with the text "Click Me".
- **QVBoxLayout *layout = new QVBoxLayout;**: Creates a vertical layout (QVBoxLayout) to arrange widgets vertically.
- **layout->addWidget(helloLabel); layout->addWidget(helloButton);**: Adds the helloLabel and helloButton to the vertical layout.
- **QWidget *centralWidget = new QWidget(this); centralWidget->setLayout(layout); setCentralWidget(centralWidget);**: Creates a central widget for the QMainWindow, sets the layout for the central widget, and sets the central widget for the main window.
- **connect(helloButton, &QPushButton::clicked, [=]() { ... });**: Connects the clicked() signal of the helloButton to a lambda function (slot). When the button is clicked, the lambda function is executed, which changes the text of helloLabel to "Button Clicked!".

Real-world scenario: Qt is used extensively in developing cross-platform desktop applications, including KDE Plasma desktop environment, VLC media player, Autodesk Maya, and many industrial control systems. Its robust feature set and cross-platform capabilities make it a popular choice for complex GUI applications that need to run on multiple operating systems.

12.2 Dear ImGui: Lightweight GUI for Tools and Immediacy

Dear ImGui (Immediate Mode GUI) is a library focused on providing a lightweight and portable GUI for C++ applications. Unlike traditional retained-mode GUI frameworks like Qt, Dear ImGui uses an immediate mode rendering approach. This means that GUI elements are drawn every frame based on the current application state, rather than being retained as persistent objects. Dear ImGui is particularly well-suited for creating tools, debugging interfaces, game development utilities, and embedded system UIs where simplicity, ease of integration, and minimal overhead are prioritized. As Johnston explains in the Dear ImGui documentation, its immediate mode paradigm offers a different approach to GUI development, emphasizing simplicity and directness (Johnston, 2024).

12.2.1 Key Features of Dear ImGui for Lightweight GUIs

Dear ImGui distinguishes itself with the following features:

- **Immediate Mode Paradigm:** GUI elements are drawn every frame, simplifying the GUI logic and making it easier to integrate into existing rendering loops. GUI state is primarily managed by the application, not the GUI library itself.
- **Lightweight and Minimal Dependencies:** Dear ImGui is designed to be lightweight, with minimal dependencies. It primarily focuses on rendering GUI elements and relies on the application to handle rendering backend integration (e.g., with OpenGL, DirectX, Vulkan, or even software renderers).
- **Ease of Integration:** Dear ImGui is designed for easy integration into existing C++ projects, especially those already using rendering libraries for graphics. It's often used in game engines, tools, and embedded systems.
- **Focus on Tooling and Debugging UIs:** Dear ImGui excels at creating utility-style interfaces, debugging tools, in-game UI

elements, and quick prototyping. It's less focused on creating complex, polished application UIs compared to frameworks like Qt.

- **Portable and Cross-Platform:** Dear ImGui is highly portable and can be used on various platforms, as long as a rendering backend is provided.

12.2.2 Getting Started with Dear ImGui: A Minimal Example with SDL2

To demonstrate Dear ImGui, we'll create a minimal example using SDL2 for window creation and input handling, and OpenGL for rendering.

Step-by-step guide:

1. **Install SDL2 and OpenGL:** Ensure you have SDL2 and OpenGL libraries installed on your system. Installation methods vary depending on your operating system. For example, on Ubuntu: `sudo apt-get install libsdl2-dev libgl1-mesa-dev`. On macOS using Homebrew: `brew install sdl2 glew`. On Windows, you might need to download SDL2 development libraries and configure your compiler to link against them.
2. **Download Dear ImGui:** Download the Dear ImGui library from the official Dear ImGui GitHub repository. You can download a ZIP archive or clone the repository.
3. **Create a Project Directory:** Create a directory for your project (e.g., `DearImGuiSDL2Example`).
4. **Copy ImGui Files:** Copy the Dear ImGui source files (`imgui.h`, `imgui.cpp`, `imgui_demo.cpp`, `imgui_draw.cpp`, `imgui_tables.cpp`, `imgui_widgets.cpp`, `imconfig.h`, `backends/imgui_impl_sdl2.cpp`, `backends/imgui_impl_opengl3.cpp`) from the Dear ImGui repository into your project directory. You can create subdirectories like `imgui/` and `imgui/backends/` to organize them.
5. **Create `main.cpp`:** Create a `main.cpp` file in your project directory with the following code:

C++

```cpp
#include <SDL.h>
#include <stdio.h>
#include "imgui.h"
#include "imgui_impl_sdl2.h"
#include "imgui_impl_opengl3.h"
```

```
int main(int argc, char* argv[])
{
   if (SDL_Init(SDL_INIT_VIDEO) != 0)
   {
      fprintf(stderr, "SDL_Init Error: %s\n", SDL_GetError());
      return 1;
   }

   SDL_GL_SetAttribute(SDL_GL_CONTEXT_FLAGS,
SDL_GL_CONTEXT_FORWARD_COMPATIBLE_FLAG);
   SDL_GL_SetAttribute(SDL_GL_CONTEXT_PROFILE_MASK,
SDL_GL_CONTEXT_PROFILE_CORE);

SDL_GL_SetAttribute(SDL_GL_CONTEXT_MAJOR_VERSION,
3);

SDL_GL_SetAttribute(SDL_GL_CONTEXT_MINOR_VERSION,
3);

   SDL_Window* window = SDL_CreateWindow(
      "Dear ImGui SDL2+OpenGL3 example",
      SDL_WINDOWPOS_CENTERED,
SDL_WINDOWPOS_CENTERED,
      1280, 720,
      SDL_WINDOW_OPENGL | SDL_WINDOW_RESIZABLE);
   if (window == nullptr)
   {
      fprintf(stderr, "SDL_CreateWindow Error: %s\n",
SDL_GetError());
      SDL_Quit();
      return 1;
   }

   SDL_GLContext gl_context = SDL_GL_CreateContext(window);
   if (gl_context == nullptr)
   {
      fprintf(stderr, "SDL_GL_CreateContext Error: %s\n",
SDL_GetError());
      SDL_DestroyWindow(window);
      SDL_Quit();
      return 1;
   }
   SDL_GL_MakeCurrent(window, gl_context);
   SDL_GL_SetSwapInterval(1); // Enable vsync
```

```
    IMGUI_CHECKVERSION();
    ImGui::CreateContext();
    ImGuiIO& io = ImGui::GetIO(); (void)io;
    ImGui::StyleColorsDark();

    ImGui_ImplSDL2_InitForOpenGL(window, gl_context);
    ImGui_ImplOpenGL3_Init("#version 130");

    bool done = false;
    while (!done)
    {
        SDL_Event event;
        while (SDL_PollEvent(&event))
        {
            ImGui_ImplSDL2_ProcessEvent(&event);
            if (event.type == SDL_QUIT)
                done = true;
            if (event.type == SDL_WINDOWEVENT &&
event.window.event == SDL_WINDOWEVENT_CLOSE &&
event.window.windowID == SDL_GetWindowID(window))
                done = true;
        }

        ImGui_ImplOpenGL3_NewFrame();
        ImGui_ImplSDL2_NewFrame();
        ImGui::NewFrame();

        ImGui::Begin("Hello, Dear ImGui!");   // Create a window called
"Hello, Dear ImGui!"
        ImGui::Text("This is some text.");             // Display some text
        ImGui::Button("Button");                       // Display a button
        ImGui::End();

        glClearColor(0.45f, 0.55f, 0.60f, 1.00f);
        glClear(GL_COLOR_BUFFER_BIT);
        ImGui::Render();

ImGui_ImplOpenGL3_RenderDrawData(ImGui::GetDrawData());
        SDL_GL_SwapWindow(window);
    }

    ImGui_ImplOpenGL3_Shutdown();
    ImGui_ImplSDL2_Shutdown();
    ImGui::DestroyContext();

    SDL_GL_DeleteContext(gl_context);
```

```
    SDL_DestroyWindow(window);
    SDL_Quit();

    return 0;
}
```

6. **Compile and Link:** Compile main.cpp, imgui.cpp, imgui_draw.cpp, imgui_tables.cpp, imgui_widgets.cpp, backends/imgui_impl_sdl2.cpp, and backends/imgui_impl_opengl3.cpp. Link with SDL2 and OpenGL libraries. The compilation and linking commands will vary depending on your operating system and compiler.
   Example compilation command (GCC on Linux):
   Bash

   ```
   g++ main.cpp imgui*.cpp imgui/backends/imgui_impl_sdl2.cpp
   imgui/backends/imgui_impl_opengl3.cpp -o dear_imgui_example -
   lSDL2 -lGL -std=c++17
   ```
7. **Run:** Execute the compiled executable (./dear_imgui_example on Linux).

Code Explanation:

- **SDL2 Initialization:** The code initializes SDL2 for window creation, OpenGL context setup, and event handling.
- **Dear ImGui Initialization:** IMGUI_CHECKVERSION(), ImGui::CreateContext(), ImGui_ImplSDL2_InitForOpenGL(), and ImGui_ImplOpenGL3_Init() initialize Dear ImGui and its SDL2 and OpenGL3 backends.
- **ImGui::NewFrame(), ImGui::Render():** ImGui::NewFrame() starts a new Dear ImGui frame. ImGui::Render() generates the draw commands for the current frame.
- **ImGui::Begin("Hello, Dear ImGui!"); ... ImGui::End();:** Defines a Dear ImGui window named "Hello, Dear ImGui!". Inside this block, Dear ImGui widgets are created.
  - ImGui::Text("This is some text.");: Displays text.
  - ImGui::Button("Button");: Displays a button.
- **Rendering:** glClearColor(), glClear(), ImGui_ImplOpenGL3_RenderDrawData(), and SDL_GL_SwapWindow() handle OpenGL rendering and window swapping to display the Dear ImGui UI.
- **Event Handling:** The SDL event loop processes events, and ImGui_ImplSDL2_ProcessEvent(&event) passes SDL events to Dear ImGui for input handling.
- **Shutdown:** ImGui_ImplOpenGL3_Shutdown(), ImGui_ImplSDL2_Shutdown(), ImGui::DestroyContext(),

SDL_GL_DeleteContext(), SDL_DestroyWindow(), and SDL_Quit() clean up resources.

Real-world scenario: Dear ImGui is widely used in game development for creating in-game debugging tools, level editors, and custom game engine UIs. It's also used in tools for graphics programming, simulations, and embedded systems where a lightweight, easily integratable GUI is needed. Examples include game engines like Blender, game development tools, and[8] hardware debugging interfaces.

12.3 WinAPI: Native Windows GUI Development

WinAPI (Windows API), also known as[9] the Windows SDK, is the native C API provided by Microsoft for developing applications on Windows. It offers direct access to the Windows operating system's functionalities, including window management, graphics, input, and system services. While WinAPI is powerful and allows for fine-grained control over Windows features, it is[10] also known for its complexity and steeper learning curve compared to higher-level frameworks like Qt. As Petzold comprehensively explains in "Programming Windows,"[11] WinAPI provides the foundational tools for building Windows applications (Petzold, 1998).

12.3.1 Key Features of WinAPI for Windows GUIs

WinAPI[12] offers a range of features for Windows GUI development:

- **Native Windows Functionality:** WinAPI provides direct access to all Windows OS features, allowing developers to create applications that are deeply integrated with the Windows platform.
- **Fine-Grained Control:** WinAPI offers a high degree of control over window creation, message handling, graphics rendering, and other GUI aspects.
- **Performance:** Applications developed[13] using WinAPI can achieve excellent performance as they directly interact with the operating system without layers of abstraction.
- **Wide Range of Controls:** WinAPI provides a set of common controls (buttons, edit boxes, list boxes, etc.) and allows for creating custom[14] window classes and controls.[15]

- **Long History and Legacy:** WinAPI has a long history and a vast amount of existing code and documentation. It is the foundation upon which many Windows applications and frameworks are built.

12.3.2 Getting Started with WinAPI: A Simple Window Example

Let's create a basic WinAPI application that displays a window with "Hello, WinAPI!" text.

Step-by-step guide:

1. **Set up a Windows Development Environment:** Ensure you have a Windows development environment set up, including a C++ compiler (like Visual Studio or MinGW-w64) and the Windows SDK. Visual Studio typically includes the Windows SDK.
2. **Create a New Project (Visual Studio):** Open Visual Studio. Go to "File" -> "New" -> "Project..." -> "Empty Project" (or "Windows Desktop Application" if you prefer a template with pre-configured settings). Choose a project name (e.g., HelloWorldWinAPI) and location. Click "Create".
3. **Add a Source File:** In Solution Explorer, right-click on "Source Files" -> "Add" -> "New Item..." -> "C++ File (.cpp)". Name the file main.cpp and click "Add".
4. **Paste the WinAPI Code:** Copy and paste the following WinAPI code into main.cpp:

   C++

```cpp
#include <windows.h>

LRESULT CALLBACK WindowProc(HWND hwnd, UINT uMsg,
WPARAM wParam, LPARAM lParam);

int WINAPI WinMain(HINSTANCE hInstance, HINSTANCE
hPrevInstance, LPSTR pCmdLine, int nCmdShow)
{
    const char CLASS_NAME[]  = "SampleWindowClass";

    WNDCLASS wc = { };

    wc.lpfnWndProc   = WindowProc;
    wc.hInstance     = hInstance;
    wc.lpszClassName = CLASS_NAME;
```

```
    wc.hbrBackground = (HBRUSH)(COLOR_WINDOW+1); // Set
background color

    RegisterClass(&wc);

    HWND hwnd = CreateWindowEx(
        0,                          // Optional window styles.
        CLASS_NAME,                     // Window class
        "Hello WinAPI!",              // Window text
        WS_OVERLAPPEDWINDOW | WS_VISIBLE,  // Window
style

        // Size and position
        CW_USEDEFAULT, CW_USEDEFAULT,
CW_USEDEFAULT, CW_USEDEFAULT,

        nullptr,       // Parent window
        nullptr,       // Menu
        hInstance,     // Instance handle
        nullptr        // Pointer to window-creation data
        );

    if (hwnd == nullptr)
    {
        return 0;
    }

    ShowWindow(hwnd, nCmdShow);

    MSG msg = { };
    while (GetMessage(&msg, nullptr, 0, 0))
    {
        TranslateMessage(&msg);
        DispatchMessage(&msg);
    }

    return 0;
}

LRESULT CALLBACK WindowProc(HWND hwnd, UINT uMsg,
WPARAM wParam, LPARAM lParam)
{
    switch (uMsg)
    {
    case WM_DESTROY:
        PostQuitMessage(0);
```

```
        return 0;

    case WM_PAINT:
        {
            PAINTSTRUCT ps;
            HDC hdc = BeginPaint(hwnd, &ps);

            FillRect(hdc, &ps.rcPaint, (HBRUSH)
(COLOR_WINDOW+1)); // Fill background again (optional)

            TextOut(hdc,
                5, 5,
                "Hello, WinAPI!", 13); // Draw text

            EndPaint(hwnd, &ps);
        }
        return 0;
    }
    return DefWindowProc(hwnd, uMsg, wParam, lParam);
}
```

5. **Build and Run (Visual Studio):** In Visual Studio, press `Ctrl+Shift+B` (or "Build" -> "Build Solution") to build the project. Then, press `Ctrl+F5` (or "Debug" -> "Start Without Debugging" or "Debug" -> "Start Debugging") to run the application.

Code Explanation:

- **#include <windows.h>**: Includes the main Windows API header file.
- **WINAPI WinMain(...)**: The entry point for WinAPI GUI applications (similar to `main()` in console applications).
- **WNDCLASS wc = { };**: Declares a `WNDCLASS` structure to define the window class.
  - `wc.lpfnWndProc = WindowProc;`: Sets the window procedure (`WindowProc`) that will handle messages for windows of this class.
  - `wc.hInstance = hInstance;`: Sets the instance handle.
  - `wc.lpszClassName = CLASS_NAME;`: Sets the class name.
  - `wc.hbrBackground = (HBRUSH)(COLOR_WINDOW+1);`: Sets the background brush for the window class.
- **RegisterClass(&wc);**: Registers the window class with the operating system.
- **HWND hwnd = CreateWindowEx(...)**: Creates the window.

- CLASS_NAME: Uses the registered window class.
- "Hello WinAPI!": Sets the window title.
- WS_OVERLAPPEDWINDOW | WS_VISIBLE: Sets window styles (overlapped window with title bar, borders, etc., and visible initially).
- CW_USEDEFAULT: Uses default size and position for the window.
- hInstance: Instance handle.

* **ShowWindow(hwnd, nCmdShow);**: Shows the window.
* **Message Loop:** The while (GetMessage(&msg, ...)) loop retrieves messages from the message queue and dispatches them to the window procedure.
    - GetMessage(&msg, ...): Retrieves a message from the message queue.
    - TranslateMessage(&msg): Processes keyboard input messages.
    - DispatchMessage(&msg): Dispatches the message to the[16] window procedure (WindowProc).
* **WindowProc(HWND hwnd, UINT uMsg, WPARAM wParam, LPARAM lParam)**: The window procedure that handles messages sent to the window.
    - switch (uMsg): Handles different message types.
        - WM_DESTROY: Handles the WM_DESTROY message (window destruction).[17] PostQuitMessage(0)[18] posts a quit message to the message queue, causing the message loop to terminate.
        - WM_PAINT: Handles the WM_PAINT message (window repaint).
            - BeginPaint(hwnd, &ps): Starts painting.
            - FillRect(...): Fills the background (optional).
            - TextOut(hdc, 5, 5, "Hello, WinAPI!", 13): Draws the text "Hello, WinAPI!" at position (5, 5).
            - EndPaint(hwnd, &ps): Ends painting.[19]
        - DefWindowProc(hwnd, uMsg, wParam, lParam): For messages not explicitly handled, calls the default window procedure[20] for default processing.

Real-world scenario: WinAPI is used to develop core Windows operating system components, system-level applications, and high-performance Windows-specific software. Applications requiring deep integration with Windows features or needing to maximize performance on the[21] Windows platform might choose WinAPI for

GUI development. Examples include parts of the Windows shell, some system utilities, and specialized Windows applications.

12.4 Choosing the Right[22] GUI Framework: A Comparative Overview

Selecting the appropriate GUI framework depends heavily on the project requirements, target platforms, and development priorities. Each of Qt, Dear ImGui, and WinAPI offers distinct advantages and disadvantages,[23] making them suitable for different scenarios.

- **Cross-Platform Compatibility:**
  - **Qt:** Excellent cross-platform support. Write code once, deploy on Windows, macOS, Linux, mobile, and embedded platforms.
  - **Dear ImGui:** Portable but requires a rendering backend implementation for each platform (OpenGL, DirectX, Vulkan, etc.). Cross-platform in terms of code portability but needs backend integration.
  - **WinAPI:** Windows-specific. Not cross-platform.

- **Complexity and Learning Curve:**
  - **Qt:** Moderate learning curve. Comprehensive framework with a large API, but well-documented and with good tooling (Qt Creator). Signals and slots mechanism requires understanding.
  - **Dear ImGui:** Very low learning curve. Simple API, easy to integrate. Immediate mode paradigm is different from traditional GUI frameworks but straightforward to grasp for basic UIs.
  - **WinAPI:** Steep learning curve. Complex C API, message-based programming model, verbose code. Requires a deeper understanding of Windows internals.
- **Performance and Resource Usage:**
  - **Qt:** Good performance, but higher overhead than Dear ImGui or raw WinAPI due to its comprehensive nature and abstraction layers. Suitable for complex applications but might be overkill for very resource-constrained systems.
  - **Dear ImGui:** Very lightweight and minimal overhead. Highly performant for rendering simple UIs. Ideal for tools, debugging interfaces, and embedded systems with limited resources.

  - **WinAPI:** Potentially highest performance for Windows-specific applications as it directly interacts with the OS. Minimal abstraction overhead.
- **Feature Set and Application Type Suitability:**
  - **Qt:** Rich feature set. Suitable for complex desktop applications, cross-platform applications, applications requiring polished UIs, and large-scale projects.
  - **Dear ImGui:** Limited feature set focused on UI rendering. Best for tools, debugging UIs, game development utilities, embedded system interfaces, and situations where rapid UI prototyping is needed. Less suitable for complex application UIs.
  - **WinAPI:** Powerful and feature-rich for Windows-specific applications. Suitable for applications requiring deep Windows integration, system-level software, and applications where maximum Windows performance is paramount.

Guidance for Choosing:

- **Choose Qt if:**
  - Cross-platform compatibility is a primary requirement.
  - You are developing a complex desktop application with a rich UI.
  - You want a comprehensive framework with a wide range of features beyond GUI.
  - You prefer a more structured, object-oriented approach to GUI development.
- **Choose Dear ImGui if:**
  - You need a lightweight GUI for tools, debugging interfaces, or in-game UIs.
  - Ease of integration and minimal overhead are important.
  - You are working on game development, graphics programming, or embedded systems.
  - You prefer a simpler, immediate mode GUI paradigm.
- **Choose WinAPI if:**
  - You are developing a Windows-specific application.
  - You need maximum performance and direct access to Windows OS features.

- You are comfortable with the complexity of the WinAPI and C-style programming.
- You are building system-level software or applications that require deep Windows integration.

12.5 Conclusion: Selecting the Right Tool for GUI Development in C++

C++ offers a spectrum of options for GUI development, each catering to different needs and priorities. Qt provides a robust, cross-platform framework for complex applications. Dear ImGui offers a lightweight and immediate mode approach ideal for tools and utilities. WinAPI provides native Windows power and control for platform-specific applications. For Computer Technology students and educators, understanding these different approaches is crucial for making informed decisions about GUI framework selection and for developing a wide range of C++ applications with effective and user-friendly interfaces. The choice ultimately depends on the specific requirements of the project, balancing factors like platform support, complexity, performance, and the nature of the user interface needed.

Chapter 13

Game Development with C++: Powering Interactive Worlds

C++ has long been a cornerstone of the game development industry, revered for its performance, control, and extensive ecosystem of libraries and engines. Its ability to handle complex computations efficiently and interact directly with hardware makes it ideally suited for the demanding nature of game development, where frame rates, responsiveness, and intricate game logic are paramount. For Computer Technology students and educators, understanding game development with C++ offers a pathway into a dynamic and creative field, equipping them with skills applicable not only to game creation but also to broader software engineering disciplines. This section delves into the world of game development with C++, exploring the use of libraries like SDL and SFML for foundational game programming, the basics of C++ scripting within powerful game engines like Unreal Engine, and the critical techniques for optimizing game performance to deliver engaging and seamless player experiences.

13.1 Using SDL and SFML: Building Blocks for Game Engines

SDL (Simple DirectMedia Layer) and SFML (Simple and Fast Multimedia Library) are popular cross-platform libraries that provide essential building blocks for game development in C++. They offer functionalities for handling graphics, input, audio, and window management, abstracting away platform-specific complexities and allowing developers to focus on game logic and design. While they are lower-level than full-fledged game engines, SDL and SFML are invaluable for learning the fundamentals of game programming and for developing 2D games or custom game engine components. As Rabbitzsch highlights in "SFML Game Development," these libraries provide a solid foundation for understanding game development principles (Rabbitzsch, 2013).

13.1.1 SDL (Simple DirectMedia Layer): Low-Level Control and Cross-Platform Access

SDL is a cross-platform library providing low-level access to audio, keyboard, mouse, joystick, and graphics hardware via OpenGL and Direct3D. It is written in C, but has C++ bindings, and is widely used in game development, emulators, and multimedia applications. SDL's strength lies in its portability and direct hardware access, making it suitable for performance-sensitive applications and for developers who prefer fine-grained control.

Key Features of SDL for Game Development:

- **Cross-Platform:** SDL supports a wide range of operating systems, including Windows, macOS, Linux, iOS, and Android, enabling developers to target multiple platforms with a single codebase.
- **Graphics and Rendering:** SDL provides functionalities for creating windows, rendering 2D graphics using hardware acceleration (OpenGL, Direct3D), and managing textures and surfaces.
- **Input Handling:** SDL offers robust input handling for keyboard, mouse, joysticks, and gamepads, allowing for responsive game controls.
- **Audio Support:** SDL provides audio playback and recording capabilities, supporting various audio formats and devices.

- **Event Handling:** SDL uses an event-driven model for managing user input, window events, and other system events, which is fundamental for game loops and interactive applications.

Getting Started with SDL: Creating a Window and Rendering a Sprite

Step-by-step guide:

1. **Install SDL2:** Download and install the SDL2 development libraries from the official SDL website. Choose the appropriate runtime binaries and development libraries for your operating system and compiler. You will need to configure your compiler to link against the SDL2 libraries.
2. **Create a Project Directory:** Create a directory for your project (e.g., SDLSpriteExample).
3. **Create main.cpp:** Create a main.cpp file in your project directory with the following code:

C++

```
#include <SDL.h>
#include <iostream>

int main(int argc, char* argv[]) {
  if (SDL_Init(SDL_INIT_VIDEO) < 0) {
    std::cerr << "SDL could not initialize! SDL_Error: " <<
SDL_GetError() << std::endl;
    return 1;
  }

  SDL_Window* window = SDL_CreateWindow(
    "SDL Sprite Example",       // window title
    SDL_WINDOWPOS_UNDEFINED,     // initial x position
    SDL_WINDOWPOS_UNDEFINED,     // initial y position
    640,                     // width, in pixels
    480,                     // height, in pixels
    SDL_WINDOW_SHOWN                // flags - shown always
  );

  if (window == nullptr) {
    std::cerr << "Window could not be created! SDL_Error: " <<
SDL_GetError() << std::endl;
    SDL_Quit();
    return 1;
  }
```

```
    SDL_Renderer* renderer = SDL_CreateRenderer(window, -1,
SDL_RENDERER_ACCELERATED);
    if (renderer == nullptr) {
        std::cerr << "Renderer could not be created! SDL_Error: " <<
SDL_GetError() << std::endl;
        SDL_DestroyWindow(window);
        SDL_Quit();
        return 1;
    }

    SDL_Surface* surface = SDL_LoadBMP("sprite.bmp"); // Load a
BMP image (replace with your sprite.bmp)
    if (surface == nullptr) {
        std::cerr << "Surface could not be created! SDL_Error: " <<
SDL_GetError() << std::endl;
        SDL_DestroyRenderer(renderer);
        SDL_DestroyWindow(window);
        SDL_Quit();
        return 1;
    }

    SDL_Texture* texture = SDL_CreateTextureFromSurface(renderer,
surface);
    SDL_FreeSurface(surface); // Surface not needed after texture
creation
    if (texture == nullptr) {
        std::cerr << "Texture could not be created! SDL_Error: " <<
SDL_GetError() << std::endl;
        SDL_DestroyTexture(texture);
        SDL_DestroyRenderer(renderer);
        SDL_DestroyWindow(window);
        SDL_Quit();
        return 1;
    }

    SDL_Rect renderQuad = { 50, 50, 200, 200 }; // Position and size
of sprite
    SDL_Rect clipRect = { 0, 0, 200, 200 };     // Clip rectangle (entire
sprite)

    bool quit = false;
    SDL_Event e;
    while (!quit) {
        while (SDL_PollEvent(&e) != 0) {
            if (e.type == SDL_QUIT) {
```

```
                quit = true;
            }
        }

        SDL_SetRenderDrawColor(renderer, 0x00, 0x00, 0x00, 0xFF); //
Black background
        SDL_RenderClear(renderer);

        SDL_RenderCopy(renderer, texture, &clipRect, &renderQuad);
// Render sprite

        SDL_RenderPresent(renderer); // Update screen
    }

    SDL_DestroyTexture(texture);
    SDL_DestroyRenderer(renderer);
    SDL_DestroyWindow(window);
    SDL_Quit();

    return 0;
}
```

4. **Prepare sprite.bmp:** Create a simple BMP image file named sprite.bmp (e.g., a small square of a solid color) and place it in the same directory as your main.cpp. You can use image editing software like GIMP or Paint to create a BMP image.
5. **Compile and Link:** Compile main.cpp and link with the SDL2 library. The compilation and linking commands will depend on your operating system and compiler.

   Example compilation command (GCC on Linux):
   Bash

   ```
   g++ main.cpp -o sdl_sprite_example -lSDL2 -std=c++17
   ```
5. **Run:** Execute the compiled executable (./sdl_sprite_example on Linux). You should see a window with your sprite rendered on a black background.

Code Explanation:

- **SDL_Init(SDL_INIT_VIDEO):** Initializes the SDL video subsystem.
- **SDL_CreateWindow(...):** Creates an SDL window with specified title, position, size, and flags.
- **SDL_CreateRenderer(...):** Creates an SDL renderer, which is used to draw graphics to the window.

SDL_RENDERER_ACCELERATED requests hardware acceleration if available.

- **SDL_LoadBMP("sprite.bmp"):** Loads a BMP image from the file sprite.bmp into an SDL surface. SDL surfaces are software representations of images.
- **SDL_CreateTextureFromSurface(...):** Creates an SDL texture from the surface. Textures are hardware-accelerated representations of images that are efficient for rendering.
- **SDL_FreeSurface(surface):** Frees the SDL surface, as it is no longer needed after the texture is created.
- **SDL_Rect renderQuad = { ... };:** Defines a rectangle (SDL_Rect) that specifies the position and size where the sprite will be rendered on the screen.
- **SDL_Rect clipRect = { ... };:** Defines a clipping rectangle, which specifies which part of the texture to render. In this case, it's the entire sprite.
- **Event Loop:** The while (!quit) loop is the main game loop.
    - **SDL_PollEvent(&e):** Polls for pending SDL events (keyboard input, mouse events, window events, etc.).
    - **if (e.type == SDL_QUIT):** Checks for the quit event (e.g., window close button).
    - **SDL_SetRenderDrawColor(...):** Sets the renderer's draw color to black.
    - **SDL_RenderClear(renderer):** Clears the renderer with the draw color (fills the screen with black).
    - **SDL_RenderCopy(renderer, texture, &clipRect, &renderQuad):** Renders the texture (sprite) to the renderer, using the clip rectangle and render rectangle to control which part of the texture is rendered and where it is rendered on the screen.
    - **SDL_RenderPresent(renderer):** Updates the screen with the rendered content.
- **Resource Cleanup:** SDL_DestroyTexture(), SDL_DestroyRenderer(), SDL_DestroyWindow(), and SDL_Quit() clean up SDL resources when the program exits.

Real-world scenario: SDL is used in many indie games, emulators, and multimedia applications where cross-platform compatibility and low-level control are important. Examples include popular indie games like *Cave Story* and *VVVVVV*, as well as various game emulators and media players. Its flexibility and performance make it a valuable tool for developers who want to build games from the ground up or create custom multimedia solutions.

13.1.2 SFML (Simple and Fast Multimedia Library): Object-Oriented Convenience

SFML is another popular cross-platform library for game development, built with C++ and offering a more object-oriented approach compared to SDL. SFML provides modules for graphics, window management, audio, network, and system functionalities. It is designed to be easy to use and provides a higher level of abstraction than SDL, making it a good choice for developers who prefer a more streamlined and object-oriented development experience. As Barbato details in "SFML Blueprints," SFML simplifies game development with its intuitive API (Barbato, 2015).

Key Features of SFML for Game Development:

- **Cross-Platform:** SFML, like SDL, supports multiple operating systems (Windows, macOS, Linux, etc.), enabling cross-platform game development.
- **Object-Oriented API:** SFML's API is designed in an object-oriented manner, making it more C++-friendly and potentially easier to learn for developers familiar with object-oriented programming.
- **Graphics and Rendering:** SFML provides classes for window management, drawing shapes, sprites, text, and managing textures and shaders. It uses OpenGL for hardware-accelerated rendering.
- **Input Handling:** SFML offers classes for handling keyboard, mouse, and joystick input, as well as touch input on mobile platforms.
- **Audio Support:** SFML provides classes for playing sounds and music, supporting various audio formats.
- **Networking:** SFML includes networking capabilities for creating multiplayer games or network-aware applications.

Getting Started with SFML: Creating a Window and Drawing a Shape

Step-by-step guide:

1. **Install SFML:** Download and install the SFML library from the official SFML website. Choose the appropriate SFML version for your operating system and compiler. You will need to configure your compiler to link against the SFML libraries.
2. **Create a Project Directory:** Create a directory for your project (e.g., SFMLShapeExample).

3. **Create main.cpp:** Create a main.cpp file in your project directory with the following code:

C++

```
#include <SFML/Graphics.hpp>

int main()
{
    sf::RenderWindow window(sf::VideoMode(640, 480), "SFML Shape
Example");

    sf::CircleShape circle(100.f); // Create a circle shape with radius 100
    circle.setFillColor(sf::Color::Green);
    circle.setPosition(220, 140);

    while (window.isOpen())
    {
        sf::Event event;
        while (window.pollEvent(event))
        {
            if (event.type == sf::Event::Closed)
                window.close();
        }

        window.clear(); // Clear the window
        window.draw(circle); // Draw the circle
        window.display(); // Update the window
    }

    return 0;
}
```

4. **Compile and Link:** Compile main.cpp and link with the SFML graphics module (and potentially other SFML modules depending on your project). The compilation and linking commands will vary depending on your operating system and compiler.
   Example compilation command (GCC on Linux):
   Bash

```
g++ main.cpp -o sfml_shape_example -lsfml-graphics -lsfml-window -
lsfml-system -std=c++17
```

5. **Run:** Execute the compiled executable (./sfml_shape_example on Linux). You should see a window with a green circle drawn in it.

Code Explanation:

- **#include <SFML/Graphics.hpp>:** Includes the SFML graphics header, which provides classes for window management, shapes, sprites, etc.
- **sf::RenderWindow window(sf::VideoMode(640, 480), "SFML Shape Example");:** Creates an SFML render window with specified video mode (width, height) and title.
- **sf::CircleShape circle(100.f);:** Creates an SFML circle shape with a radius of 100 pixels.
- **circle.setFillColor(sf::Color::Green);:** Sets the fill color of the circle to green.
- **circle.setPosition(220, 140);:** Sets the position of the circle in the window.
- **Game Loop:** The while (window.isOpen()) loop is the main game loop.
    - o **window.pollEvent(event):** Polls for SFML events (window events, input events).
    - o **if (event.type == sf::Event::Closed):** Checks for the window close event.
    - o **window.clear():** Clears the window with the default clear color (usually black).
    - o **window.draw(circle):** Draws the circle shape to the window.
    - o **window.display():** Updates the window to display the drawn content.

Real-world scenario: SFML is used in a variety of 2D games and multimedia applications. Its object-oriented design and ease of use make it a popular choice for game development education, indie game projects, and rapid prototyping. While perhaps less prevalent in AAA game development compared to custom engines or Unreal Engine, SFML remains a valuable library for 2D game development and for learning game programming concepts in C++.

13.2 Unreal Engine Basics (C++ Scripting): Power and Flexibility

Unreal Engine is a leading game engine widely used in the industry for developing high-fidelity games across various platforms, from PC and consoles to mobile and VR/AR. While Unreal Engine provides a visual scripting system called Blueprint, C++ scripting is a powerful and essential aspect of Unreal Engine development, offering deeper control, performance optimization, and the ability to create complex game logic and engine extensions. For aspiring game developers, understanding Unreal Engine C++ scripting is crucial for unlocking the full potential of this industry-standard engine. As Gregory explains in "Game Engine Architecture," modern game engines like Unreal Engine rely heavily on C++ for their core functionalities (Gregory, 2018).

13.2.1 Key Concepts of Unreal Engine C++ Scripting

Unreal Engine's C++ scripting system is built upon a set of core concepts and conventions:

- **Reflection System:** Unreal Engine uses a powerful reflection system that allows C++ classes, properties, and functions to be exposed to the engine and to Blueprint visual scripting. This enables seamless integration between C++ code and the engine's editor and runtime environment. Macros like UCLASS(), UFUNCTION(), UPROPERTY() are used to mark C++ code for reflection.
- **Actors and Components:** Actors are the fundamental building blocks of game worlds in Unreal Engine. They are objects that can be placed in a level and possess behavior. Components are reusable modules that provide specific functionalities to Actors (e.g., rendering, physics, audio). C++ is used to create custom Actors and Components with specific game logic and behaviors.
- **Game Framework Classes:** Unreal Engine provides a set of core game framework classes that define the structure of a game, including GameMode (manages game rules and gameplay flow), PlayerController (handles player input), Pawn or Character (represent game characters), and GameState (stores game state information). C++ is used to extend and customize these framework classes to implement game-specific logic.
- **Unreal Header Tool (UHT):** UHT is a preprocessor that parses Unreal Engine C++ header files and generates reflection metadata.

This metadata is used by the engine for various purposes, including Blueprint integration, property serialization, and garbage collection.

- **Garbage Collection:** Unreal Engine has its own garbage collection system to automatically manage memory for reflected UObjects (objects derived from UObject, the base class for most Unreal Engine objects). This simplifies memory management for game developers.
- **Blueprint Integration:** C++ code in Unreal Engine is designed to work seamlessly with Blueprint visual scripting. C++ classes and functions can be exposed to Blueprint, allowing designers and other team members to extend and customize C++ logic visually.

13.2.2 Getting Started with Unreal Engine C++ Scripting: Creating a Basic Actor

Let's create a simple C++ Actor in Unreal Engine that logs a message to the output log when the game starts.

Step-by-step guide:

1. **Install Unreal Engine:** Download and install the Unreal Engine from the official Unreal Engine website. Follow the installation instructions for your operating system.
2. **Create a New C++ Project:** Open the Unreal Engine Launcher. Go to the "Library" tab and launch Unreal Engine. In the "New Project Categories" window, select "Games" and then "Blank" template. Choose "C++" as the project type. Give your project a name (e.g., MyCppActorProject) and choose a project location. Click "Create Project".
3. **Add a New C++ Class (Actor):** In the Unreal Editor, go to "File" -> "New C++ Class...". In the "Choose Parent Class" window, select "Actor". Name your class MyTestActor and click "Create Class". Visual Studio (or your configured C++ IDE) will open with the newly created C++ class files (MyTestActor.h and MyTestActor.cpp).
4. **Modify MyTestActor.h:** In MyTestActor.h, add the UCLASS() macro above the class declaration. This macro marks the class for Unreal Engine's reflection system.

```
C++

#pragma once

#include "CoreMinimal.h"
```

```
#include "GameFramework/Actor.h"
#include "MyTestActor.generated.h"

UCLASS() // Add UCLASS() macro
class MYCPPACTORPROJECT_API AMyTestActor : public AActor
{
   GENERATED_BODY()

public:
   // Sets default values for this actor's properties
   AMyTestActor();

protected:
   // Called when the game starts or when spawned
   virtual void BeginPlay() override;

public:
   // Called every frame
   virtual void Tick(float DeltaTime) override;

};
```

5. **Modify MyTestActor.cpp:** In MyTestActor.cpp, add code to the BeginPlay() function to log a message to the output log when the Actor is spawned in the game world.

```
C++

#include "MyTestActor.h"
#include "Kismet/GameplayStatics.h" // Include GameplayStatics
for logging

// Sets default values
AMyTestActor::AMyTestActor()
{
    // Set this actor to call Tick() every frame.  You can turn this off to
improve performance if you don't need it.
   PrimaryActorTick.bCanEverTick = true;

}

// Called when the game starts or when spawned
void AMyTestActor::BeginPlay()
{
   Super::BeginPlay();
```

```
    // Log a message to the output log
    UE_LOG(LogTemp, Warning, TEXT("Hello from MyTestActor C++ Actor!"));
}

// Called every frame
void AMyTestActor::Tick(float DeltaTime)
{
    Super::Tick(DeltaTime);

}
```

6. **Compile and Run in Unreal Editor:** In the Unreal Editor, click "Compile" to compile your C++ code. Once compilation is successful, drag and drop your MyTestActor from the "Content Browser" into the level viewport to place an instance of your Actor in the game world. Press "Play" to run the game in the editor.
7. **Check Output Log:** Open the "Output Log" window in the Unreal Editor (Window -> Developer Tools -> Output Log). You should see the message "Hello from MyTestActor C++ Actor!" printed in the log when the game starts.

Code Explanation:

- **UCLASS() Macro:** The UCLASS() macro in MyTestActor.h marks the AMyTestActor class as a UObject, making it part of Unreal Engine's reflection system and enabling features like garbage collection and Blueprint integration.
- **GENERATED_BODY() Macro:** The GENERATED_BODY() macro is essential for UObjects. It generates necessary code for reflection and other engine functionalities.
- **BeginPlay() Function:** The BeginPlay() function is an override of a virtual function inherited from AActor. It is called when the Actor is spawned into the game world at the beginning of gameplay.
- **UE_LOG(LogTemp, Warning, TEXT("Hello from MyTestActor C++ Actor!"));:** Uses the UE_LOG macro to print a message to the Unreal Engine output log.
    - LogTemp: Specifies the log category (temporary log messages).
    - Warning: Specifies the log verbosity level (Warning, Error, etc.).
    - TEXT("..."): The message to log, wrapped in the TEXT() macro for proper Unicode handling in Unreal Engine.

- **Compilation and Editor[11] Integration:** After compiling the C++ code in Unreal Engine, the MyTestActor class becomes available in the Unreal Editor. You can place instances of this Actor in levels, modify its properties (if you expose any using UPROPERTY()), and interact with it using Blueprint visual scripting.

Real-world scenario: Unreal Engine C++ scripting is used extensively in professional game development for creating core gameplay systems, AI logic, physics interactions, custom game mechanics, and engine extensions. Almost all complex gameplay logic and engine features in AAA games developed with Unreal Engine are implemented using C++. Examples include character controllers,[12] AI systems, networking code, rendering pipelines, and custom tools for game designers. C++ scripting provides the performance and flexibility needed to create sophisticated and optimized game experiences within the Unreal Engine framework.

13.3 Performance Optimization for Games: Achieving Smooth Gameplay

Performance optimization is a critical aspect of game development. Games are real-time interactive applications that require consistent frame rates and responsiveness to provide a smooth and enjoyable player experience. Inefficient code or unoptimized game assets can lead to performance bottlenecks, resulting in low frame rates, stuttering, and a poor player experience. For Computer Technology students and educators involved in game development, understanding performance optimization techniques is paramount. As Eberly emphasizes in "Game Physics," performance optimization is often a trade-off between visual fidelity and computational cost (Eberly, 2010).

13.3.1 Identifying Performance Bottlenecks: Profiling and Measurement

The first step in performance optimization is to identify performance bottlenecks – the sections of code or game systems that are consuming the most processing time and causing performance issues. Profiling tools are essential for this process.

Techniques for Profiling and Bottleneck Identification:

- **Profiling Tools:** Use profilers to measure the execution time of different parts of your game code. Profilers can provide detailed information about function call counts, execution times, memory allocations, and CPU/GPU utilization.
    - **Unreal Engine Profiler:** Unreal Engine has a built-in profiler that can be accessed within the editor (Session Frontend -> Profiler). It provides detailed performance insights into various engine subsystems, including rendering, game logic, AI, and physics.
    - **External Profilers:** Platform-specific profilers like *perf* (Linux), *VTune Amplifier* (Intel), *Xcode Instruments* (macOS), and *Visual Studio Profiler* (Windows) can provide system-level performance data and insights into CPU and GPU usage.
- **Frame Rate Counters (FPS):** Displaying an FPS counter in your game is a simple but effective way to monitor overall performance and detect frame rate drops.
- **Custom Timers and Benchmarks:** Implement custom timers in your code to measure the execution time of specific functions or code blocks. This is useful for isolating and benchmarking particular algorithms or systems.
- **GPU Profiling:** Use GPU profiling tools (e.g., RenderDoc, NVIDIA Nsight Graphics, AMD Radeon GPU Profiler) to analyze GPU performance, identify rendering bottlenecks, and optimize shaders and rendering techniques.

Real-world scenario: Game developers routinely use profilers throughout the game development process. During development, profilers are used to identify performance-critical areas and guide optimization efforts. In QA and testing phases, profilers help to ensure that the game meets performance targets on target hardware and to diagnose performance issues reported by testers. Profiling is an iterative process, where developers profile, optimize, re-profile, and repeat until satisfactory performance is achieved.

13.3.2 Algorithm and Data Structure Optimization: Efficient Logic

Choosing efficient algorithms and data structures is crucial for game performance, particularly in systems that are executed frequently, such as game logic, AI, physics, and collision detection.

Optimization Techniques:

- **Algorithm Complexity:** Select algorithms with lower time complexity for performance-critical tasks. For example, use O(log n) or O(n) algorithms instead of O(n^2) or O(n^3) algorithms where possible, especially for large datasets or frequently executed code.
- **Data Structure Choice:** Choose data structures that are optimized for the operations you need to perform most often. For example, use hash tables (unordered_map in C++) for fast lookups, vectors or arrays for sequential data access, and spatial data structures (e.g., quadtrees, octrees, BVHs) for efficient spatial queries in games with large worlds.
- **Pre-computation and Caching:** Pre-compute results or data that are used repeatedly and store them in caches to avoid redundant computations. For example, pre-calculate lighting or visibility information, or cache frequently accessed game data.
- **Avoid Unnecessary Operations:** Minimize unnecessary computations, memory allocations, and function calls in performance-critical code paths.

Real-world scenario: In games, AI pathfinding algorithms, collision detection routines, and physics simulations are often performance-intensive. Game developers carefully optimize these systems by selecting efficient algorithms and data structures. For example, using A* pathfinding algorithm instead of Dijkstra's algorithm in large game worlds, or using bounding volume hierarchies (BVHs) for efficient collision queries.

13.3.3 Rendering Optimization: Efficient Graphics Pipeline

Rendering is often a major performance bottleneck in games, especially in visually rich and complex games. Optimizing the rendering pipeline is crucial for achieving high frame rates and visually appealing graphics.

Rendering Optimization Techniques:

- **Reduce Draw Calls:** Minimize the number of draw calls (API calls to render objects). Batch rendering techniques (e.g., instancing, draw call merging) can significantly reduce draw call overhead by rendering multiple objects in a single draw call.
- **Level of Detail (LOD):** Implement level of detail (LOD) techniques to render less detailed versions of objects when they are

far away from the camera. This reduces the polygon count and rendering workload for distant objects.

- **Occlusion Culling:** Use occlusion culling techniques to avoid rendering objects that are hidden behind other objects and are not visible to the camera. This reduces the number of objects that need to be rendered.
- **Shader Optimization:** Optimize shaders to reduce GPU workload. Minimize complex computations in shaders, reduce texture lookups, and use efficient shader instructions.
- **Texture Optimization:** Optimize textures by using compressed texture formats, mipmaps, and texture atlases. Compressed textures reduce memory usage and bandwidth. Mipmaps improve rendering quality for distant textures. Texture atlases reduce draw calls by packing multiple textures into a single texture.
- **Shadow Optimization:** Shadows can be computationally expensive. Optimize shadow rendering by using shadow mapping techniques effectively, reducing shadow resolution, or using simpler shadow algorithms where appropriate.
- **Post-Processing Effects Optimization:** Post-processing effects (e.g., bloom, depth of field, motion blur) can add visual polish but also increase GPU workload. Optimize post-processing effects by reducing their complexity, using lower resolution buffers, or selectively applying effects only where needed.

Real-world scenario: Modern games employ a wide range of rendering optimization techniques to achieve high visual fidelity while maintaining smooth frame rates. Techniques like level of detail, occlusion culling, shader optimization, and texture compression are standard practices in game rendering pipelines. Game engines like Unreal Engine and Unity provide built-in tools and features to assist developers in optimizing rendering performance.

13.3.4 Memory Management: Reducing Memory Footprint and Allocations

Efficient memory management is crucial in game development, especially for games targeting platforms with limited memory resources (e.g., mobile devices, consoles). Excessive memory usage can lead to performance issues, crashes, and reduced game stability.

Memory Management Optimization Techniques:

- **Minimize Dynamic Memory Allocation:** Reduce dynamic memory allocation, especially in performance-critical code paths and during gameplay. Dynamic allocation can be slow and lead to memory fragmentation. Prefer static or stack-based allocation where possible.
- **Object Pooling:** Use object pooling for frequently created and destroyed objects (e.g., projectiles, particle effects, enemies). Object pools reuse pre-allocated objects instead of allocating and deallocating memory repeatedly, reducing allocation overhead and fragmentation.
- **Data Packing and Alignment:** Pack data structures efficiently to reduce memory footprint (as discussed in section 11.4.5).
- **Memory Streaming and Loading Strategies:** Implement efficient memory streaming and loading strategies to load game assets (textures, models, audio) on demand and unload assets that are no longer needed. This reduces the overall memory footprint of the game.
- **Memory Profiling and Leak Detection:** Use memory profiling tools to identify memory leaks and areas of excessive memory allocation. Fix memory leaks and optimize memory usage to prevent memory-related issues.

Real-world scenario: Memory management is a critical consideration in game development across all platforms. Mobile games, in particular, must be highly memory-efficient to run smoothly on devices with limited RAM. Game developers use techniques like object pooling, data packing, and asset streaming to optimize memory usage and ensure that games run within memory constraints. Memory leaks are rigorously tracked and fixed during development to prevent crashes and instability.

13.3.5 Code Optimization: Writing Efficient C++ Code

Writing efficient C++ code is a fundamental aspect of game performance optimization. The techniques discussed in section 11.4 (Writing Performant C++ Code) are directly applicable to game development.

Key Code Optimization Techniques for Games:

- **Algorithm and Data Structure Selection:** Choose efficient algorithms and data structures (as discussed in 13.3.2).

- **Compiler Optimizations:** Enable compiler optimizations (-O2, -O3, LTO, PGO).
- **Inline Functions:** Use inline functions for small, frequently called functions.
- **Loop Optimization:** Optimize loops for performance (loop unrolling, cache-friendly access, vectorization).
- **Data Alignment and Packing:** Consider data alignment and packing for memory access and footprint efficiency.
- **Minimize Virtual Function Calls (where appropriate):** Virtual function calls can have a small performance overhead compared to direct function calls. In performance-critical code paths, consider using non-virtual functions or static polymorphism (templates, CRTP) if dynamic polymorphism is not strictly necessary.
- **Branch Prediction Optimization:** Structure code to minimize branch mispredictions, which can cause pipeline stalls in modern processors. Use techniques like conditional moves or branchless code where possible.

Real-world scenario: Game codebases are often very large and complex. Game developers invest significant effort in writing efficient C++ code and applying various code optimization techniques to ensure that game logic, AI, physics, and other systems run smoothly and efficiently. Code reviews, static analysis, and performance testing are integral parts of the game development process to maintain code quality and performance.

By mastering these performance optimization techniques, Computer Technology students and educators can develop games that are not only visually impressive and engaging but also run smoothly and efficiently across target platforms, providing players with a polished and enjoyable gaming experience. Performance optimization is an ongoing process in game development, requiring continuous profiling, analysis, and refinement throughout the development cycle.

Chapter 14

Web and Networking with C++: Connecting the World

The internet and web technologies have become integral to modern computing, and the ability to develop networked applications and web services is a crucial skill for Computer Technology professionals. C++, renowned for its performance and control, is a powerful language for building robust and efficient web and networking solutions. While often perceived as a language for system-level programming or game development, C++ offers a rich ecosystem for web and networking tasks, ranging from low-level socket programming to high-level web application frameworks. For Computer Technology students and educators, understanding web and networking with C++ is essential for creating a wide spectrum of applications, from high-performance network servers to sophisticated web services. This section explores fundamental networking concepts in C++ using libraries like boost::asio and raw sockets, delves into HTTP client and server development with libraries like cpp-httplib and libcurl, and introduces web application development using frameworks such as Crow and CppCMS.

14.1 Basics of Networking with C++: Establishing Connections

Networking forms the backbone of modern communication, enabling data exchange between computers across local networks or the internet. In C++, networking capabilities are often accessed through libraries that provide abstractions over operating system-level network interfaces. Understanding the basics of networking in C++ involves grasping fundamental concepts like sockets, network protocols, and asynchronous operations. Libraries like `boost::asio` and raw sockets offer different levels of abstraction for network programming, catering to varying needs and complexities. As Stevens and colleagues detail in "UNIX Network Programming, Volume 1, Networking APIs: Sockets and XTI," a solid understanding of socket APIs is foundational for network programming (Stevens, Fenner, & Rudoff, 2004).

14.1.1 Boost.Asio: A Cross-Platform Networking Library

Boost.Asio is a powerful, cross-platform C++ library for network and low-level I/O programming. It provides a consistent asynchronous model for various I/O operations, including sockets, timers, serial ports, and more. Boost.Asio simplifies network programming by abstracting away platform-specific details and offering a modern, efficient, and portable approach to handling network connections and data transfer. Its asynchronous nature is particularly beneficial for building scalable and responsive network applications.

Key Features of Boost.Asio for Networking:

- **Cross-Platform Asynchronous I/O:** Boost.Asio provides a consistent API for asynchronous I/O operations across different operating systems (Windows, Linux, macOS, etc.). Asynchronous operations allow programs to perform other tasks while waiting for I/O operations to complete, improving responsiveness and efficiency.
- **Sockets (TCP and UDP):** Boost.Asio offers classes for working with TCP and UDP sockets, the fundamental building blocks of network communication. It simplifies socket creation, binding, listening, accepting connections, and sending/receiving data.

- **Timers:** Boost.Asio includes timers that can be used to schedule events or implement timeouts in network applications.
- **Resolvers:** Boost.Asio provides resolvers for translating hostnames to IP addresses, essential for establishing connections to remote servers.
- **Strand-Based Concurrency:** Boost.Asio promotes a strand-based concurrency model, which simplifies concurrent programming by ensuring that handlers for asynchronous operations are executed sequentially within a strand, avoiding race conditions and simplifying synchronization.

Getting Started with Boost.Asio: A Simple TCP Echo Server

Let's create a basic TCP echo server using Boost.Asio that listens for incoming connections and echoes back any data received from clients.

Step-by-step guide:

1. **Install Boost Library:** Ensure you have the Boost C++ library installed on your system. Installation methods vary depending on your operating system. For example, on Ubuntu: `sudo apt-get install libboost-all-dev`. On macOS using Homebrew: `brew install boost`. On Windows, you can download Boost from the official Boost website.
2. **Create a Project Directory:** Create a directory for your project (e.g., `AsioEchoServer`).
3. **Create `server.cpp`:** Create a `server.cpp` file in your project directory with the following code:

```
C++

#include <boost/asio.hpp>
#include <iostream>

using boost::asio::ip::tcp;

int main() {
   try {
      boost::asio::io_context io_context;
      tcp::acceptor acceptor(io_context, tcp::endpoint(tcp::v4(), 13)); //
Listen on port 13

      std::cout << "Echo server started, listening on port 13..." <<
std::endl;

      for (;;) {
```

```
        tcp::socket socket = acceptor.accept(); // Accept incoming
connection

        std::cout << "Connection accepted from: " <<
socket.remote_endpoint() << std::endl;


        boost::asio::streambuf buffer;
        boost::asio::read_until(socket, buffer, '\n'); // Read until
newline

        std::string message = boost::asio::buffer_cast<const
char*>(buffer.data());
        std::cout << "Received message: " << message;

        boost::asio::write(socket, boost::asio::buffer(message)); //
Echo back the message
        std::cout << "Echoed message back to client." << std::endl;
      }
  } catch (std::exception& e) {
    std::cerr << "Exception: " << e.what() << std::endl;
  }

  return 0;
}
```

4. **Compile and Link:** Compile server.cpp and link with the Boost.Asio library. The compilation and linking commands will depend on your operating system and compiler.
   Example compilation command (GCC on Linux):
   Bash

   ```
   g++ server.cpp -o asio_echo_server -lboost_system -std=c++17
   ```
5. **Run the Server:** Execute the compiled executable (./asio_echo_server on Linux). The server will start listening on port 13.
6. **Test with a Client (e.g., telnet or netcat):** Open a terminal and use telnet or netcat to connect to localhost on port 13 and send a message.

Using telnet:

Bash

```
telnet localhost 13
Trying 127.0.0.1...
Connected to localhost.
Escape character is '^]'.
Hello Server!\n
Hello Server!
Connection closed by foreign host.
```

Using netcat (nc):

Bash

```
nc localhost 13
Hello from netcat!\n
Hello from netcat!
```

Code Explanation:

- **#include <boost/asio.hpp>**: Includes the Boost.Asio header file.
- **using boost::asio::ip::tcp;**: Simplifies code by bringing boost::asio::ip::tcp into the current namespace.
- **boost::asio::io_context io_context;**: Creates an io_context object, which is the core of Boost.Asio and provides I/O services.
- **tcp::acceptor acceptor(io_context, tcp::endpoint(tcp::v4(), 13));**: Creates a TCP acceptor to listen for incoming connections on port 13 (TCP IPv4).
- **acceptor.accept();**: Accepts an incoming connection, creating a new tcp::socket for communication with the client. This is a blocking operation, waiting for a connection.
- **boost::asio::streambuf buffer;**: Creates a streambuf to store data received from the client.
- **boost::asio::read_until(socket, buffer, '\n');**: Reads data from the socket into the buffer until a newline character (\n) is encountered. This is also a blocking operation.
- **std::string message = boost::asio::buffer_cast<const char*>(buffer.data());**: Converts the data in the buffer to a std::string.
- **boost::asio::write(socket, boost::asio::buffer(message));**: Writes the received message back to the client socket (echoing the message).
- **Error Handling:** The try-catch block handles potential exceptions during network operations.

Real-world scenario: Boost.Asio is used in a wide range of high-performance network applications, including network servers, clients, chat applications, and custom network protocols. Its efficiency, cross-platform nature, and asynchronous capabilities make it a popular choice for developing robust and scalable networking solutions in C++. Examples include high-frequency trading platforms, game servers, and communication systems.

14.1.2 Raw Sockets: Low-Level Network Control

Raw sockets provide the most direct and low-level access to network protocols and interfaces in C++. Unlike libraries like Boost.Asio that offer abstractions, raw sockets allow developers to interact directly with network layers, crafting custom network packets and protocols. While powerful, raw socket programming is more complex and often requires a deeper understanding of network protocols and operating system specifics. They are typically used for specialized networking tasks, network analysis tools, and protocol development. As Comer discusses in "Internetworking with TCP/IP, Volume I: Principles, Protocols, and Architecture," understanding raw sockets is crucial for in-depth network protocol analysis and development (Comer, 2018).

Key Features of Raw Sockets:

- **Low-Level Protocol Access:** Raw sockets allow direct access to network protocols like IP, ICMP, TCP, and UDP, enabling developers to craft custom packets and headers.
- **Protocol Development and Analysis:** They are essential for developing new network protocols, network analysis tools (e.g., packet sniffers), and network security applications.
- **Operating System Dependency:** Raw socket programming is highly operating system-dependent. Code written for raw sockets on one OS might not be directly portable to another.
- **Privilege Requirements:** Creating and using raw sockets often requires elevated privileges (e.g., root or administrator access) as they bypass standard operating system network security mechanisms.
- **Complexity:** Raw socket programming is more complex than using higher-level libraries. Developers need to handle packet construction, protocol details, and error handling at a lower level.

Example Scenario (Conceptual): Building a Custom Packet Sniffer (Illustrative - Requires Elevated Privileges)

Creating a fully functional packet sniffer with raw sockets is complex and platform-dependent, often requiring significant system-level programming knowledge and elevated privileges. However, a conceptual outline can illustrate the basic principles.

Conceptual Steps (Illustrative - Not a Complete, Runnable Example):

1. **Create a Raw Socket:** Use the `socket()` system call with `AF_PACKET` (or `AF_INET` with `SOCK_RAW` and specific protocol) to create a raw socket. The exact parameters depend on the desired protocol and operating system.
2. **Bind to Network Interface (Optional):** Bind the raw socket to a specific network interface if you want to capture packets only on that interface.
3. **Set Socket Options (e.g., Promiscuous Mode):** For packet sniffing, set the socket to promiscuous mode to capture all packets on the network interface, not just those destined for the local machine. This typically requires root/administrator privileges.
4. **Receive Packets:** Use `recvfrom()` or similar system calls to receive raw network packets from the socket.
5. **Packet Decoding and Analysis:** Decode the raw packet data to analyze network protocols, headers, and payloads. This requires detailed knowledge of network protocol structures (e.g., Ethernet, IP, TCP, UDP headers).
6. **Display or Process Packets:** Display the captured packet information or process it for network analysis, security monitoring, or other purposes.

Code Snippet (Illustrative - Highly Simplified and Platform-Dependent):

C++

```
// WARNING: Conceptual snippet - not a complete, runnable example.
// Raw socket programming is complex and OS-dependent.
// Requires elevated privileges to run.

#include <sys/socket.h>
#include <netinet/in.h>
#include <netinet/ip.h>
```

```
#include <stdio.h>

int main() {
  int raw_socket = socket(AF_INET, SOCK_RAW, IPPROTO_TCP); //
Example: Raw TCP socket (OS-dependent)
  if (raw_socket == -1) {
    perror("Socket creation failed");
    return 1;
  }

  char buffer[65535]; // Buffer to hold packet data
  sockaddr_in source_addr;
  socklen_t addr_len = sizeof(source_addr);

  printf("Listening for raw packets...\n");

  while (true) {
    int bytes_received = recvfrom(raw_socket, buffer, sizeof(buffer), 0,
(sockaddr*)&source_addr, &addr_len);
    if (bytes_received > 0) {
      iphdr* ip_header = (iphdr*)buffer; // Interpret buffer as IP header
(example)
      printf("Received packet, IP protocol: %u, Source IP: ...\n", ip_header-
>protocol); // Example analysis
      // ... Further packet decoding and analysis ...
    }
  }

  return 0;
}
```

Caution: Raw socket programming is advanced and requires careful handling of network protocols and security considerations. Incorrectly implemented raw socket applications can have security vulnerabilities or disrupt network operations. For most general networking tasks, higher-level libraries like Boost.Asio are recommended due to their ease of use, portability, and safety.

Real-world scenario: Raw sockets are used in network security tools (e.g., Wireshark, Nmap), network protocol analyzers, and specialized network applications that require fine-grained control over network packets. For example, network intrusion detection systems might use raw sockets to monitor network traffic for malicious patterns. Security researchers and network administrators often use raw socket tools for network diagnosis and security auditing.

14.2 HTTP Libraries in C++: Web Communication Simplified

HTTP (Hypertext Transfer Protocol) is the foundation of the World Wide Web, defining how web browsers and servers communicate. In C++, HTTP libraries simplify the process of making HTTP requests (as a client) and handling HTTP requests (as a server). Libraries like cpp-httplib and libcurl provide convenient APIs for working with HTTP, abstracting away the complexities of socket programming and protocol details. They are essential for developing web clients, interacting with RESTful APIs, and building web servers or web-enabled applications in C++. As Fielding and colleagues define in RFC 2616, HTTP is a request-response protocol operating in the application layer of the Internet protocol suite (Fielding et al., 1999).

14.2.1 cpp-httplib: A Lightweight HTTP Library

cpp-httplib is a header-only C++ library for HTTP client and server functionality. It is designed to be lightweight, easy to use, and requires no external dependencies beyond standard C++ libraries. cpp-httplib is well-suited for projects where simplicity and minimal dependencies are prioritized, such as embedded systems, small utilities, or when integrating HTTP capabilities into existing C++ applications without adding heavy framework dependencies.

Key Features of cpp-httplib:

- **Header-Only Library:** cpp-httplib is distributed as a header-only library, simplifying integration into C++ projects. No separate compilation or linking is typically required.
- **HTTP Client and Server:** It provides both HTTP client and server functionalities within a single library.
- **Simple and Intuitive API:** cpp-httplib offers a straightforward and easy-to-use API for making HTTP requests and handling server requests.
- **Modern HTTP Features:** Supports modern HTTP features like HTTPS, Keep-Alive connections, request/response headers, and various HTTP methods (GET, POST, PUT, DELETE, etc.).

- **Lightweight and Minimal Dependencies:** Has minimal dependencies, relying primarily on standard C++ libraries and basic socket functionalities.

Getting Started with cpp-httplib: Making an HTTP GET Request

Let's use cpp-httplib to make an HTTP GET request to a public API endpoint (e.g., a simple JSON placeholder API) and print the response body.

Step-by-step guide:

1. **Download cpp-httplib:** Download the httplib.h header file from the cpp-httplib GitHub repository. It's a single header file library. Place httplib.h in your project directory or in a location where your compiler can find it (e.g., include directory).
2. **Create a Project Directory:** Create a directory for your project (e.g., cppHttplibGetRequest).
3. **Create get_request.cpp:** Create a get_request.cpp file in your project directory with the following code:

C++

```
#include "httplib.h" // Include httplib.h
#include <iostream>

int main() {
  httplib::Client cli("http://jsonplaceholder.typicode.com"); // Create
HTTP client

  auto res = cli.Get("/todos/1"); // Make a GET request to
/todos/1

  if (res) {
    if (res->status == 200) {
      std::cout << "Status: " << res->status << std::endl;
      std::cout << "Body:\n" << res->body << std::endl; // Print
response body
    } else {
      std::cerr << "HTTP Request failed, status code: " << res-
>status << std::endl;
    }
  } else {
    std::cerr << "HTTP Request error" << std::endl;
    auto err = res.error();
```

```
        std::cerr << "Error code: " << err << std::endl;
    }

    return 0;
}
```

4. **Compile and Link (No Linking Needed - Header-Only):** Compile get_request.cpp. Since cpp-httplib is header-only, you typically don't need to link against any libraries.
   Example compilation command (GCC on Linux):
   Bash

   ```bash
   g++ get_request.cpp -o cpp_httplib_get_request -std=c++17
   ```
5. **Run:** Execute the compiled executable (./cpp_httplib_get_request on Linux). The program will make an HTTP GET request to jsonplaceholder.typicode.com/todos/1 and print the HTTP status code and response body (which will be a JSON string).

Code Explanation:

- **#include "httplib.h"**: Includes the httplib.h header file.
- **httplib::Client cli("http://jsonplaceholder.typicode.com");**: Creates an httplib::Client object, specifying the base URL of the API endpoint.
- **auto res = cli.Get("/todos/1");**: Makes an HTTP GET request to the path /todos/1 relative to the base URL. The Get() method returns a httplib::Result object, which represents the HTTP response.
- **if (res)**: Checks if the request was successful (i.e., if res is not null).
- **if (res->status == 200)**: Checks if the HTTP status code is 200 (OK), indicating a successful response.
- **std::cout << "Body:\n" << res->body << std::endl;**: Prints the response body (res->body), which contains the JSON data returned by the API.
- **Error Handling:** The code includes basic error handling to check for request failures and non-200 status codes.

Real-world scenario: cpp-httplib is useful for developing simple HTTP clients and servers in C++ applications. It can be used for tasks like interacting with REST APIs, fetching data from web services, or creating basic web interfaces for command-line tools or embedded systems. Its lightweight nature makes it suitable for resource-constrained environments.

14.2.2 libcurl: A Versatile and Feature-Rich HTTP Library

libcurl is a highly versatile and feature-rich, multi-protocol file transfer library. While it supports many protocols beyond HTTP (FTP, SMTP, etc.), it is widely used as a robust HTTP client library in C++ and other languages. libcurl is known for its extensive feature set, reliability, and wide platform support. It is suitable for complex HTTP interactions, handling various authentication methods, cookies, SSL/TLS, and more. As Stenberg and contributors detail in the libcurl documentation, it is a powerful tool for a wide range of network transfer tasks (Stenberg et al., 2024).

Key Features of libcurl for HTTP:

- **Multi-Protocol Support:** libcurl supports a wide range of protocols, including HTTP, HTTPS, FTP, SMTP, POP3, and more.
- **Feature-Rich HTTP Client:** Offers extensive features for HTTP client development, including support for various HTTP methods, headers, cookies, authentication (Basic, Digest, NTLM, etc.), redirects, proxies, SSL/TLS, and more.
- **Wide Platform Support:** libcurl is highly portable and supports a vast number of platforms, making it suitable for cross-platform applications requiring advanced HTTP capabilities.
- **Performance and Reliability:** libcurl is known for its performance and reliability, having been used in countless applications and systems over many years.
- **C API (with C++ Bindings):** libcurl is primarily a C library, but C++ bindings are available, allowing for integration into C++ projects.

Getting Started with libcurl: Making an HTTPS GET Request

Let's use libcurl to make an HTTPS GET request to a secure API endpoint (e.g., `https://api.github.com/users/github`) and print the response body.

Step-by-step guide:

1. **Install libcurl:** Ensure you have libcurl development libraries installed on your system. Installation methods vary depending on your operating system. For example, on Ubuntu: `sudo apt-get install libcurl4-openssl-dev`. On macOS using Homebrew: `brew install curl`. On Windows, you might need to download libcurl

binaries and development files and configure your compiler to link against them.

2. **Create a Project Directory:** Create a directory for your project (e.g., LibcurlHttpsGetRequest).
3. **Create https_get.cpp:** Create a https_get.cpp file in your project directory with the following code:

```
C++

#include <iostream>
#include <curl/curl.h> // Include curl header

size_t WriteCallback(char *contents, size_t size, size_t nmemb,
std::string *output) {
    size_t total_size = size * nmemb;
    output->append(contents, total_size);
    return total_size;
}

int main() {
    CURL *curl;
    CURLcode res;
    std::string response_body;

    curl_global_init(CURL_GLOBAL_DEFAULT); // Initialize curl

    curl = curl_easy_init();
    if (curl) {
        curl_easy_setopt(curl, CURLOPT_URL,
"https://api.github.com/users/github"); // Set URL
        curl_easy_setopt(curl, CURLOPT_WRITEFUNCTION,
WriteCallback); // Set write callback
        curl_easy_setopt(curl, CURLOPT_WRITEDATA,
&response_body); // Set write callback data

        res = curl_easy_perform(curl); // Perform the request

        if (res == CURLE_OK) {
            long http_code = 0;
            curl_easy_getinfo(curl, CURLINFO_RESPONSE_CODE,
&http_code);
            std::cout << "Status: " << http_code << std::endl;
            std::cout << "Body:\n" << response_body << std::endl; //
Print response body
        } else {
```

```
        std::cerr << "curl_easy_perform() failed: " <<
curl_easy_strerror(res) << std::endl;
      }

      curl_easy_cleanup(curl); // Cleanup curl object
    }
    curl_global_cleanup(); // Global cleanup

    return 0;
}
```

4. **Compile and Link:** Compile https_get.cpp and link with the libcurl library. The compilation and linking commands will depend on your operating system and compiler.
   Example compilation command (GCC on Linux):
   Bash

   ```
   g++ https_get.cpp -o libcurl_https_get -lcurl -std=c++17
   ```
5. **Run:** Execute the compiled executable (./libcurl_https_get on Linux). The program will make an HTTPS GET request to api.github.com/users/github and print the HTTP status code and response body (JSON data).

Code Explanation:

- **#include <curl/curl.h>**: Includes the libcurl header file.
- WriteCallback **Function:** A callback function (WriteCallback) is defined to handle the response data received from the server. libcurl calls this function as data is received. It appends the received data to the response_body string.
- **curl_global_init(CURL_GLOBAL_DEFAULT);**: Initializes libcurl.
- **curl = curl_easy_init();**: Initializes a libcurl "easy" handle, which is used for performing individual HTTP requests.
- **curl_easy_setopt(curl, CURLOPT_URL, "https://api.github.com/users/github");**: Sets the URL for the HTTP request.
- **curl_easy_setopt(curl, CURLOPT_WRITEFUNCTION, WriteCallback);**: Sets the write callback function to WriteCallback.
- **curl_easy_setopt(curl, CURLOPT_WRITEDATA, &response_body);**: Sets the data pointer that will be passed to the write callback function (&response_body).
- **res = curl_easy_perform(curl);**: Performs the HTTP request.
- **if (res == CURLE_OK)**: Checks if the request was successful (CURLE_OK indicates success).

- **curl_easy_getinfo(curl, CURLINFO_RESPONSE_CODE, &http_code);**: Gets the HTTP response code.
- **std::cout << "Body:\n" << response_body << std::endl;**: Prints the response body.
- **Error Handling:** The code checks for errors from curl_easy_perform() and prints an error message if the request fails.
- **curl_easy_cleanup(curl);**: Cleans up the libcurl "easy" handle.
- **curl_global_cleanup();**: Performs global libcurl cleanup.

Real-world scenario: libcurl is a workhorse in network programming, used in countless applications for various network transfer tasks, including HTTP communication. Web browsers, download managers, command-line tools like curl, and many backend systems rely on libcurl for its robust and feature-rich HTTP client capabilities. It is often used when complex HTTP interactions, protocol features, and broad protocol support are required.

14.3 Writing Web Applications with C++: Frameworks for Server-Side Development

While C++ is often used for backend services and APIs, it can also be used to build complete web applications, including server-side logic and dynamic content generation. Web application frameworks in C++ provide structure, abstractions, and tools to simplify web development, handling routing, request processing, templating, and other common web development tasks. Frameworks like Crow and CppCMS offer different approaches to C++ web development, balancing performance, ease of use, and feature sets.

14.3.1 Crow: A Lightweight and Fast Web Framework

Crow is a lightweight, header-only C++ web framework that emphasizes speed and ease of use. It is designed for building RESTful APIs and web applications with minimal overhead. Crow's simplicity and performance make it suitable for microservices, backend APIs, and situations where a fast and lean web framework is desired. As the Crow documentation highlights, it aims to provide a "C++ microframework for web" (Crow Framework, 2024).

Key Features of Crow:

- **Header-Only:** Crow is a header-only library, simplifying project integration and deployment.
- **Lightweight and Fast:** Designed for performance and minimal overhead.
- **RESTful API Support:** Well-suited for building RESTful APIs and web services.
- **Routing:** Provides a simple and expressive routing system for mapping URLs to C++ handlers.
- **Request and Response Handling:** Simplifies handling HTTP requests and generating responses.
- **JSON Support:** Built-in support for JSON serialization and deserialization.
- **Middleware Support:** Allows for adding middleware to handle request processing steps (e.g., authentication, logging).

Getting Started with Crow: A Simple "Hello World" Web Application

Let's create a basic "Hello World" web application using Crow that responds to HTTP GET requests at the root path (/).

Step-by-step guide:

1. **Download Crow:** Download the crow_all.h header file from the Crow GitHub repository. It's a single header file library. Place crow_all.h in your project directory or in a location where your compiler can find it (e.g., include directory).
2. **Create a Project Directory:** Create a directory for your project (e.g., CrowHelloWorld).
3. **Create server.cpp:** Create a server.cpp file in your project directory with the following code:

```
C++

#include "crow_all.h" // Include crow_all.h

int main() {
  crow::SimpleApp app; // Create Crow application

  CROW_ROUTE(app, "/")
  ([](){
    return "Hello World from Crow!"; // Return "Hello World!" for
root path
```

```
    });

    app.port(18080).multithreaded().run(); // Run server on port 18080
}
```

4. **Compile and Link (No Linking Needed - Header-Only):** Compile `server.cpp`. Since Crow is header-only, you typically don't need to link against any libraries.
   Example compilation command (GCC on Linux):
   Bash
   ```
   g++ server.cpp -o crow_hello_world -std=c++17
   ```
5. **Run the Server:** Execute the compiled executable (`./crow_hello_world` on Linux). The server will start listening on port 18080.
6. **Access in a Web Browser or with `curl`:** Open a web browser and navigate to `http://localhost:18080/` or use `curl` from a terminal.
   Using a web browser: Open `http://localhost:18080/` in your browser. You should see "Hello World from Crow!" displayed in the browser.

   Using `curl`:
   Bash
   ```
   curl http://localhost:18080/
   Hello World from Crow!
   ```

Code Explanation:

- **`#include "crow_all.h"`**: Includes the `crow_all.h` header file, which includes all Crow components.
- **`crow::SimpleApp app;`**: Creates a `crow::SimpleApp` object, which represents the Crow web application.
- **`CROW_ROUTE(app, "/")`**: Defines a route for the root path (`/`). The `CROW_ROUTE` macro associates a URL path with a handler function (lambda function in this case).
- **`([](){ return "Hello World from Crow!"; });`**: This is a lambda function that serves as the handler for GET requests to the root path. It simply returns the string "Hello World from Crow!".
- **`app.port(18080).multithreaded().run();`**: Configures and starts the Crow web server.
  - `app.port(18080)`: Sets the server to listen on port 18080.
  - `.multithreaded()`: Enables multithreading for handling multiple requests concurrently.

   - .run(): Starts the web server and begins listening for incoming HTTP requests.

Real-world scenario: Crow is suitable for building microservices, lightweight APIs, and web utilities where performance and simplicity are key. It can be used for backend services in web applications, RESTful API endpoints, and embedded web servers. Its header-only nature and minimal dependencies make it easy to deploy and integrate into various environments.

14.3.2 CppCMS: A Feature-Rich Web Application Framework

CppCMS (C++ Content Management System) is a more comprehensive and feature-rich C++ web application framework compared to Crow. It provides a broader set of functionalities for building complex web applications, including templating, form handling, session management, and more. CppCMS is designed for performance and scalability, suitable for building dynamic websites, web portals, and content-driven web applications. As Kucherawy details in the CppCMS documentation, it aims to be a "high performance C++ Web Development Framework" (CppCMS Framework, 2024).

Key Features of CppCMS:

- **Feature-Rich Framework:** CppCMS offers a wide range of features for web application development, including:
   - **Templating Engine:** For generating dynamic HTML content.
   - **Form Handling:** For processing user input from web forms.
   - **Session Management:** For managing user sessions and state.
   - **Localization (i18n):** Support for internationalization and localization.
   - **URL Dispatcher:** A flexible URL routing system.
   - **Cache System:** Built-in caching mechanisms for performance optimization.
   - **ORM (Object-Relational Mapping):** For database interaction (optional).
- **Performance-Oriented:** Designed for high performance and scalability.

- **Asynchronous Request Handling:** Supports asynchronous request processing for improved concurrency.
- **Mature and Stable:** CppCMS is a mature and stable framework that has been used in various web projects.

Example Scenario (Conceptual): Building a Simple Web Page with CppCMS (Illustrative - Requires Setup)

Creating a full CppCMS application requires more setup and project structure compared to header-only frameworks. A conceptual outline and code snippet can illustrate the basic principles of CppCMS.

Conceptual Steps (Illustrative - Not a Complete, Runnable Example):

1. **Install CppCMS:** Install the CppCMS library and development tools on your system. Installation typically involves compiling CppCMS from source or using pre-built packages if available for your distribution.
2. **Create a CppCMS Project Structure:** CppCMS projects typically have a specific directory structure for controllers, views (templates), and configuration files.
3. **Define a Controller:** Create a C++ class that inherits from `cppcms::application` to act as a controller for your web application. Controllers handle incoming HTTP requests and generate responses.
4. **Implement Actions (Request Handlers):** Define action methods within your controller class to handle specific URL paths or HTTP methods (e.g., `index()` action for the root path).
5. **Create Views (Templates):** Create template files (e.g., using CppCMS's template engine) to define the HTML structure of your web pages. Templates can embed C++ code to dynamically generate content.
6. **Configure URL Dispatcher:** Configure the URL dispatcher to map URLs to controller actions.
7. **Run the CppCMS Application:** Compile and run your CppCMS application, which will start a web server and handle incoming requests.

Code Snippet (Illustrative - Highly Simplified Controller Example):

```
C++

// WARNING: Conceptual snippet - not a complete, runnable example.
// CppCMS setup and project structure are more involved.

#include <cppcms/application.h>
#include <cppcms/http_response.h>

class HelloWorldApp : public cppcms::application {
public:
  void main(std::string /*url*/) override {
    response().out() << "<html>\n"
                "<head><title>Hello CppCMS</title></head>\n"
                "<body>\n"
                "  <h1>Hello World from CppCMS!</h1>\n"
                "</body>\n"
                "</html>\n";
  }
};

int main() {
  try {
    cppcms::service srv(cppcms::json_config("config.json")); // Load config
(config.json needs to be created)

srv.applications_pool().mount(cppcms::application_factory<HelloWorldApp>(
));
    srv.run();
  } catch (std::exception const &e) {
    std::cerr << e.what() << std::endl;
  }
  return 0;
}
```

Caution: Building a complete CppCMS application involves more steps than this simplified example. You would need to set up a proper project structure, create a configuration file (`config.json`), compile and link against CppCMS libraries, and potentially use a more sophisticated build system (like CMake). Refer to the CppCMS documentation for detailed setup and usage instructions.

Real-world scenario: CppCMS is used for building high-performance web applications, content management systems, and web portals where performance, scalability, and a comprehensive feature set are important. It is suitable for projects requiring dynamic content generation, database interaction, and robust web framework capabilities. While perhaps less widely adopted than some other web frameworks, CppCMS offers a powerful option for C++ developers building web applications.

14.4 Conclusion: C++ in the Web and Networking Landscape

C++ plays a significant role in web and networking, offering a range of tools and libraries for various tasks. From low-level socket programming with Boost.Asio and raw sockets to high-level web application development with frameworks like Crow and CppCMS, C++ provides the performance, control, and flexibility needed for building robust and efficient network solutions. For Computer Technology students and educators, mastering these C++ networking and web development skills opens doors to a wide array of opportunities in areas ranging from backend services and APIs to high-performance web applications and specialized network tools. Choosing the right approach and library depends on the specific project requirements, balancing factors like performance needs, complexity, cross-platform requirements, and the desired level of abstraction.

Chapter 15

Deploying C++ Applications: From Development to Distribution

The journey of a C++ application extends beyond development and testing to the critical phase of deployment, where the software is packaged, distributed, and made available to end-users. Effective deployment strategies are paramount for ensuring a seamless user experience, maintaining software integrity, and facilitating updates and maintenance. For Computer Technology students and educators, understanding the intricacies of C++ application deployment is essential, as it bridges the gap between theoretical coding and real-world software delivery. This section explores key aspects of C++ application deployment, encompassing packaging techniques for different operating systems, cross-compilation for platform versatility, the use of containerization with Docker for simplified deployment, and best practices for software distribution to ensure a robust and user-friendly delivery process.

15.1 Packaging Applications: Tailoring for Target Platforms

Packaging applications is the process of bundling all necessary components—executables, libraries, configuration files, and resources—into a single distributable file format tailored for a specific operating system. This ensures that the application can be easily installed and run on the target platform without requiring users to manually manage dependencies or configurations. Different operating systems employ distinct packaging formats, and understanding these formats is crucial for C++ developers aiming for cross-platform compatibility or platform-specific distribution. As Loukides and Oram note in "Building Open Source Hardware," proper packaging is essential for user adoption and ease of distribution (Loukides & Oram, 2010).

15.1.1 MSI (Microsoft Installer): Standard for Windows

MSI (Microsoft Installer) is the standard installation package format for Windows-based applications. MSI packages are designed to provide a robust and consistent installation experience, handling file copying, registry modifications, and dependency management. Creating MSI packages for C++ applications ensures seamless integration with the Windows environment and simplifies installation for Windows users.

Creating an MSI Package for a C++ Application using WiX Toolset

WiX (Windows Installer XML) Toolset is a powerful, open-source toolset for creating MSI installation packages. It uses XML-based configuration files to define the installation process.

Step-by-step guide:

1. **Install WiX Toolset:** Download and install the WiX Toolset from the official WiX website. Choose the appropriate installer for your Windows version.
2. **Create a Project Directory:** Create a directory for your MSI project (e.g., `MyCppAppInstaller`). Inside this directory, create a subdirectory named `Source` and place your C++ application's executable (`MyCppApp.exe`) and any required DLLs or resources within the `Source` subdirectory.

3. **Create Product.wxs:** Create a Product.wxs file (a WiX XML source file) in your project directory. This file will define the MSI package structure. Example Product.wxs content:

XML

```
<?xml version="1.0" encoding="UTF-8"?>
<Wix xmlns="http://schemas.microsoft.com/wix/2006/wi">
  <Product Id="*" Name="My C++ Application" Version="1.0.0.0"
Manufacturer="Your Manufacturer" UpgradeCode="YOUR-
UPGRADE-GUID-HERE">
    <Package InstallerVersion="200" Compressed="yes"
InstallScope="perMachine" />

    <MajorUpgrade DowngradeErrorMessage="A newer version of
[ProductName] is already installed." />
    <MediaTemplate EmbedCab="yes" CompressionLevel="high"
EmbedCompressed="yes" />

    <Feature Id="ProductFeature" Title="Main Application"
Level="1">
      <ComponentGroupRef Id="ProductComponents" />
    </Feature>
  </Product>

  <Fragment>
    <Directory Id="TARGETDIR" Name="SourceDir">
      <Directory Id="ProgramFilesFolder">
        <Directory Id="INSTALLFOLDER"
Name="MyCppApp">
          <ComponentGroup Id="ProductComponents">
            <Component Id="MyCppAppExeComponent"
Guid="YOUR-COMPONENT-GUID-EXE">
              <File Id="MyCppAppExe"
Source="$(var.ProjectDir)\Source\MyCppApp.exe" KeyPath="yes"
/>
            </Component>
            </ComponentGroup>
        </Directory>
      </Directory>
    </Directory>
  </Fragment>
</Wix>
```

Important:

- Replace "YOUR-UPGRADE-GUID-HERE" with a unique GUID (Globally Unique Identifier) for your application's UpgradeCode. Generate a new GUID using a GUID generator tool (many are available online or within development environments like Visual Studio). This GUID is crucial for upgrades and uninstallation.
- Replace "YOUR-COMPONENT-GUID-EXE" with a unique GUID for the MyCppAppExeComponent Component. Generate a new GUID.
- Adjust Name, Manufacturer, Version, and Directory names as needed for your application.
- Add more <Component> elements within <ComponentGroup Id="ProductComponents"> to include any DLLs, resource files, or other components your application requires. Ensure each <Component> has a unique Guid.

4. **Compile Product.wxs to MSI:** Open a command prompt in your project directory (where Product.wxs is located). Use the WiX compiler (candle.exe) and linker (light.exe) to compile Product.wxs into an MSI file. You might need to adjust paths based on your WiX installation directory.

Bash

```bash
"%WIX%\candle.exe" Product.wxs -arch x64  -dProjectDir="." -o obj\
"%WIX%\light.exe" obj\Product.wixobj -o MyCppAppInstaller.msi
```

   - "%WIX%\candle.exe" and "%WIX%\light.exe": Assume the WiX Toolset binaries are in the %WIX% environment variable. If not, you'll need to provide the full paths to candle.exe and light.exe (typically in C:\Program Files (x86)\WiX Toolset v[version]\bin).
   - -arch x64: Specifies the target architecture (e.g., x64 for 64-bit Windows). Adjust as needed (e.g., -arch x86 for 32-bit).
   - -dProjectDir=".": Defines a preprocessor variable ProjectDir to the current directory (.). This is used in Product.wxs to refer to the project's source files.
   - -o obj\: Specifies the output directory for object files (obj).
   - -o MyCppAppInstaller.msi: Specifies the output MSI file name (MyCppAppInstaller.msi).

5. **Run the MSI Installer:** After successful compilation, you will find MyCppAppInstaller.msi in your project directory. Double-

click this MSI file to run the installer and install your C++ application.

Code Explanation:

- Product.wxs **(WiX XML):** Defines the MSI package structure using XML.
    - <Product>: Root element, defines product information (Name, Version, Manufacturer, UpgradeCode).
    - <Package>: Defines package properties (InstallerVersion, Compressed, InstallScope).
    - <MajorUpgrade>: Handles major upgrades, preventing downgrades.
    - <MediaTemplate>: Configures media embedding and compression.
    - <Feature>: Defines installable features (in this case, a single "Main Application" feature).
    - <ComponentGroupRef>: References a group of components to be installed.
    - <Directory Id="TARGETDIR">...: Defines the directory structure for installation. TARGETDIR is the root, ProgramFilesFolder refers to the Program Files directory,[1] and INSTALLFOLDER is the application's installation directory within Program Files.
    - <ComponentGroup Id="ProductComponents">...: Defines a group of components to be installed.
    - <Component Id="MyCppAppExeComponent">...: Defines a component for the application's executable.
        - <File Id="MyCppAppExe" Source="...">: Specifies the file to be installed (MyCppApp.exe) and its source location ($(var.ProjectDir)\Source\MyCppApp.exe). KeyPath="yes" indicates[2] this file is crucial for component detection.
- candle.exe **(WiX Compiler):** Compiles the Product.wxs XML source file into an object file (Product.wixobj).
- light.exe **(WiX Linker):** Links the object file and creates the final MSI installer file (MyCppAppInstaller.msi).

Real-world scenario: MSI packages are the standard for distributing Windows desktop applications. Software vendors and IT departments widely use MSI for deploying applications across Windows environments due to its robust installation, uninstallation, and update capabilities. Enterprise deployment tools often rely on MSI packages for automated software distribution and management.

15.1.2 DEB (Debian Package): Package Format for Debian and Ubuntu

DEB is the package format used by Debian-based Linux distributions, including Ubuntu, Linux Mint, and others. DEB packages are archives that contain application files, metadata (package name, version, dependencies), and installation scripts. Creating DEB packages for C++ applications ensures easy installation and integration within Debian-based Linux systems.

Creating a DEB Package for a C++ Application using dpkg-deb
dpkg-deb is a command-line tool used to create and manipulate DEB packages.

Step-by-step guide:

1. **Install dpkg-dev:** Ensure you have the dpkg-dev package installed on your Debian-based system.
   Bash

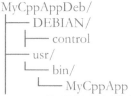

   ```
   sudo apt-get update
   sudo apt-get install dpkg-dev
   ```
2. **Create a Project Directory:** Create a directory for your DEB project (e.g., MyCppAppDeb). Inside this directory, create the following structure:

   - DEBIAN/: This directory *must* be named DEBIAN (all caps) and contains control files for the package.
     - control: This file contains metadata about the package (package name, version, description, dependencies).
   - usr/bin/: This is where the application executable will be installed (typically /usr/bin/ on Linux systems).
     - MyCppApp: Place your compiled C++ executable (e.g., MyCppApp) here. Ensure it's executable (chmod +x usr/bin/MyCppApp).

3. **Create DEBIAN/control file:** Create a control file inside the DEBIAN directory with the following content. Adjust the values as needed for your application.

```
Package: mycppapp
Version: 1.0.0
Architecture: amd64
Maintainer: Your Name <your.email@example.com>
Description: My C++ Application
This is a sample DEB package for a C++ application.
```

Explanation of control file fields:

- Package: The name of your package (lowercase, no spaces, e.g., mycppapp). This is used for installation and removal.
- Version: The version of your application (e.g., 1.0.0).
- Architecture: The target architecture (e.g., amd64 for 64-bit x86, i386 for 32-bit x86, arm64, armhf).
- Maintainer: Your name and email address.
- Description: A short description of your application. The indented lines after the first line are a long description.
- You can add more fields to the control file, such as Depends (for package dependencies), Section, Priority, etc., as needed. Refer to the Debian Policy Manual for details.

4. **Build the DEB Package:** Open a terminal in the MyCppAppDeb directory (the directory containing the DEBIAN directory). Use the dpkg-deb command to build the DEB package.

Bash

```
dpkg-deb --build MyCppAppDeb
```

This command will create a DEB package file named MyCppAppDeb.deb in the parent directory of MyCppAppDeb.

5. **Install the DEB Package (Optional):** You can test the DEB package by installing it using dpkg -i or apt install ./MyCppAppDeb.deb.

Bash

```
sudo dpkg -i MyCppAppDeb.deb
# Or using apt:
# sudo apt install ./MyCppAppDeb.deb
```

This will install MyCppApp executable to /usr/bin/. You can then run it from the terminal by typing MyCppApp. To uninstall, use sudo apt-get remove mycppapp.

Code Explanation:

- **DEB Package Structure:** The DEB package is essentially an archive with a specific directory structure. The DEBIAN directory is crucial and contains control files. The usr/ directory (and other standard Linux directory prefixes like opt/, etc/, var/) mirrors the filesystem structure where files will be installed.
- **DEBIAN/control File:** This file provides essential metadata about the package, allowing package managers like apt and dpkg to manage the package correctly.
- **dpkg-deb --build MyCppAppDeb:** This command uses dpkg-deb to create a DEB archive from the MyCppAppDeb directory. It packages the contents of MyCppAppDeb into a MyCppAppDeb.deb file.

Real-world scenario: DEB packages are fundamental for software distribution on Debian and Ubuntu systems, which are widely used for servers, desktops, and embedded systems. Software repositories (like Ubuntu repositories) distribute software as DEB packages. Many Linux applications, server software, and development tools are distributed as DEB packages for Debian-based distributions.

15.1.3 RPM (RPM Package Manager): Package Format for Red Hat and Fedora

RPM (RPM Package Manager, originally Red Hat Package Manager) is another prominent package format used by Red Hat Enterprise Linux, Fedora, CentOS, SUSE Linux Enterprise, and other Linux distributions. RPM packages, similar to DEB, contain application files, metadata, and installation scripts. Creating RPM packages is essential for distributing C++ applications on RPM-based Linux systems.

Creating an RPM Package for a C++ Application using rpmbuild
rpmbuild is the primary tool for building RPM packages. RPM building is typically more structured than DEB building and relies on a "spec file" to define the package.

Step-by-step guide:

1. **Install rpm-build:** Ensure you have the rpm-build package installed on your RPM-based system (e.g., Fedora, CentOS, Red Hat).
   Bash

```
sudo dnf install rpm-build  # For Fedora, CentOS, RHEL (using dnf)
# sudo yum install rpm-build  # For older CentOS, RHEL (using yum)
```

2. **Create RPM Build Directories:** RPM build process uses a specific directory structure. Create the necessary directories in your home directory (or another suitable location).

   Bash

   ```
   mkdir -p ~/rpmbuild/{BUILD,RPMS,SOURCES,SPECS,SRPMS}
   ```

   - BUILD/: Used for the build process (compiling, etc.).
   - RPMS/: Where the built binary RPM packages (.rpm files) are placed.
   - SOURCES/: Where source code archives, patches, and other source files are placed.
   - SPECS/: Where spec files (.spec files) are placed. Spec files define how the RPM package is built.
3. **Place Application Files in SOURCES/:** Place your compiled C++ executable (MyCppApp) and any required resources in the ~/rpmbuild/SOURCES/ directory. You can also create a source archive (e.g., .tar.gz) containing your application files and place that in SOURCES/. For this example, let's assume you place the executable directly in SOURCES/ and name it MyCppApp.
4. **Create a Spec File (.spec):** Create a spec file (e.g., mycppapp.spec) in the ~/rpmbuild/SPECS/ directory. This file defines how RPM should build your package. Example mycppapp.spec content:

   RPM spec files

   ```
   Name:        mycppapp
   Version:     1.0.0
   Release:     1%{?dist}
   Summary:      My C++ Application

   License:     GPLv3+  ; Or your application's license
   URL:         http://example.com/mycppapp ; Replace with your
   application's URL
   Source0:      %{name}  ; Assumes executable is directly in
   SOURCES/ and named 'mycppapp'

   BuildArch:     x86_64 ; Or 'i686', 'noarch', etc.

   %description
   This is a sample RPM package for a C++ application.

   %prep
   ```

```
# No preparation needed for this simple example

%build
# No build step needed as we are packaging a pre-compiled executable

%install
mkdir -p %{buildroot}%{_bindir}
install -m 0755 %{SOURCE0} %{buildroot}%{_bindir}/%{name}

%files
%{_bindir}/%{name}

%changelog
* Thu Mar 07 2025 Your Name <your.email@example.com> - 1.0.0-1
- Initial package build.
```

Explanation of Spec File Sections:

- Name, Version, Release, Summary, License, URL, Source0, BuildArch: Metadata about the package (name, version, release number, summary, license, URL, source file, architecture).
- %description: Long description of the package.
- %prep: Section for preparation steps (e.g., unpacking source archives). Empty in this example.
- %build: Section for build steps (compiling the application). Empty in this example as we are packaging a pre-compiled executable.
- %install: Section for installation steps.
  - mkdir -p %{buildroot}%{_bindir}: Creates the destination directory for binaries (%{_bindir} typically expands to /usr/bin). %{buildroot} is a temporary root directory used during package building.
  - install -m 0755 %{SOURCE0} %{buildroot}%{_bindir}/%{name}: Installs the executable (%{SOURCE0}, which is mycppapp from SOURCES/) to the destination binary directory, making it executable (-m 0755).
- %files: Section that lists the files included in the RPM package.
  - %{_bindir}/%{name}: Includes the installed executable.
- %changelog: Changelog information for the package.

5. **Build the RPM Package:** Open a terminal and use the rpmbuild command to build the RPM package from the spec file.
   Bash

   ```
   rpmbuild -ba ~/rpmbuild/SPECS/mycppapp.spec
   ```
   This command will build both binary RPM (.rpm) and source RPM (.src.rpm) packages. The binary RPM package (mycppapp-1.0.0-1.[architecture].rpm) will be placed in ~/rpmbuild/RPMS/[architecture]/ (e.g., ~/rpmbuild/RPMS/x86_64/).
6. **Install the RPM Package (Optional):** You can test the RPM package by installing it using rpm -i or yum localinstall or dnf install.
   Bash

   ```
   sudo rpm -i ~/rpmbuild/RPMS/x86_64/mycppapp-1.0.0-
   1.x86_64.rpm
   # Or using yum/dnf:
   # sudo yum localinstall ~/rpmbuild/RPMS/x86_64/mycppapp-1.0.0-
   1.x86_64.rpm
   # sudo dnf install ~/rpmbuild/RPMS/x86_64/mycppapp-1.0.0-
   1.x86_64.rpm
   ```

   This will install MyCppApp executable to /usr/bin/. You can then run it from the terminal by typing mycppapp. To uninstall, use sudo rpm -e mycppapp or sudo yum remove mycppapp or sudo dnf remove mycppapp.

Code Explanation:

- **RPM Build Directory Structure:** RPM build process relies on a predefined directory structure (rpmbuild/BUILD, RPMS, SOURCES, SPECS).
- **Spec File (.spec):** The spec file is the central control file for RPM building. It defines package metadata, build and install steps, and the list of files to include in the package.
- **rpmbuild -ba ~/rpmbuild/SPECS/mycppapp.spec:** This command uses rpmbuild to build the RPM package based on the instructions in the mycppapp.spec file. -ba option means "build both binary and source RPMs".

Real-world scenario: RPM packages are the standard for distributing software on Red Hat-based Linux distributions, which are widely used in enterprise environments and for servers. Red Hat, Fedora, CentOS, and SUSE repositories distribute software as RPM packages. Many enterprise Linux applications, server software, and development tools are distributed as RPM packages for RPM-based distributions.

15.2 Cross-Compilation Techniques: Building for Different Architectures

Cross-compilation is the process of compiling code on one platform (the host system) to create executables that will run on a different platform (the target system). This is essential when developing C++ applications for embedded systems, mobile devices, or platforms different from the development environment. Cross-compilation allows developers to build applications for various architectures without needing to set up native build environments for each target platform. As Yaghmour explains in "Building Embedded Linux Systems," cross-compilation is a cornerstone of embedded systems development (Yaghmour, 2003).

15.2.1 Toolchains and Setups for Cross-Compilation

Cross-compilation relies on specialized toolchains – sets of compilers, linkers, and utilities specifically built to target a particular architecture. A cross-compilation toolchain typically includes:

- **Cross-Compiler:** A compiler that runs on the host system but generates machine code for the target architecture (e.g., arm-linux-gnueabihf-g++ for ARM Linux).
- **Cross-Linker:** A linker that links object files compiled for the target architecture.
- **Target System Libraries:** Libraries (e.g., standard C++ library, system libraries) compiled for the target architecture. These are often provided as part of the toolchain or need to be obtained separately.
- **Sysroot:** A directory containing the target system's root filesystem, including libraries and headers. This is used during compilation and linking to resolve dependencies against the target system's environment.

Conceptual Example: Cross-Compiling for ARM Linux using GCC

Let's conceptually outline cross-compiling a simple "Hello World" C++ program for ARM Linux from an x86-64 Linux host.

Conceptual Steps:

1. **Obtain an ARM Cross-Compilation Toolchain:** Download or build an ARM cross-compilation toolchain for your host system. Pre-built toolchains are often available from Linux distribution repositories or toolchain providers (e.g., Linaro, ARM). For example, on Debian/Ubuntu, you might install a toolchain like `gcc-arm-linux-gnueabihf`.
   Bash
   ```
   sudo apt-get update
   sudo apt-get install gcc-arm-linux-gnueabihf g++-arm-linux-gnueabihf
   ```
2. **Create `hello.cpp`:** Create a simple `hello.cpp` file:
   C++
   ```
   #include <iostream>

   int main() {
     std::cout << "Hello ARM Linux from cross-compiled C++!" <<
   std::endl;
     return 0;
   }
   ```
3. **Cross-Compile using the Toolchain:** Use the ARM cross-compiler (`arm-linux-gnueabihf-g++`) to compile `hello.cpp`. You might need to specify the sysroot and other compiler/linker flags depending on your toolchain and target system.
   Bash
   ```
   arm-linux-gnueabihf-g++ hello.cpp -o hello_arm -static # Example
   command
   ```
   - `arm-linux-gnueabihf-g++`: The ARM cross-compiler.
   - `hello.cpp`: Source file.
   - `-o hello_arm`: Output executable name (`hello_arm`).
   - `-static`: (Optional, for simplicity in this example) Statically link libraries to avoid runtime dependency issues on the target system (for a basic example). In real-world scenarios, you might need to handle dynamic linking and library dependencies more carefully.

   - You might need to add flags like --sysroot=[path-to-sysroot] to specify the target system's sysroot if your toolchain requires it.
4. **Transfer and Run on ARM Target:** Transfer the cross-compiled executable hello_arm to your ARM Linux target system (e.g., using scp, adb push for Android, etc.). Make it executable (chmod +x hello_arm) and run it on the ARM target.

Bash

```
./hello_arm
```

You should see the output "Hello ARM Linux from cross-compiled C++!" on the ARM target system.

Code Explanation:

- **Cross-Compiler (arm-linux-gnueabihf-g++):** Replaces the standard host compiler (g++). It's configured to generate ARM architecture machine code.
- -static **(Optional):** In this simplified example, static linking is used to bundle all necessary libraries into the executable. For more complex applications, you'd typically use dynamic linking and ensure that required shared libraries are available on the target system.
- **Sysroot (Potentially Required):** For more complex projects, you might need to specify the sysroot to tell the compiler and linker where to find the target system's libraries and headers. The sysroot path depends on your toolchain and target system setup.

Real-world scenario: Cross-compilation is essential for developing software for embedded systems (like Raspberry Pi, IoT devices), mobile platforms (Android, iOS), and game consoles where the development environment is often different from the target platform. Embedded Linux development, Android NDK development, and game development for consoles heavily rely on cross-compilation toolchains.

15.2.2 CMake for Cross-Compilation: Managing Build Systems

CMake is a cross-platform build system generator that can simplify cross-compilation setup. CMake can be configured to use cross-compilation toolchains and manage build processes for different target architectures.

Using CMake for Cross-Compilation
Step-by-step guide:

1. **Install CMake:** Ensure you have CMake installed on your host system.
   Bash

   ```
   sudo apt-get install cmake  # Debian/Ubuntu
   brew install cmake          # macOS (Homebrew)
   # ... (Windows - download from CMake website)
   ```
2. **Create a Project Directory:** Create a directory for your CMake project (e.g., CMakeCrossCompile).
3. **Create CMakeLists.txt:** Create a CMakeLists.txt file in your project directory. Example CMakeLists.txt for a simple executable:
   CMake

   ```
   cmake_minimum_required(VERSION 3.15) # Or your required
   CMake version
   project(HelloCrossCompile)

   add_executable(hello_crosscompile hello.cpp)
   ```
4. **Create a Toolchain File (arm-linux-gnueabihf.cmake):** Create a CMake toolchain file (e.g., arm-linux-gnueabihf.cmake) in your project directory or a location CMake can find. This file describes the cross-compilation toolchain. Example arm-linux-gnueabihf.cmake for an ARM Linux toolchain:

   CMake

   ```
   set(CMAKE_SYSTEM_NAME Linux)
   set(CMAKE_SYSTEM_PROCESSOR arm)
   set(CMAKE_SYSTEM_VERSION 1) # Or your target system
   version

   set(CMAKE_C_COMPILER   arm-linux-gnueabihf-gcc)
   set(CMAKE_CXX_COMPILER arm-linux-gnueabihf-g++)

   # Set sysroot if needed (adjust path accordingly)
   # set(CMAKE_SYSROOT /path/to/your/arm-linux-gnueabihf-
   sysroot)

   set(CMAKE_FIND_ROOT_PATH_MODE_PROGRAM NEVER)
   set(CMAKE_FIND_ROOT_PATH_MODE_LIBRARY ONLY)
   set(CMAKE_FIND_ROOT_PATH_MODE_INCLUDE ONLY)
   set(CMAKE_FIND_ROOT_PATH_MODE_PACKAGE ONLY)
   ```
   - Adjust CMAKE_C_COMPILER, CMAKE_CXX_COMPILER, and CMAKE_SYSROOT

paths to match your toolchain installation. The example assumes the toolchain executables are in your PATH.
    - CMAKE_FIND_ROOT_PATH_MODE_*: These settings control how CMake searches for libraries and headers. NEVER for host programs, ONLY for target libraries and includes.

5. **Create hello.cpp:** Create the hello.cpp source file (same as in the previous example).
6. **Configure and Build with CMake:** Open a terminal in your project directory. Create a build directory (e.g., build_arm). Configure CMake, specifying the toolchain file. Then build the project.

   Bash

   ```
   mkdir build_arm
   cd build_arm
   cmake .. -DCMAKE_TOOLCHAIN_FILE=../arm-linux-
   gnueabihf.cmake
   make
   ```
    - cmake ..: Runs CMake configuration, using the CMakeLists.txt in the parent directory (..).
    - -DCMAKE_TOOLCHAIN_FILE=../arm-linux-gnueabihf.cmake: Specifies the toolchain file to use for cross-compilation.
    - make: Builds the project using make (or your configured build tool).
7. **Find the Cross-Compiled Executable:** The cross-compiled executable (hello_crosscompile) will be in the build_arm directory (or a subdirectory depending on your CMake setup).
8. **Transfer and Run on ARM Target:** Transfer and run hello_crosscompile on your ARM Linux target system as described in the previous example.

Code Explanation:

- **CMakeLists.txt:** Standard CMake project file, defines the project and executable.
- **Toolchain File (arm-linux-gnueabihf.cmake):** Configures CMake for cross-compilation. It sets:
    - CMAKE_SYSTEM_NAME, CMAKE_SYSTEM_PROCESSOR, CMAKE_SYSTEM_VERSION: Target system information.
    - CMAKE_C_COMPILER, CMAKE_CXX_COMPILER: Paths to the cross-compilers.

  - CMAKE_SYSROOT (Optional): Path to the target system's sysroot.
  - CMAKE_FIND_ROOT_PATH_MODE_*: CMake library/header search modes for cross-compilation.
- **CMake Configuration:** cmake .. -DCMAKE_TOOLCHAIN_FILE=../arm-linux-gnueabihf.cmake configures CMake to use the specified toolchain file, setting up the build system for cross-compilation.

Real-world scenario: CMake is widely used in C++ projects, including cross-platform and embedded development. It simplifies managing build processes for complex projects and handling cross-compilation for different target architectures. Many open-source projects and professional software development workflows use CMake for build system generation and cross-compilation management.

15.3 Using Docker for Deployment: Containerization for Consistency

Docker is a containerization platform that simplifies application deployment by packaging applications and their dependencies into containers. Containers are lightweight, portable, and isolated environments that ensure applications run consistently across different systems, regardless of the underlying infrastructure. Docker is increasingly popular for deploying C++ applications, especially for server-side applications and microservices, as it addresses many deployment challenges related to dependency management, environment consistency, and scalability. As Turnbull describes in "The Docker Book," containerization revolutionizes application deployment and management (Turnbull, 2014).

15.3.1 Benefits of Containerization with Docker for C++ Applications

- **Environment Consistency:** Docker containers encapsulate the application and its entire runtime environment (libraries, dependencies, configuration). This ensures that the application runs consistently across development, testing, and production environments, eliminating "it works on my machine" issues.

- **Dependency Isolation:** Containers isolate application dependencies from the host system and other containers. This avoids dependency conflicts and simplifies dependency management, especially for C++ applications that might rely on specific library versions or system configurations.
- **Portability:** Docker containers are portable and can be easily moved and deployed across different Docker-compatible platforms (Linux, Windows, macOS, cloud providers). This simplifies deployment to various environments.
- **Scalability:** Docker facilitates scaling applications by easily creating and managing multiple container instances. Container orchestration tools like Docker Compose and Kubernetes further enhance scalability and management of containerized applications.
- **Simplified Deployment Pipelines:** Docker simplifies CI/CD (Continuous Integration/Continuous Deployment) pipelines. Docker images can be built automatically in CI systems and deployed consistently to various environments.
- **Resource Efficiency:** Docker containers are lightweight and share the host OS kernel, making them more resource-efficient than traditional virtual machines.

15.3.2 Dockerizing a Simple C++ Application

Let's Dockerize a simple "Hello World" C++ application.

Step-by-step guide:

1. **Install Docker:** Install Docker Desktop (for Windows, macOS) or Docker Engine (for Linux) on your development machine. Follow the installation instructions for your operating system from the official Docker website.
2. **Create a Project Directory:** Create a directory for your Docker project (e.g., DockerCppApp).
3. **Create hello.cpp:** Create hello.cpp in your project directory (same "Hello World" program as before).
4. **Create Dockerfile:** Create a Dockerfile in your project directory. This file defines how to build the Docker image for your C++ application. Example Dockerfile content:
   Dockerfile

```
FROM ubuntu:latest  # Base image: Ubuntu latest

WORKDIR /app # Set working directory inside the container
```

```
COPY . /app # Copy project files into /app

RUN apt-get update && apt-get install -y g++ # Install g++ compiler
RUN g++ hello.cpp -o hello_app # Compile the C++ application

CMD ["./hello_app"] # Command to run when the container starts
```

Explanation of Dockerfile instructions:

- FROM ubuntu:latest: Specifies the base image for the Docker image. Here, we use the latest Ubuntu image from Docker Hub.
- WORKDIR /app: Sets the working directory inside the container to /app. Subsequent commands will be executed in this directory.
- COPY . /app: Copies all files from the current directory (where the Dockerfile is located) on the host machine to the /app directory inside the container.
- RUN apt-get update && apt-get install -y g++: Executes commands inside the container during image build. This line updates[5] the package lists and installs the g++ C++ compiler.[6]
- RUN g++ hello.cpp -o hello_app: Compiles the hello.cpp source code inside the container, creating an executable named hello_app.
- CMD ["./hello_app"]: Specifies the command to run when a container is started from this image. Here, it runs the compiled hello_app executable.

5. **Build the Docker Image:** Open a terminal in your project directory (where the Dockerfile is located). Build the Docker image using the docker build command.
   Bash

   ```
   docker build -t my-cpp-app .
   ```

   - docker build: Docker command to build an image.
   - -t my-cpp-app: Tags the image with the name my-cpp-app. You can choose a different name.
   - .: Specifies the build context as the current directory (where the Dockerfile is).

6. **Run the Docker Container:** Run a container from the built Docker image using the docker run command.
   Bash

   ```
   docker run my-cpp-app
   ```

   You should see the output "Hello World from Dockerized C++!" printed to your terminal.

Code Explanation:

- **Dockerfile:** Defines the steps to create a Docker image. It specifies the base image, copies application code, installs dependencies (g++ compiler in this case), compiles the application within the container, and sets the command to run when the container starts.
- **docker build -t my-cpp-app .:** Builds a Docker image named my-cpp-app based on the Dockerfile in the current directory. Docker builds images in layers, caching intermediate steps for faster rebuilds.
- **docker run my-cpp-app:** Runs a container from the my-cpp-app image. Docker creates an isolated container environment based on the image, and the CMD instruction in the Dockerfile is executed inside the container.

Real-world scenario: Docker is widely adopted for deploying microservices, web applications, and backend services. It is used extensively in cloud environments, CI/CD pipelines, and development workflows to ensure consistent and reproducible deployments. Containerizing C++ applications with Docker simplifies deployment, dependency management, and scaling, making it a valuable tool for modern software development and operations.

15.4 Best Practices for Distributing Software: Reaching Your Users Effectively

Distributing software effectively involves more than just packaging and deployment. It encompasses considerations like versioning, updates, security, and choosing appropriate distribution channels to reach your target audience. Adhering to best practices ensures a positive user experience, maintains software quality, and facilitates long-term software maintenance and evolution. As Hunt and Thomas advise in "The Pragmatic Programmer," automating the build and release process is crucial for efficient software delivery (Hunt & Thomas, 1999).

15.4.1 Versioning and Updates: Managing Software Evolution

- **Semantic Versioning:** Adopt a clear versioning scheme, such as Semantic Versioning (SemVer) (major.minor.patch), to communicate the nature of changes in each release. SemVer helps users understand the compatibility and scope of updates.

- **Release Notes:** Provide clear and concise release notes with each software update, detailing new features, bug fixes, and any important changes. Release notes inform users about what's new and improved in each version.
- **Automated Update Mechanisms:** Implement automated update mechanisms where feasible, allowing users to easily update to newer versions of the software. Auto-updates streamline the update process and ensure users are running the latest, most secure versions. For desktop applications, consider using update frameworks or mechanisms provided by operating systems or third-party libraries. For web services, CI/CD pipelines and container orchestration tools facilitate automated deployments of new versions.
- **Backward Compatibility:** Strive for backward compatibility whenever possible to minimize disruption for existing users when releasing updates. Clearly communicate any breaking changes and provide migration paths if necessary.

15.4.2 Security Considerations in Software Distribution

- **Code Signing:** Sign your software packages (MSI, DEB, RPM, executables) with digital signatures to verify their authenticity and integrity. Code signing assures users that the software comes from a trusted source and has not been tampered with.
- **Secure Distribution Channels:** Distribute software through secure channels (HTTPS websites, official repositories, app stores) to prevent man-in-the-middle attacks and ensure users download legitimate copies of the software.
- **Vulnerability Management:** Establish a process for handling security vulnerabilities. Promptly release security updates when vulnerabilities are discovered and communicate security advisories to users.
- **Regular Security Audits:** Conduct regular security audits and penetration testing of your software to identify and address potential security weaknesses.

15.4.3 Choosing Distribution Channels: Reaching Your Audience

- **Website Downloads:** For many desktop applications and open-source software, distributing software directly from your project website is a common approach. Provide clear download links for different platforms and package formats.

- **Operating System Repositories:** For Linux distributions, distributing packages through official or community repositories (e.g., Debian repositories, Fedora repositories, PPAs for Ubuntu) makes software easily accessible to Linux users through standard package managers (apt, dnf, yum).
- **App Stores:** For mobile applications (Android, iOS) and desktop applications on some platforms (e.g., Windows Store, macOS App Store), app stores provide a centralized distribution platform, discovery mechanisms, and often handle updates and payments.
- **Package Managers (e.g., NuGet, Conan, vcpkg):** For C++ libraries and development tools, package managers like Conan, vcpkg, and NuGet (for Windows C++ development) simplify dependency management and distribution of reusable components.

15.5 Conclusion: Mastering C++ Application Deployment

Deploying C++ applications effectively requires a comprehensive understanding of packaging formats, cross-compilation, containerization, and best practices for software distribution. By mastering these techniques, Computer Technology students and educators can ensure that their C++ creations reach users reliably, securely, and efficiently across diverse platforms and environments. Choosing the appropriate deployment strategies and tools depends on the specific application, target audience, and deployment environment. A well-executed deployment process is crucial for the success and long-term maintainability of any C++ software project.

Bibliography

1. Abrahams, D., & Gurtovoy, A. (2004). C++ template metaprogramming: Concepts, tools, and techniques from generative programming. Addison-Wesley.

2. Barbato, R. (2015). SFML Blueprints. Packt Publishing.

3. Blanchette, J., & Summerfield, M. (2008). C++ GUI Programming with Qt 4. Prentice Hall.

4. Boehm, H. J. (2018). Foundations of multithreaded, parallel, and distributed programming. Cambridge University Press.

5. Bulka, D., & Mayhew, D. (2000). Efficient C++: Performance programming techniques. Addison-Wesley.

6. Butenhof, D. R. (2004). Programming in C++: Style and coding rules. Prentice Hall PTR.

7. Comer, D. E. (2018). Internetworking with TCP/IP, Volume I: Principles, Protocols, and Architecture (6th ed.). Pearson.

8. CppCMS Framework. (2024). CppCMS - High Performance C++ Web Development Framework. Retrieved from http://cppcms.com/wikipp/en/page/Main

9. Crow Framework. (2024). Crow C++ Microframework for Web. Retrieved from https://crowcpp.org/

10. Czarnecki, K., & Eisenecker, U. W. (2000). Generative programming: Methods, tools, and applications. Addison-Wesley.

11. Dos Reis, G., D'Angelo, J., & Vandevoorde, D. (2017). C++ templates: The definitive guide (2nd ed.). Addison-Wesley.

12. Duffy, B. (2021). Concurrent Programming in C++20: Get up to speed with the new features of concurrent programming in C++20. Packt Publishing.

13. Eberly, D. (2010). Game physics (2nd ed.). CRC Press.

14. Eckel, B. (2000). Thinking in C++ (2nd ed.). Prentice Hall.

15. Eigen. (n.d.). Eigen C++ library. Retrieved from https://eigen.tuxfamily.org/

16. Fielding, R., Gettys, J., Mogul, J., Frystyk, H., Masinter, L., Leach, P., & Berners-Lee, T. (1999). RFC 2616 - Hypertext Transfer Protocol -- HTTP/1.1. Internet Engineering Task Force (IETF).

17. Fowler, M., & Foemmel, M. (2006). Continuous integration. Addison-Wesley Signature Series.

18. Friedl, J. E. F. (2006). Mastering regular expressions (3rd ed.). O'Reilly Media.

19. Furr, A., & Davies, P. (2005). Embedded systems architecture. Newnes.

20. Gamma, E., Helm, R., Johnson, R., & Vlissides, J. (1995). Design patterns: Elements of reusable object-oriented software. Addison-Wesley.

21. Garcia, R., Gregor, D., & Dos Reis, G. (2017). Effective C++ in an embedded environment. Addison-Wesley.

22. Gonzalez, L., & Seijo, D. (2019). Conan C++ Package Manager: Create and manage reusable components with C++ and Conan. Packt Publishing.

23. Google. (n.d.). Chrome OS. Retrieved from https://www.google.com/chromeos/

24. Gregory, J. (2018). Game engine architecture (3rd ed.). CRC Press.

25. Gurtovoy, N., & Alexandrescu, A. (2001). Modern C++ design: Generic programming and design patterns applied. Addison-Wesley.

26. Hunt, A., & Thomas, D. (1999). The pragmatic programmer: From journeyman to master. Addison-Wesley.

27. Johnston, O. (2024). Dear ImGui. Retrieved from https://github.com/ocornut/imgui

28. Josuttis, N. M. (2012). C++ standard library tutorial and reference (2nd ed.). Addison-Wesley Professional.

29. Koenig, A., & Moo, B. E. (2000). Accelerated C++: Practical programming by example. Addison-Wesley.

30. Koeninger, B., Muskalla, P., & Petrović, G. (2013). Modern C++ design: Generic programming and design patterns applied. Addison-Wesley.

31. Koopman, P. (2012). Embedded systems design with platform FPGAs: Principles and practices. McGraw-Hill Education.

32. Lakos, J. O. (1996). Large-scale C++ software design. Addison-Wesley.

33. Libeskind-Hadas, R., & Zobel, D. (1998). Programming with libraries. John Wiley & Sons, Inc.

34. Lippman, S. B., Lajoie, J., & Moo, B. E. (2012). C++ primer (5th ed.). Addison-Wesley.

35. Loukides, M., & Oram, A. (2010). Building open source hardware: DIY manufacturing for hackers and makers. O'Reilly Media.

36. Maguire, S. (1993). Writing solid code: Microsoft's techniques for developing bug-free C programs. Microsoft Press.

37. Martin, B. G., & Hoffman, P. (2023). Mastering CMake: A comprehensive guide to build systems and cross-platform software compilation (2nd ed.). Kitware, Inc.

38. Martin, R. C. (2008). Clean code: A handbook of agile software craftsmanship. Prentice Hall.

39. McConnell, S. (2004). Code complete: A practical handbook of software construction (2nd ed.). Microsoft Press.

40. McKinnell, J. (2020). Asynchronous C++20: Core techniques in modern C++ concurrency. Apress.

41. McKenney, P. E. (2011). Is parallel programming hard, and, if so, what can you do about it?. Cambridge University Press.

42. Meyer, B. (1997). Object-oriented software construction (2nd ed.). Prentice Hall PTR.

43. Meyers, S. (2001). Effective STL: 50 specific ways to improve your use of the standard template library. Addison-Wesley.

44. Meyers, S. (2005). Effective C++: 55 specific ways to improve your programs and designs (3rd ed.). Addison-Wesley.

45. Meyers, S. (2014). Effective modern C++: 42 specific ways to improve your use of C++11 and C++14. O'Reilly Media.

46. Patterson, D. A., & Hennessy, J. L. (2021). Computer organization and design RISC-V edition: The hardware/software interface. Morgan Kaufmann.

47. Petzold, C. (1998). Programming Windows (5th ed.). Microsoft Press.

48. Prata, S. (2014). C++ primer plus (6th ed.). Addison-Wesley Professional.

49. Rabbitzsch, J. (2013). SFML Game Development. Packt Publishing.

50. Reinders, J. (2007). Intel threading building blocks: Outfitting C++ for multi-core architecture. O'Reilly Media, Inc.

51. Ritchie, D. M. (1993). The development of the C language. ACM SIGPLAN Notices, 28(3), 201-208.

52. Sanderson, C., & Curtin, R. R. (2016). Armadillo: A template-based C++ library for linear algebra. Journal of Open Source Software, 1(2), 26.

53. Stenberg, D., et al. (2024). libcurl - Curl home page. Retrieved from https://curl.se/

54. Stevens, W. R., Fenner, A., & Rudoff, A. M. (2004). UNIX Network Programming, Volume 1, Networking APIs: Sockets and XTI (3rd ed.). Addison-Wesley.

55. Stroustrup, B. (1980). A preliminary design of C with classes. Bell Laboratories.

56. Stroustrup, B. (1994). The design and evolution of C++. Addison-Wesley.

57. Stroustrup, B. (2013). The C++ programming language (4th ed.). Addison-Wesley.

58. Stroustrup, B. (2018). A tour of C++ (2nd ed.). Addison-Wesley.

59. Sutter, H., & Alexandrescu, A. (2005). C++ coding standards: 101 rules, guidelines, and best practices. Addison-Wesley Professional.

60. Turner, S. E. (2018). Effective performance engineering: Tools and techniques for programmers. Addison-Wesley Professional.

61. Turnbull, J. (2014). The Docker book: Containerization using Docker. James Turnbull.

62. Vandevoorde, D., & Josuttis, N. M. (2003). C++ templates: The complete guide. Addison-Wesley Professional.

63. Vandevoorde, D., Josuttis, N. M., & Gregor, D. (2017). C++ templates: The complete guide (2nd ed.). Addison-Wesley Professional.

64. Westfall, C. (2022). Effective CMake: Practical techniques and patterns to make the most of CMake. Pragmatic Bookshelf.

65. Williams, A. (2019). C++ concurrency in action: Practical multithreading. Manning Publications.

66. Yaghmour, K. (2003). Building embedded Linux systems: Concepts, techniques, and methods. O'Reilly Media.

About The Author

Early Life and Education

Mark John Lado was born on September 24, 1992, in Danao City, Philippines. From an early age, he exhibited a keen interest in technology and education, which would later shape his career. He pursued his Bachelor of Science in Information Systems (BSIS) at Colegio de San Antonio de Padua, where he graduated with a strong foundation in technology and systems analysis. His academic journey continued as he earned a Master's degree in Information Technology (MIT) from the Northern Negros State College of Science and Technology in Sagay City, Philippines. Currently, he is pursuing his Doctorate in Information Technology at the State University of Northern Negros, reflecting his commitment to lifelong learning and professional growth.

Professional Career

Mark has built a diverse and impactful career in education and technology. He currently serves as an Instructor in the College of Technology and Engineering at Cebu Technological University, a role he has held since October 2022. Prior to this, he was a Faculty member in Business Education and Information Systems at Colegio de San Antonio de Padua from 2018 to 2022. His earlier roles include working as a Part-Time Information Technology Instructor at the University of the Visayas - Danao Branch and as an ICT Coordinator at Carmen Christian School Inc. in 2017.

Research and Innovation

Mark is an active researcher with a focus on applying technology to solve real-world problems. Some of his notable projects include:

1. "Development of a Microprocessor-Based Sensor Network for Monitoring Water Parameters in Tilapia Traponds"
2. "A Wireless Digital Public Address with Voice Alarm and Text-to-Speech Feature for Different Campuses", which was published in Globus: An International Journal of Management & IT

His research contributions highlight his dedication to innovation and his ability to bridge theoretical knowledge with practical applications.

Authorship and Publications

Mark is a prolific author, having written and published multiple books on technology topics. His works include:

1. Mastering CRUD with Flask in 5 Days; Build Python Web Applications - From Novice to...
2. Flask, PostgreSQL, and Bootstrap: Building Data-Driven Web Applications with CRUD...
3. From Model to Web App: A Comprehensive Guide to Building Data-Driven Web...
4. The Beginner's Guide Computer Systems; Principles, Practices, and Troubleshooting:...
5. Flask Web Framework Building Interactive Web Applications with SQLite Database: A...
6. Mastering PC Troubleshooting & Operating Systems: The Modern Landscape of PC...
7. Mastering Flask in 5 Days; From Zero to Deployment: Building Your First Web App:...
8. Data Modeling and Process Analysis; Essential for Technology Analysts and AI...
9. The Echo of the Past; Information Networks from Stone to Silicon and Beyond AI: How...
10. Cybersecurity Essentials Protecting Your Digital Life, Data, and Privacy in a...
11. Mastering PC Troubleshooting and Operating Systems: The Future-Ready...
12. From Idea to Manuscript: A Step-by-Step Guide to Writing Your Nonfiction Book
13. Microprocessor Magic: Unlocking the Potential of Building Projects from Scratch

14. Data Modeling and Process Analysis: A Comprehensive Guide – Volume I
15. Python Data Science Essentials: A Comprehensive Guide to Mastering...
16. Mastering PC Troubleshooting and Operating Systems: A Comprehensive Guide
17. Cybersecurity Confidence: 8 Steps to Master Digital Security and Boost Productivity
18. Embedded Systems: From Historical Development to Modern-Day Applications

These books are widely recognized and serve as valuable resources for students, hobbyists, and professionals in the IT field. His publications are available on platforms like Amazon and ThriftBooks, further extending his reach and impact

Certifications and Professional Development

Mark has pursued several certifications to enhance his expertise, including:

- Computer Hardware Servicing from Cebu Technological University
- Consumer Electronics Servicing from TESDA

These certifications underscore his commitment to continuous professional development and staying updated with emerging technological trends.

Contributions to IT Education

As an active member of the Philippine Society of Information Technology Educators (PSITE), Mark contributes to advancing IT education standards in the Philippines. His teaching, research, and authorship have made him a respected figure in the academic and IT communities. He is known for his adaptability to emerging technologies, such as AI-driven systems and cybersecurity, ensuring that his work remains relevant and impactful.

Personal Interests

Outside of his professional life, Mark enjoys reading books, spending time at the beach, and engaging in physical activities like inline skating and biking. These hobbies not only help him unwind but also contribute to his overall well-being and creativity.

Legacy and Impact

Mark John Lado's dedication to education, research, and professional excellence has made him a valuable asset to the IT community. His contributions have empowered countless students and professionals, preparing them for the challenges of a rapidly evolving technological landscape. His unwavering passion for technology and continuous pursuit of learning ensure that his legacy will endure for years to come.

For more details about his work, you can visit his official website
https://markjohnlado.com/

or explore his publications on Amazon Author Page
https://www.amazon.com/stores/author/B0BZM8PM6R

I highly recommend reading this book to further enhance your skills and deepen your understanding of the subject.

https://a.co/d/iJmBV7K

https://a.co/d/b1W3F8n

https://a.co/d/izTWNbO

https://a.co/d/6HHyUFk

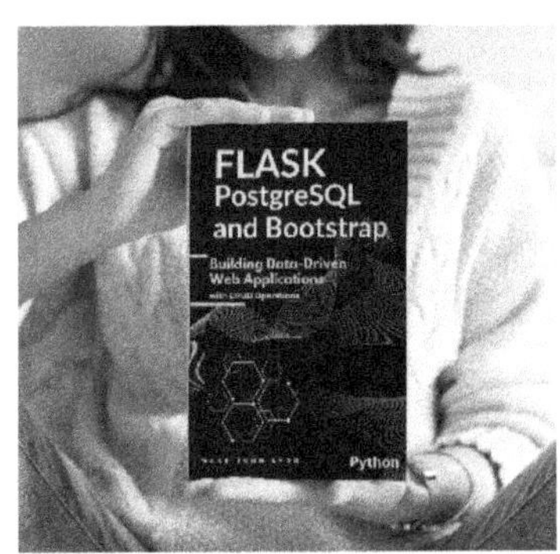

www.ingramcontent.com/pod-product-compliance
Lightning Source LLC
LaVergne TN
LVHW051427050326
832903LV00030BD/2957

* 9 7 9 8 3 1 3 7 4 5 8 6 2 *